*Founding Sins*

# Founding Sins

*How a Group of Antislavery Radicals Fought to Put Christ into the Constitution*

JOSEPH S. MOORE

OXFORD
UNIVERSITY PRESS

Oxford University Press is a department of the University of Oxford. It furthers the University's objective of excellence in research, scholarship, and education by publishing worldwide.

Oxford New York
Auckland Cape Town Dar es Salaam Hong Kong Karachi
Kuala Lumpur Madrid Melbourne Mexico City Nairobi
New Delhi Shanghai Taipei Toronto

With offices in
Argentina Austria Brazil Chile Czech Republic France Greece
Guatemala Hungary Italy Japan Poland Portugal Singapore
South Korea Switzerland Thailand Turkey Ukraine Vietnam



Published in the United States of America by
Oxford University Press
198 Madison Avenue, New York, NY 10016



Library of Congress Cataloging-in-Publication Data
Moore, Joseph S. (Joseph Solomon), 1977–
Founding sins : how a group of antislavery radicals fought to put Christ into the constitution / Joseph S. Moore.
pages cm
Includes bibliographical references and index.
ISBN 978–0–19–026924–1 (cloth : alk. paper)
1. Religious right—United States—History. 2. Church and state—United States—History. 3. Covenanters—United States. I. Title.
BR516.M6657 2016
322'.10973—dc23
2015009829

1 3 5 7 9 8 6 4 2
Printed in the United States of America
on acid-free paper

*To Mom, who taught me to love reading words*

*And to Dad, who taught me to have words of my own*

*We the People of the United States, humbly acknowledging Almighty God as the source of all authority and power in civil government, the Lord Jesus Christ as the Ruler among the nations, his revealed will as the supreme law of the land, in order to constitute a Christian government, and in order to form a more perfect union. . . .*

—PROPOSED AMENDMENT TO THE CONSTITUTION,
introduced in memorial by
Senator Charles Sumner, 1864[1]

# *Contents*

# *Acknowledgments*

EVEN A SHORT book acquires a long list of people deserving thanks. This book is the product of many acts of kindness I received along the way. The following are inadequate acknowledgments of many debts long overdue and never fully paid.

I was generously supported in my research by Harvard University's International Seminar on the History of the Atlantic World, Duke University's John Hope Franklin Research Center, the Organization of American Historians–Immigration and Ethnic History Society John Higham Travel Grant, and the University of North Carolina at Greensboro's Allen W. Trelease Graduate Fellowship and Atlantic World Research Network. An invitation to speak at the University of Edinburgh's Institute for Advanced Studies in the Humanities helped hone my words. Courtesy appointments gave precious time to work on ideas surrounded by engaging scholars. The University of Notre Dame's History Department and the Keough-Naughton Institute for Irish Studies were generous with their time and encouragement. The Institute for Irish Studies at Queen's University Belfast, especially Dominic Bryan and Valerie Miller, gave me invaluable space to work.

On both sides of the Atlantic Ocean, the staffs and volunteers of many libraries and archives were unendingly helpful: the British Library, National Library of Scotland, New College Library at the University of Edinburgh, Public Record Office of Northern Ireland, the Hesburgh Libraries at the University of Notre Dame, David M. Rubenstein Rare Book and Manuscript Library at Duke University, Reformed Presbyterian Theological Seminary, Clifford E. Barbour Library at Pittsburgh Theological Seminary, Special Collections of McCain Library at Erskine College and Theological Seminary, John Bulow Campbell Library at Columbia Theological Seminary, Vermont State Archives and Records

Administration, Selma Public Library and Old Depot Museum, South Caroliniana Library at the University of South Carolina, and South Carolina Department of Archives and History. Special thanks go to Edith Brawley, Thomas Reid, and Mary Morrow.

Gardner-Webb University provided the perfect place to inspire and be inspired by students, faculty, and friends. Ben and Sarah Gaskins housed me for late-night work sessions and encouraged me with daily conversations worth taking a break to have. Elizabeth Amato, Walter Dalton, Donna Spivey Ellington, Michael Kuchinsky, Robert Munoz, Donna Schronce, Dianne Sykes, Timothy Vanderburg, and David Yelton are wonderful colleagues. I received exceptional institutional support from Earl Leininger, Benjamin Leslie, and Frank Bonner. Dean Mary Roby's fantastic staff at the Gardner-Webb library made this work doable, especially Kevin Bridges. Jasmine Stevenson and Stephanie McKellop (a tremendous scholar in her own right) did great work tracking down references.

I have been the beneficiary of many historians who took the time to talk with me about extreme Presbyterians when they could have been attending to much more pressing matters. Mark A. Noll encouraged my work long before I was encouraged it would go anywhere. Vernon and Georganne Burton warmly opened their home to me while researching in South Carolina. Kaarin Michaelsen graciously hosted my research time in London. In emails and conversations, Eric Burin, John Fea, Lacy Ford, Charles Irons, Richard MacMaster, Thomas Kidd, and Paul Thompson turned me on to good sources and helpful concepts on American religious history and the history of antislavery. The late Eugene Genovese commented on an early draft on southern antislavery religion. Andrew Holmes, David Gleeson, Patrick Griffin, Kerby Miller, James Smyth, and David Wilson gave valuable insights on Irish religious and ethnic history. William Roulston introduced me to researching Irish history on the ground in Belfast. Donald Smith generously shared his remarkable database of information on Vermont and the early American backcountry. Mary Cayton, T. Michael Parrish, and Jewel Spangler provided helpful critiques. Led by Sarah Griffith, the Charlotte historians' monthly gathering gave comments on chapters that moved the argument forward. Faculty at the University of North Carolina at Greensboro helped birth this project from a vague idea to what it has become. Thanks go especially to Charles C. Bolton, Thomas Jackson, Lisa Levenstein, and Loren Schweninger for their suggestions on various stages of this research.

I have met some truly excellent historians of the Covenanters and Presbyterians whose work is both thought-provoking and groundbreaking. I am honored to be part of this cohort of thinkers: Craig Gallagher, Peter Gilmore, Michael Griggs, Daniel Ritchie, Emily Moberg Robinson, Rankin Sherling, and Valerie Wallace. I am doubly thankful to Emily, both for her profound scholarship and for her insightful editing suggestions. Tribute is due to the host of historians who came before us without whom today's efforts would be impossible: Ray A. King, Reid W. Stewart, Lowry Ware, William L. Fisk, Robert Lathan, and William M. Glasgow.

I have forged several important friendships along the path of researching, thinking, and rethinking this book, and each led to invaluable feedback, encouragement, and ideas I could not have found on my own. These compatriots of history will hold my affection long after the research is done and include Christopher Cameron, Christopher Graham, Luke Harlow, Allison Madar, Jane G. V. McGaughey, and Ben Wright. Will Duffy sparked new thoughts on old ideas. Steve Contianos was always there to keep me grounded in the real world.

Some mentors are that in more than name. Robert M. Calhoon, to whom I owe so very much, made my career possible. He is both a professional guide and personal friend.

My family is supportive in every way, even if they remain a bit quizzical as to why I traverse the globe ever in search of one more archive. Joseph S. Moore gave me far more than his name—he gave me the love of history. Louise Moore, who has been enjoying us for more than eighty years, lovingly supported many early trips. I am thankful for my beautiful wife, Mary Julia. She epitomizes the passionate pursuit of perfection and, in so doing, inspires me to seek the same. My daughter, Charlotte, distracted me endlessly to do things more fun with someone far more important. I wish I had indulged that impulse more often.

Finally, I am eternally grateful to Michael and Rachel Moore. This book is for my parents. They spent money they did not have to buy for a toddler they were not expecting books he could not yet read from the mail-order Children's Book of the Month Club. The rest is history.

# *The Presbyterian Fringe: Abbreviations, Terms, and Language*

In order to treat Covenanters as a broad cultural phenomenon, every effort has been made to minimize or shorten organizational labels. A guide to these groups, their monikers, and their abbreviations is provided here.

## *Anti-political Engagement*

These groups took official stances against participating in political elections, juries, and other governmental activity as a witness against non-Presbyterian states and secular governments.

| | |
|---|---|
| *RPs* | —Reformed Presbyterians |
| | —Cameronians |
| | —Society People |
| | —Hard-liners |
| | —Old Light (occasionally also as Old School) |
| | —Synod of the Reformed Presbyterian Church |
| *Anti-Burghers* | —Seceders who found the Burgher Oath of Scotland unacceptable |

## *Pro-political Engagement*

These groups took official stances allowing for various levels of political participation with non-Presbyterian states and secular governments.

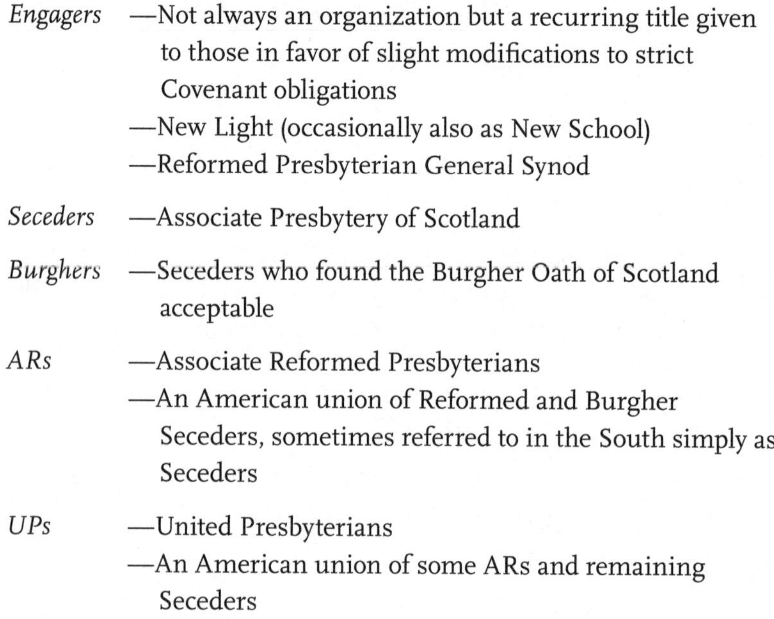

| | |
|---|---|
| *Engagers* | —Not always an organization but a recurring title given to those in favor of slight modifications to strict Covenant obligations<br>—New Light (occasionally also as New School)<br>—Reformed Presbyterian General Synod |
| *Seceders* | —Associate Presbytery of Scotland |
| *Burghers* | —Seceders who found the Burgher Oath of Scotland acceptable |
| *ARs* | —Associate Reformed Presbyterians<br>—An American union of Reformed and Burgher Seceders, sometimes referred to in the South simply as Seceders |
| *UPs* | —United Presbyterians<br>—An American union of some ARs and remaining Seceders |

Original spelling, italics, and capitalization have been retained where it is not overly confusing, although some words have been modernized for clarity. This is especially true of passages from seventeenth-century Scotland as well as personal letters. Editorial clarifications within quotes are bracketed.

# *Founding Sins*

# *Introduction*

THE UNITED STATES was not founded as a Christian nation, because slavery was in the Constitution and Jesus was not. The people who said this, rather loudly and for quite a long time, were called the Covenanters. Whereas today most religious conservatives insist that America's Founders created a Christian nation, Covenanters were the most conservative Christians in early America, and they vehemently disagreed. Christian America advocates such as David Barton and Glenn Beck are anxious to blame the mythology of a secular founding on liberals who distort the past from the left. Yet, in the actual past, the most strident critique of America's failure to be a Christian nation came from the right.

Conservative Christians today do not have history *wrong* so much as they have it *backward*. The United States was not founded as a Christian nation only to later lose its way. In fact, the United States is a more Christian nation today than it was when the Founders wrote the Constitution. We trust God on our coins (1864) and paper money (1955). The Post Office no longer opens on Sunday (1912). Students pledge allegiance to a nation "under God" (1954) and spend government loans and grants to study theology at religious schools (1944, 1965). An entire government office focuses on helping religious charities use tax money (2001). Presidents Bush and Obama both called for national days of prayer each year they were in office, something President Jefferson refused to do and President Madison did once but later regretted. All of this represents the creation of something new, not the continuation of something old.[1]

When the Founders failed to found a Christian nation it was not by accident. They were intentionally dismissing those who sought to mix God and government in the new nation in old, European ways. That failure was loudly protested. In the thick of America's first culture wars were the Covenanters, an assortment of radical Scotch-Irish Presbyterian sects sharing the conviction that all nations must be in an explicit covenant with God. For more than 200 years, these fringe Presbyterians loudly demanded that the United States repent of the founding sins embedded in its Constitution. Although almost entirely forgotten today, Covenanters' efforts to Christianize America after the fact came shockingly close to succeeding then. In the process Covenanters fought the English in multiple revolutions, confronted the Founders and their godless Constitution, took up arms against the federal government in the Whiskey Rebellion, offended both George Washington and Thomas Jefferson, served as conductors on the Underground Railroad, aided in the founding of the American Colonization Society, fought in the Civil War, mounted a star-studded national campaign to amend the Constitution to include the authority of Jesus, inspired secular Americans to label themselves "liberals," and ultimately displayed to the modern fundamentalist movement the acceptable limits of reform. Along the way they met with, and in some cases persuaded, evangelists such as George Whitefield, Founding Fathers such as Benjamin Franklin, abolitionists such as John Brown, presidents such as Abraham Lincoln, and Supreme Court justices such as William Strong. Prompted by the Covenanters, Lincoln considered asking Congress to amend the Constitution to acknowledge God; he deleted the paragraph from his State of the Union only after his shocked Cabinet told him it was a horrible idea. By the time they were done, Covenanters had inserted their cause into almost every prominent event in American history—and very nearly into the Constitution itself.[2]

Unlike today, in the original Christian America debate the most conservative Christians argued that the Founding Fathers failed. Covenanter critiques centered on two interrelated themes. The first was the absence of Jesus Christ in the Constitution: an affront to God's name and an open statement of rebellion against his reign over the people. The second was human slavery and its long wake of American racism: a desecration of God's image. Even as America changed and as life in America changed the Covenanters, these arguments maintained a remarkable continuity among their religious adherents in both the North and the South, spanning the years from the Early Republic to the Civil War era and Reconstruction and into the twentieth century. The Covenanters' insistence on God in the law and humanity's equality before it gave purpose and energy to their fight against America's twin founding sins.

Like most extremist arguments, Covenanter political logic was deceptively simple. A nation was its laws, and law was rooted in the authority of God. The English Magna Carta's preamble issued laws "at the prompting of God." In America's great charter, however, God was neither prompting nor prompted. He was not there at all. Therefore, the Constitution had a "We the People" problem. Taking the law out of God's hands was "an assumption of unlawful authority," one Covenanter wrote, on par with leadership by a wanton, raging horde. According to the Covenanters, the US Constitution's preamble displayed the true nature of America's religious rebellion: the public, which lacked the rightfully constituted authority to institute power, had replaced a lawful judge (God) with itself. Any nation founded by casting off a Christian British government in favor of a rebellious "We the People" was bound to present problems for anyone hoping for a Christian America.[3]

Covenanters insisted that while "the People" were of broadly Christian heritage, this did not make the United States a Christian nation. Their fellow citizens often disagreed. Especially after the religious revivals of the Second Great Awakening, many Americans became convinced that since they lived in a country of Christians, they therefore lived in a Christian country. The widespread popularity of this argument from population drove nineteenth-century Covenanters into frenzied denial. A Christian culture, even a Christian majority, did *not* equate to a Christian nation, they insisted. Moreover, these "People" were, in fact, deeply divided or apathetic about religion. As one evangelical minister complained just after the founding, the three most common denominations in post-Revolutionary America were "Deists, Nothingarians, and anythingarians." Defining the nation by its people and cultures, rather than its stated laws, obscured more than it clarified because "the People" were not religiously whole. To say that the Covenanters attacked the idea of Christian America is not to undermine the very real ways that early Americans intertwined their faith with their citizenship. Yet the Covenanters' critical distinction—that by the standards of its own time the newly born United States was simultaneously a Christian civilization and a secular nation—has been lost on our contemporary debates.[4]

Covenanters saw the church and state as brothers of the same father who possessed different talents. The one instituted the father's spiritual will; the other, his physical will. Since both sprang from God's will, both sat beneath the authority of Christ and should reflect the same moral standard. State laws should reflect biblical morality. The state could not force religious belief; that was a matter of the heart and the church. It could, however, coerce religious obedience, suppress immorality, and keep people from offending God's name and commands because these were issues of the body, not the mind. This distinction was largely lost on their detractors—another reason Covenanter political theology was a hard sell in America. It also caused at least one historian to refer to them as a Presbyterian Taliban.[5]

To square the circle on national religious identity, Covenanters argued, "the People" should look backward rather than forward. The secular American state was a new and dangerous departure from traditional Christian Europe. Thus, the Covenanters did not hold up 1787 nearly as highly as they did 1643, when Scotland and England pledged themselves to become explicitly Protestant nations with clear enforcement of Presbyterian morality. These Christian realms, if only briefly a reality, dominated Covenanters' political sensibility. They were not so much interested in creating a Christian America as in recreating a Christian Scotland in America. This accounts for much of what made Covenanter logic and tactics different from those of Christian conservatives today.

Another difference was their position on race. Covenanters rejected slavery and racism in the very era both emerged as common sense to most Americans. In this, they represent another peculiar historical anomaly. America's first Christian nationalists were also some of its most radical racial egalitarians. Their antislavery views predated even those of the Quakers. Unlike the Quakers, these were Christian militants, protecting their Underground Railroad stations with both prayer and gunfire. Perhaps most interesting, the pained Covenanter attempts to maintain an antislavery witness in the South stumbled through stages of radicalism and moderation into the Civil War before finally being absorbed into the white southern mainstream. Such views were difficult to maintain in North and South. Their long staying power in Covenanter circles, predating and outlasting most other forms of racial egalitarianism, indicates the ferocity with which they were held even where they eventually gave way. Covenanter racial views eventually experienced widespread acceptance in American life, while their political perspective did not. This was an outcome they would never have predicted. To the Covenanter mind, the one must necessarily flow from the other. American racism sprang out of its lack of Christian law.

A study of the Covenanters is an entrée into understanding what role religion could and could not play in early American government. This is not a book about the Founders and Christian America advocates per se but, rather, about one particular group of their detractors. It places forgotten Covenanter voices back into the debate over America's founding. In the past, they were dismissed but not ignored. That dismissal tells a story about what early Americans believed when they wrote, debated, ratified, and modified the US Constitution. We can also learn much by observing how far Americans were willing to entertain the twin ideas of abolishing slavery and secularism from the Constitution.

*Founding Sins* traces this history across three centuries and the multiple countries and states Covenanters tried to redeem for God. Chapter 1 reveals the roots of Covenanters' attempts to create a Presbyterian empire in Britain, lingering resentment over that failure, and origins of their early abolitionism. Chapter 2 traces their migration to colonial America and subsequent confrontations with both the British Empire and Founding Fathers. Chapter 3 locates Covenanters in the Early Republic and their in utero formulation as a distinctly American political movement protesting issues such as Sunday mail delivery and memorialization of the Founders. Chapter 4 examines their attacks, both headlong and oblique, on slavery in the North and South through the Civil War era. Chapter 5 charts the high and low tides of Covenanter influence in America, as their surprisingly fruitful efforts to amend the Constitution and maintain racial radicalism in the South both failed dramatically and dwindled to sideshows on the twentieth-century political stage. The afterword briefly traces the Covenanters' lingering influence on the rise of Christian nationalist thought in the twentieth century. To date, no work has brought this story together.[6]

Who was, and who was not, a Covenanter? *Founding Sins* takes a broadly inclusive view of the term, explained over the course of the book. All Presbyterians of whatever denomination professing the 1638 National Covenant and the 1643 Solemn League and Covenant as models for Christian statehood are included. Many Covenanter groups held those documents in various stages of high regard. Reformed Presbyterians (RPs), Associate Presbyterians, and their American hybrids such as Associate Reformed Presbyterians (ARs) and United Presbyterians (UPs) all valued the legacy of such historic statements to give insight into their own peculiar political circumstances. Many Covenanters were in fact embedded within mainline Presbyterianism itself. In effect, such peoples believed that every nation (especially Scotland, Britain, and the United States) *should* be in covenant with God. They disagreed among themselves on *how* this should be accomplished and how much one could participate in a godless political system in order to reform it. In many ways and times, each of these small groups explicitly claimed that their Covenanter heritage applied to their current circumstances even as they diverged sharply from one another as to how. To keep up with the various group names as they appear and change, a glossary is provided.[7]

Over the course of the book, several interrelated insights emerge. First, the Christian America debate is much older than is often remembered. The United States rebelled *against* a Christian kingdom and established a secular republic. From that moment forward, Americans disagreed vehemently about what such actions meant. Second, Covenanters served as the shock troops of Christian America's assault on the national government. Whereas other Christian conservatives belatedly arrived at the idea of a national solution to moral waywardness, Covenanters always made federal power the object of their efforts. Third, the Christianization of the state and questioning of racial slavery were once deeply intertwined. Dividing these two issues obscures the way certain reformers saw them as parts of a whole. Finally, the Christian Amendment movement was more than the product of nineteenth-century angst about immigration and Reconstruction. Rather, it hailed from a long and deep Atlantic history too often left submerged beneath the surface. The Covenanters sustained decidedly Old World logic in a new nation for a remarkably long time. Their religion was itself constrained, changed, and sometimes abandoned. This was to be expected. They met the inevitable resistance that came from flying in the face of the American consensus that God and government should not mix. Why and how they did so is a story worth remembering.[8]

Covenanters discovered, pressed, and exceeded the limits of Christian nationalism from the Early Republic through the turn of the twentieth century. True, despite the great cacophony of religious vantage points among Americans in the Revolutionary generation and beyond, a general Christian consensus could be found in the country. But that consensus could be taken too far. The Covenanters pushed up to and beyond that boundary, thus setting the limits of Christian nationalism in America. Those who, like this Presbyterian fringe, stood outside that consensus held visions of an explicitly Christian nation other Americans sought to avoid. What is missing in historical narratives is any sense that these actors were part of a distinct voice that contemporaries heard, understood, and rejected. It is a voice largely forgotten today. Once we hear it again, we can give those who ask about America's Christian founding an older answer. The United States clearly was not founded as a Christian nation; had it been, Jesus Christ would be found in the Constitution and slavery would be absent. There were those in the historical moment, however, who desperately wished it were otherwise. Their message, and its rejection, speaks loudly about how much religion early Americans were willing to allow in their politics.

# *I*

# *Presbyterian Empire*

*The* Pope *and* Calvin, *I'll oppose*
*Because I think them both our Foes*
*The Church and State have suffer'd more*
*By Calvin, than the scarlet Whore.*
Popish *and* Presbyterian *Zeal*
*Both bitter Foes to* Britain's *Weal*
*The* Pope *wou'd of our Faith bereave us*
*But still our* Monarchy *would leave us*
*Not so the* Presbyterian *Crew*
*That ruin'd* Church *and* Monarch *too.*

—JONATHAN SWIFT[1]

COVENANTERS FOUNDED A Christian nation in Scotland in 1638. Five years later they forged a Presbyterian empire with England. Just eight years after that they lost it all. The memory of their short-lived success, and the dream that it might happen again, lasted long and far enough to reach early America.

Before they crossed the Atlantic and became America's other Puritans, Covenanters took their name from the 1638 Scottish political alliance between factions arrayed against King Charles I. This coalition was sealed in a pact, called the National Covenant. That document signed the nation over to God—a God who, they were sure, was himself an adamant Presbyterian. A similar covenant, called the Solemn League and Covenant, was forced on England in 1643. In theory, this committed the entire British Isles to a Presbyterian empire. Most Englishmen took implementing the agreement as lightly as the Scots took it seriously. In the wars, defeats, and peace that followed, even most Scots abandoned strict commitment to these documents' religious nationalism as impracticable.

The most religiously zealous, however, believed that once a nation signed itself over to God, it was morally perilous to take it back.

So it was that the term *Covenanters* went from representing the nation of Scots to signifying Scotland's most fervent religious radicals. Quickly upon the restoration of Charles II to the throne in 1660, Covenanters became outlaws whose visions of a godly Protestant Britain looked very much like religious rebellion. Led by elders in secret cell groups for worship, Covenanters continued preaching that nations should adhere to strict Scriptural laws. They threatened armed resistance against government forces, assassinated church officials, and enforced stringent personal morality on individual members of each local society. The covenants of 1638 and 1643, accompanied by heroic stories of those who died serving the cause, inspired quests for national morality in Scotland, Ireland, and America for generations afterward.

This chapter narrates the series of events in which Covenanters came to rule over Scotland, fall from power, and eventually occupy the fringes of Presbyterianism in the Atlantic world. Rooted in Scotland, they first colonized Ireland rather than Massachusetts and immigrated to America throughout the eighteenth and nineteenth centuries rather than the 1600s. In that long process, Covenanters became to Presbyterianism what the Separatist Pilgrims were to English Puritanism—the fringe of an already outlying sect. They were religious purists who sought to recreate a heavenly ideal in their present world. Covenanters traveled by different routes to the New World than other Puritans, and those routes mattered.[2]

## *The Scottish Reformation of Soul and State*

In the sixteenth century the world suddenly got cold and dry. By the seventeenth century, from China to France and across the Atlantic as far as the Americas, social instability swiftly followed climate change. The Ming dynasty collapsed in China, the Fronde Revolt shook France, and the entire globe underwent torrents of prolonged violence. People began looking for divine explanations for their long winters, crop failures, and hunger. Witches were burned, inquisitions were empowered, and the Protestant Reformation unraveled centuries of Roman Catholic control across Europe. The worst of the crisis, ecologically and politically, climaxed in the 1630s–40s. In Scotland, these years birthed the Covenanters.[3]

Scotland first began convulsing in fits of religious fervor in 1560, when a Reform Parliament rejected the authority of the pope and established a Protestant national church, called the Kirk. Mary Queen of Scots was less than pleased, especially when she was informed that although she could consider herself as a queen in matters of state, she was but "a servant and no queen" once she entered the realm of church business. From the beginning, then, church and state in Scotland coexisted in uneasy peace.[4]

Over the course of several decades, Scottish Reformers organized local kirks on a model called Presbyterianism. Rooted in the teachings of Geneva's Protestant reformer John Calvin, Presbyterianism radically transformed the nature of religious life in Scotland. Presbyterianism was an almost bottom-up religion. It used a series of church courts to oversee religious affairs. These courts were responsive to local voices. In this structure, common people in good standing would elect their local elders, a word translated from the Greek *presbytos* from which the system derived its name. The elders would meet in local courts called sessions, which oversaw kirk affairs. Each session sent representatives to a higher court called the presbytery, where regional issues were resolved. Each presbytery, in turn, sent representatives to a higher regional body called a synod. The various synods sent representatives to a national meeting called the General Assembly, which served as the highest religious court for the land. In essence, it was a conglomerate meeting of lower court judges who formed at once a supreme court and legislature on matters of religion. Most importantly, the whole thing stood on the superstructure of local kirk members choosing their own elders.

Presbyterianism was politics in local life. As late as 1745 there were still less than 3,000 Scots who could vote in national elections. In contrast, from 1560 forward most male commoners in good moral standing voted for their church leaders democratically. Elections for elders happened every two to four years on average. Those elected made important decisions that affected everyday life for common people. Kirk elders' primary focus was not with the theological debates between divines or the political conflicts of nations but on local concerns such as fair dealings, sex, marriage, neighborhood disputes, and who could be conscripted for military service. Parliament was distant, occasional, and unrepresentative. The kirk session was close, regular, highly representative for its time and dealt with issues that were of pressing concern to constituents. Electing elders was, therefore, deeply political. Any perceived encroachment from outside forces on the community's autonomy was an attack on multiple levels at religious and political life.[5]

How, then, were kirk and state to interact? Scottish churchmen began with an important assumption. The realm was Christian. There were two Christian kingdoms within that Christian realm: the secular one, with the "power of the Sword," and the spiritual one, with the "power of the keys" to Heaven. Though different, "these two kinds of power have both one authority, one ground, one final cause," and they "tend to one end." Both state power and kirk power sprang from the same divine source and enforced one eternal truth, but each used its power in particular ways. Each Christian Scot, then, experienced God's authority in two institutions: the Christian state and the Christian kirk.[6]

The person for whom this was most complicated, and most important, was the monarch. All Christians, kings and queens included, sat beneath God's spiritual authority in the church. The monarch could not be the church's subject and its head at the same time. Since the monarch was a subject of the church, it was assumed that he or she would rule as a Christian monarch should. Just as a blacksmith could be punished by the local session for dishonesty in business, so the king should tend to his duties with godliness or risk the ire of the national General Assembly. Only a Christian, and by this they meant Presbyterian, ruler should rule a Christian land. And he or she should rule like a Christian. That meant ruling as the church said. Theologically, the church and state represented co-arms of God's authority in the world, mutually supportive of the other, with neither side interfering in the role of its counterpart. That was the theory.[7]

In practice, the Scots' particular arrangement of God's two kingdoms placed the church slightly above the state. The regent became the long arm of church law but was prevented from interfering in the issues of religious dogma and debate. The monarch's role was to uplift the church by providing for it financially, protecting it defensively, and prosecuting for it judicially. The church's role was to demand Christian behavior of all citizens, including the king. If the church deemed the state out of line, the state could be reined in. Just one year after the Scottish Parliament codified this system in *The Second Book of Discipline*, Scottish divine George Buchanan laid out the implications of such logic in *De Jure Regni Apud Scotos*. Dedicated to the king, *De Jure Regni* acknowledged that of "the punishment of *Caligula, Nero* or *Domitian*, I think there will be none that will not confess they were justly punished." The issue at hand for kirk leaders was how to distinguish a tyrant Christians could rightly kill from a "lawful King" they could not. Any encroachment by the king on the authority of the church, the realm of "King Jesus," was a good indication.[8]

From the beginning, Scottish kings did just that. The preface to the 1578 *Second Book of Discipline* blamed Scotland's growing economic problems on political leaders' "Course of Conformity," which found political unity at the expense of religious purity. This pursuit of "perpetual moderation" was signaled out as the error of the day. Through the political skill of James VI, the Scottish Kirk began to lose ground to the state across the early seventeenth century. In 1635 famine swept Scotland, followed shortly by two years of plague. Simultaneously, James's heir, Charles I, ordered the Scottish Parliament to bring the Kirk into greater unity with the English Church's government. Gone were the ruling elders, sessions, and presbyteries, and in their place was a full-fledged top-down system in which the people would answer to pastors appointed and overseen by bishops. This hierarchy stopped with the king. Then, in 1637, news arrived that Archbishop William Laud's English-style prayer book would be the new worship manual for Scottish churches. The Scots were less concerned by what it said than by what it meant. Harvests were small, sickness was everywhere, the people could not vote, the elders could not rule, and Christ was not king in his kirk. In their minds, such calamities were related. The time had come for a rebellion of the godly to reconstitute a Holy Scotland.[9]

## *The Covenanter Revolution of 1638*

There was no time like the Sabbath to start a rebellion, and that is what happened in Edinburgh's St. Giles Cathedral on July 23, 1637. When the service opened with the new liturgy, the common women in the front began to hurl footstools at the church official reading from the book. The footstools did not belong to the commoners but, rather, to the wealthy women who used them as props during long worship services. It was a visible sign that the riotous behavior underway would be no respecter of persons. The churchmen ran away, pummeled by an angry mob of Edinburgh commoners. Scotland had just begun a religious revolution.[10]

Behind the riot was a well-orchestrated coalition of Scottish leaders intent on resisting Charles I's increased efforts to consolidate power to himself by removing it from others. Ministers who led the Kirk's zealot wing joined moderate churchmen who resented English encroachments.

Lairds, Scotland's lesser nobility, had been inflamed since 1625, when Charles rashly attempted to consolidate their lands under his ownership. City and town leaders, called burghers, also joined. They remained infuriated at the Crown's interference with local elections in 1634. Charles had also intervened in the economics of Scottish trade, thereby alienating the merchant class. In fact, it was nearly impossible to find a social group he had not angered in his first decade of rule. Having sought to unify Scotland and England as kingdoms under his sole authority, Charles instead pulled off the nearly miraculous task of unifying Scotland's factions by becoming their common enemy.

Presbyterianism became Scotland's common banner. Meeting in a committee of the rebellious, leaders appointed a well-connected lawyer named Archibald Johnston of Wariston to compose a document that would bind the factions together in common cause. Wariston recalled the Scottish history of banding, a practice of social contracting that had religious as well as revolutionary implications. Banding had been outlawed as seditious by Parliament in 1585. After much wrangling in committee, Wariston's banding document was agreed upon and signed in February 1638 by representatives of the "Nobleman, Barons, Gentlemen, Burgesses, Ministers, and Commons." Everyone simply called it the National Covenant.[11]

The 1638 National Covenant signed Scotland over to God on behalf of its entire people. It therefore behooved leaders to gain all of Scotland's approval. Copies went out for signatures, and the masses subscribed by the tens of thousands. Towns doubled the signing ceremony with a communion service, as did the people of Perth. Many did so in tears, and there were scattered accounts of signing in blood. Kirk elders led their people in signing and, per Presbyterian doctrine, were not loathe to coerce the unwilling. One of the first acts of the ministers was to reinstate the meetings of the Presbyterian-styled General Assembly, which Crown officials labeled "most unlawful and disorderly." Across Scotland in 1638, revolution was revival.[12]

The National Covenant included dangerous language regarding the king, loyalty, and conscience rooted in federal theology. The signatories were persuaded that the "quietness and stability of our Religion and Kirk,. doth depend on the safety & good behavior of the King's Majesty." The king held that majesty so long as he served "the maintenance of the Kirk, and the ministration of Justice amongst us." Though the covenant declared fealty to Charles as long as he was the Christian monarch the Scots sought, implicit in the page's pregnant silence was a declaration that the Covenanters were the king's own rebels, so devoted to godly monarchy that they would rebel against the Crown itself if it failed the nation's God.[13]

Citizenship and Presbyterianism were dependent on one another, according to the National Covenant. It declared, "None shall be reputed as loyal and faithful subjects" who did not "give their Profession and make their profession of the said true religion." In addition to binding kings and citizens, the National Covenant also bound local magistrates to rule in a Christian manner. Sheriffs and other public officials were commanded to root out heretics. They also had to protect Holy Scotland from the corruption of sinful association with less Christian nations and ensure that her "laws, ancient privileges, offices and liberties" remained unsullied by the questionable religious practices of people such as the English. The overriding message was that protecting the purity of national religion was the obligation of both king and kirk.[14]

The National Covenant was a declaration of religious and political independence with implications for all of Europe. Calvinists celebrated it as a marriage of heaven and earthly realms, a moment of such historic importance that one poet predicted that "yeares from hence shall date their tyme / In Almanackes." Others were less laudatory, seeing the document for the rebellious instrument it was. In Ireland, the Lord Deputy Thomas Wentworth issued what became known as the Black Oath, a renunciation of the National Covenant. Long imprisonments and fines as high as £5,000 per person for refusing to swear the Black Oath led entire Scottish communities in Ulster to flee back to Scotland.[15]

The National Covenant sparked years of civil war in Britain, the execution of King Charles I and his Lord Deputy Wentworth, the rise of Oliver Cromwell, the violent uprising and then subduing of Ireland, a new and grander covenant, the rejection of both covenants, and conflict between religion and politics that would not find resolution for fifty years. None of this was visible in the heady religious fervor of 1638. In the tumultuous years immediately following the National Covenant things went remarkably well for God's chosen Scottish nation; in a series of conflicts called the Bishops' Wars, the Covenanter army successfully invaded England and forced a humiliating peace on the Crown.[16]

By the early 1640s, however, the Covenanter alliance had a new problem on its hands—running a country together. Factionalism threatened the movement nearly from the beginning, when fierce parliamentary debates erupted in 1640–41. Moderates feared the zealots' cherished practice of holding conventicles in the fields and private worship services in homes, carried over from the days on the political fringe. This division was masked again with the eruption of civil war to the south between the English Parliament and Charles I. Both sides jockeyed for Scotland's favor or, at the least, begged its neutrality. When the English parliamentary forces sent negotiators to form a civil alliance, they found that the Scots wanted a religious covenant as well as a political one. Chief among Scottish demands was a clear statement not just for Protestantism but for "true religion." English Protestants, even the Puritan zealots, tended to organize congregations independent of either bishop or presbytery. The Parliamentarians and Scots now encountered a dilemma. Both were Protestant, most were antibishop, and all had a strong religious zealot wing to appease. But the two groups of zealots, English Puritans and Scottish Covenanters, were not on the same page.

The English invited the Scots to send some of their most respected Presbyterian ministers to Westminster, where an assembly of divines was currently hammering out what an English reformed Protestant church would look like. The Covenanters sent a delegation of their most notable thinkers, including Samuel Rutherford and George Gillespie. The products of this convention, the *Westminster Confession of Faith* and its accompanying catechisms and worship and disciplinary directories, became the touchstone documents of orthodox Presbyterianism. These documents would not emerge until 1646.

## *The Presbyterian Empire of 1643*

The more immediate need was for political union, and the Scots would accept nothing less than another covenant to make both England and Scotland Presbyterian. Signed in 1643, the Solemn League and Covenant created, in theory, a British Presbyterian empire. The Scots reversed themselves. Where they had been against religious conformity when forced upon them from the south, now they were for it. Presbyterian unity, they stated, would bring "the peace and tranquility of Christian kingdoms and commonwealths." They also vowed to extirpate false religions, lest the one part of the nation suffer under the plagues brought on by the sins of the other. What Charles I sought to do to the Scots, Covenanters now sought to do to the English.[17]

More ambitiously, the Solemn League and Covenant sought to bring about Christ's reign in Scotland, England, and the world beyond the Isles forever. As Wariston told the Westminster Assembly, the Covenanters' ultimate purpose was to set "the Crown of Christ in this Island, to be propagat from Island to Continent. Until King Jesus be set down on his throne, with his scepter in his hand," all across Europe. Gillespie made these visions part of the apocalypse when he assured Parliament that the reign of Revelation's beast came to an end in 1643. The Scots pushed the case for pan-Presbyterian Britain with surprising effectiveness, won widespread support in the 1646 common council elections, and mounted a petition campaign asking Parliament to repress both Catholic and sectarian Protestant heresies. The Church of England was, for a short period, overtly Presbyterian. It continued to tolerate Independent congregations that were not allowed in Scotland, however, and in the long term, the English took implementing the Solemn League as lightly as the Scots took it seriously.[18]

Covenanter churchmen began to work out a theory of Presbyterian empire almost from the beginning. Of primary concern was how to establish God's church independent of the king's theoretical ability to corrupt it and how to justify the very real rebellion now going on against the king when he did so. Samuel Rutherford, the most prominent Covenanter theorist, addressed these issues in his 1644 *Lex, Rex,* which meant simply "The law, the king"—a tellingly heavy wordplay. Rutherford asserted that the king was underneath the law as all people were, simply because "all civil power is immediately from God in its root." Building on Buchanan's theories justifying overthrowing tyranny, Rutherford reasoned that if the king used civil law to violate God's law, he voided any obligation of obedience from the Christian people of the realm.[19]

Unlike John Locke and Thomas Hobbes, the era's other great political theorists, Rutherford vested the right to rule not with the people in general but with God's people specifically. The people who, by social contract, placed the king on his throne were the people who filled kirk pews on Sunday mornings. In this sense, the church raised up one of its own to govern in things civil, even while that person remained under the Kirk's spiritual authority. As Rutherford explained, "*Kings* are under the coactive power of *Christ's* keys of discipline and *Prophets* and *Pastors,* as Ambassadors of *Christ,* have the *keys of the kingdom of God.*" The church had the power to "open and let in believing Princes," as well as "to shut them out, if they rebel against *Christ.*" In theory the two sides were equal, since the magistrate could always jail a pastor if he violated some civil law—but that civic statute had to pass muster with kirk officials. For all their talk about the separate nature of the two kingdoms, church and state, Covenanters placed one kingdom squarely on top of the other. Covenanter two-kingdoms theology was, in effect, the Protestant version of Roman Catholic church–state doctrine; it simply replaced a pope with a presbytery, a point on which detractors were quick to pounce.[20]

Such ideas could quickly degenerate into theocracy, as they did when Rutherford's fellow divine George Gillespie argued that the magistrate was obligated to submit to the Kirk and to enforce its moral teachings in the civic sphere. According to Gillespie's popular 1646 tract *Aaron's Rod Blossoming*, the ideal model of government was Old Testament Israel, which he called the Jewish church. There, priests had been given great authority over the people—but politicians had not been given authority over Scriptural interpretation. Thus, Gillespie argued, "the Jewish church was formerly distinct from the Jewish state or Common-wealth." This Old Testament separation of church and state did not preclude interaction; rather, it encouraged it on the church's terms. Jesus sat as the supreme leader of two halves of the world, so both church and state answered to him. Yet the only way for the state to submit itself to Jesus's headship was to go through the church, thus solidifying its submission to spiritual authority.[21]

Covenanters also found tolerance intolerable. One divine thought the "absurdity" of governments "tolerating gross heresy" so foreign to religious reason that it bordered on insanity. The logic of Christian persecution was as old as Saint Augustine and held that heresy, like a wild animal, must be caged or killed for the safety of those who might become its prey. Rutherford, pen always at the ready, created one of the seventeenth century's most remarkable statements on the intersection of church, state, and individual freedom in his 1649 *A Free Disputation against Pretended Liberty of Conscience*. The book tellingly began with a quote from Psalm 119:45, "I will walk at Liberty, for I seek thy precepts." Liberty was tied directly to how morally one's life was lived. Thus freedom was interwoven intimately with tyranny. Covenanters condemned Catholicism's doctrinal domination not because it was tyrannical per se but because they did not think that it was biblical tyranny. Freedom from papal oppression did not mean that the English tendency to indulge in the "other extremity of wild toleration"—what Rutherford called the "abominable Liberty of conscience"—should be embraced. Just as the king did not have the right to rule outside of God's way, so, Rutherford insisted, individuals could not live "as if our conscience had a Prerogative Royal" to reject "the revealed will of God." Tolerance would put the individual's conscience in the role of "Rule, Umpire, Judge, Bible and his *God*." Where would it end? The proliferation of religious sects would lead to "many Religions, many faiths, many sundry Gospels in one Christian society." There was only one God, one faith, and one salvation. "Ergo," Rutherford insisted, "toleration is not of God." Toleration, another minister taught, was nothing more than "legal license,—openly and obstinately to pervert, contradict and revile the declarations of God" so long as one did not disturb the internal peace of the nation. How could this be, however, when God condemned sin in a society and brought judgment down on those who reviled him? Kings must "promote godliness in a politicke way by their sword." Too much tolerance was a national security issue for Christian governments.[22]

None of these theories, then, were in the least democratic. In fact, Covenanters held that democracy was either "ridiculous nonsense" or "absolute untruth." Place the masses in control of themselves, and they would inevitably fall prey to their sinful natures. It was not monarchy Covenanters feared but degenerate monarchy. A strong but immoral king would try to unseat Christ from his throne, but a strong and moral ruler would have the inclination to support God's law on earth along with the power to enforce it. A strong and upright Christian monarchy would, they explained, still benefit the common people by providing a stable environment to do business, raise a family, and worship God. One application of this was the Covenanter insistence on government salaries for pastors, which took on the air of a seventeenth-century civil rights argument. As early as 1646, Covenanter Thomas Edwards decried that maidservants, desperate for salvation, "out of their wages do allow so much yearly as five or six shillings to their Ministers." Many "poor godly persons" who endeavored to join English churches were turned away because of their poverty, while "persons of great rank and quality" could afford Puritan membership. Being served by a religious minister should be, Covenanters argued, a civil right independent of the ability to pay. Without a pastor provided for them by the government, the poor could lose their place at the communion table.[23]

Rutherford and Gillespie took these antidemocratic, antitoleration, two-kingdoms views into the decade-long Westminster Assembly's efforts to forge a pan-British Protestantism. The documents they produced had a short life in English religion but cast a long shadow over Presbyterianism in Scotland, Ireland, and America. These six publications included the *Confession of Faith*, catechisms for adults and children, the *Directory for the Public Worship of God*, a manual of Presbyterian governance, and an English translation of the book of Psalms built for singing, called a Psalter. These documents became the touchstones of Presbyterianism. They created a church sweeping in scope, covering every aspect of life from birth to death, integrating relationships local and national, and clarifying fine points of theology in language that shaped generations of Presbyterians.[24]

For contemporaries, the political implications of the Westminster documents created far more contentiousness than did the doctrinal. When the English Parliament printed the *Confession of Faith*, they left out chapters stating that churches could censure individuals and the sections stating that resisting a godly king, even in print, constituted rebellion against God. These assertions reflected Rutherford and Gillespie's earlier theories that the state played a role in restricting blasphemy and heresy at the church's direction. Furthermore, though the Westminster Assembly established a limited freedom of conscience for the individual, it did not extend to anything that contradicted the word of God. The individual did not have the right under "the pretense of Christian liberty" to "practice any sin, or cherish any lust." Liberty meant that the church and its people were free from oppressive, ungodly, or Catholic states as well as from any person or ruler who went too far with his or her own freedoms. In short, the *Confession* as the Covenanters understood it offered freedom to do the right thing without the freedom to be wrong.[25]

## *The Engagement Controversy and the Killing Time*

Neither the National Covenant nor the Solemn League and Covenant disavowed kingship in itself, only particular kings who would not subscribe to the covenants. Losing the war badly, Charles I surrendered to the Scots; he felt that they would treat him more fairly than the English parliamentary forces. He also pledged to swear allegiance to the Solemn League and Covenant on the condition that the Scots help him regain England and that no one be forced to subscribe to the covenants against his or her conscience. This threw the Covenanter factions into confusion. Many Scots felt that they had won. Charles was now a Covenanter king. They promptly turned south to invade England. These elements were called Engagers. Non-Engagers were less convinced of Charles's sincerity and were reticent to turn on their avowedly Presbyterian allies to the south.

The issue split the Covenanter alliance. The hard-liners had never made up more than one-third of the clergy, though their following among the commons was stronger. Moderates, whose allegiance to the covenants had always been motivated more by economic and class antagonisms than by religious zealotry, were happy to have the king on their side. The issue threatened to throw Scotland into its own civil war.[26]

It took an English Puritan, Oliver Cromwell, to reunite Covenanter Scotland. In 1649, after defeating the Engager army and overseeing the king's legal trial, the Cromwell-led Parliament beheaded the king. The Covenanters' goal had never been regicide; the point was to convert the king, not do away with him. Now a general whose most recent victory was against a Protestant Scottish army had executed a king committed to the covenants. When the heir to the throne, Charles II, swore the Solemn League and Covenant in 1650, Scottish factions united again in a Covenanter army that marched south to meet the English New Model Army. As one historian noted, this misnamed Third English Civil War was partially "a war of religion between the saints of a British Israel and Judah, fought over the reading of a Covenant which had bound them together." Cromwell's Puritans promptly crushed the Covenanter army at Dunbar and then at Worcester. By the end of 1651 Scotland was defenseless, and the Covenanter alliance was a mere puppet for parliamentary rule out of Westminster.[27]

In *Leviathan*, Thomas Hobbes surveyed the smoldering aftermath of more than a decade of religious war with unguarded disdain for the Scottish Presbyterians. The Wars of the Three Kingdoms saw civil violence on all sides, not least from the Covenanter forces. Scottish soldiers had somewhat routinely executed servants of opposing noblemen and "made a lamentable Slaughter of Women, Pedees, and Cook-boys" following armies they defeated. Hobbes believed that even Covenanter civilians committed atrocities, killing passing stragglers as "acceptable Sacrifices" to "the God of the Covenant." He blamed the religious zealotry of the Covenanters for starting it all, as "some men have pretended for their disobedience to their Sovereign, a new Covenant, made not with men, but with God." This was, Hobbes said, a pretense only the most fanatical could not see through. If the Scots created a national contract with God, he wondered, who had signed for God?[28]

Hobbes was not the only person weary of King Covenant's reign. During a decade of war, hard-liners pushed moderate ministers out of their local kirks. This move, known as the Remonstrance, looked hauntingly like interference in local affairs from distant Edinburgh. As the war years closed badly for the Scots, religious zealotry was wearing thin on many who stood to lose from continual antagonism with Cromwell's England. When Charles II successfully regained the throne in 1660, fears that the new king had been lukewarm in his allegiance to the Solemn League and Covenant were quickly proved correct. Charles began pushing hard-line ministers out of their pulpits in 1661, just as those zealots had done to their opponents a decade before. Bishops were restored to both kingdoms in 1662, as was the right of wealthy patrons to appoint the local kirk minister over the protests of the local congregation. The government declared it seditious to worship anywhere other than the local church, outlawing conventicles and house churches. Swearing the covenants was labeled treason. Owning a copy of the documents was banned. Nobles, wealthy supporters, and moderate ministers, whose loyalty had always been rooted in less religious causes, quickly disassociated from the coalition's zealous members. In ten years, the Covenanters had gone from ruling Scotland to running from it.

A measure of this change can be seen in the shifting usage of the term *Covenanter* in the early 1660s. Once a term of Scottish national unity, the word suddenly took on the mantle of religious extremism unmoored from sanity. Scots such as George Mackenzie saw Covenanters as "the mad-cap Zealots of this bigot Age." Archbishop James Sharp, who would later become a victim of Covenanter vigilante justice, dismissed humorously in 1661 rumors he was "an apostate covenanter," with the joke that "sure the next will be that I am turned phanatick & enemy to the King." To be a Covenanter, he knew, was to be a traitor and a terrorist. Labels such as "phanaticks" and "covenant-mongers" stuck in the public mind. Critics pointed out that Covenanters, no longer Reformation heroes, once gladly enslaved the consciences of unwilling Scots and Englishmen. For the next two decades, political and religious pressure pressed down on kirk members to renounce their former political religion. Surely, prevailing wisdom dictated, sustaining "phanatick" religion after decades of destruction served no purpose.[29]

Yet the covenants were perpetually binding, which complicated the process of renouncing them. Signatories of the Solemn League had explicitly bound "we and our posterity after us." Once a nation had been sworn over to God for eternity, the devout failed to see how it could be taken back. The Bible, many authors insisted, was riddled with covenants that obliged those who never took them down through the generations. Moses spoke to those who were unborn or minors when their parents left Egypt as if their parents' covenant was their own. Violation of a covenant of peace with the Gibeonites brought a plague to Israel even though the agreement was hundreds of years old. Obligations were also passed through the sacrament of baptism. Actions performed by parents in their representative capacity were considered virtually done by their child. Thus, when their parents' generation swore Scotland and England over to God, the children and future generations inherited this promise and the obligation of upholding a Christian, Presbyterian Britain.[30]

As they moved to the fringe of Scottish religious life, adherents to what became known as the Good Old Cause became conditionally British. If Scotland could not swear loyalty to the covenants, then Covenanters would reject loyalty to Scotland. Nearly thirty years removed from 1638, this strident adherence to an old and overthrown political arrangement struck the majority of Scots as odd and out of touch with modern political realities. Covenanters were the outlying elements of a best-forgotten idea that led to nothing but chaos, bigotry, religious tyranny, and war.[31]

Returning the "phanatick" genie back to the bottle proved difficult in some areas, however, especially the southwest Lowlands and across the Irish Sea in Ulster. The political strength and ideological heft of the Covenanter movement always sprang from its popular appeal in those areas. A visiting English bishop was startled by how well the common people knew their political theology. "We were indeed amazed," he remarked, "to see a poor commonality so capable to argue upon points of Government on the bounds to be set to the power of princes in matters of religion." Increased government efforts to lessen the power of kirk elders sparked resentment among the laity that eventually required military occupation to quell.[32]

Religious resistance took the form of secret church services. Called conventicles, these meetings often occurred in the countryside, with pike-wielding guards posted to warn of oncoming government soldiers. Thousands, and at times tens of thousands, of Scots attended. Crown officials rightly saw these meetings as subversive activities where armed religious radicals met in secret to discuss the faults of King Charles II's administration. Ministers of the covenants were known as "hill preachers" and wore masks to conceal their identities from government spies. Condemnation of ungodly politics emanating from Edinburgh and London was woven into the very fabric of their sermons. While preaching on the beast in the book of Daniel that subdued three kings, one minister taught that these were the three horns of Revelation's beast—"three of her horns, *England, Scotland,* and *Ireland,*" were bound to be sawed off for unrighteousness.[33]

Charles II, a king whose father had been beheaded by radical Puritans, was not prone to sit idly by as field-preaching Presbyterians denounced his reign and denied his power. Conventicles were outlawed across the three kingdoms as "Rendezvous of Rebellion." The Crown outlawed "the bearing of, and shooting with fire-arms" without a government license, as it was assumed that gatherings of armed locals could only lead to treason. The problem became more acute in 1666, when England went to war with the Netherlands. Since Dutch Protestants offered safe haven for Covenanter ministers, and since they were government outlaws anyway, many Covenanter students did their theological study there. Such treasons only exacerbated government angst. Fines were instated for nonattendance at the regular kirk meetings overseen by moderate ministers and bishops. Military units went out to the fields to arrest suspected participants, and laypeople complained that "three or four Redcoats have and may still dissipate Thousands" with their superior weaponry. When this did not work, soldiers were quartered in the homes of families who had signed the covenants, and fines were greatly increased. Eventually, the punishments assigned to conventiclers were indistinguishable from those for any seditious activity, including forfeiture of one-quarter of all possessions, loss of freedom, and exile.[34]

When they could not worship out of doors, Covenanter families gathered in small numbers in local homes, connected by a cell group structure to other followers. There, away from the watchful eyes of the law, they could sing the Psalms, read the Bible, and tell stories of the glorious past of a once Holy Scotland. Meeting together allowed Covenanters to encourage one another with the memory that they had once ruled Scotland: they should not be disheartened, as they would surely rule again. Their performance of political faith was crucial. By repeating weekly that the covenants applied to the kingdoms of the world, people who were unborn in 1638 and rarely traveled beyond their village came to believe it was so. The more times they met, the truer God's claim to Scotland became. The meetings' devotional activities were also remarkably egalitarian. The role of president rotated weekly among the men, and men and women of all ages were included in public reading of the Bible and popular religious texts. In these meetings, which came to be known as society meetings, kirk discipline was also handed out to keep the attendees' personal lives in line. Discipline was doubly important, as government spies attempted to infiltrate these seditious cell groups.[35]

Crown officials worried that these closed-door meetings fomented unrest and rebellion. Events in 1666 proved them right. That year, soldiers arrested a farmer in the town of Dalry, impounded his corn, and threatened to strip him naked and roast him alive. Four conventicler outlaws rescued the man, tied up the soldiers, and made their escape. Galvanized by these events, white-hot local anger with government officials boiled over into a full-fledged revolt called the Pentland Rising. Hundreds of commoners gathered with what poor arms they could acquire and prayed that the king would restore the covenants. Angered by fines for conventicles, bishops who forced pastors on local kirks, and a steadily worsening economic climate, the army swelled to 1,000 ill-fed, underarmed men. They marched on Edinburgh anyway. Predictably, government troops dispersed this Covenanter army quickly. Those not killed were exiled to the New World.

So began what one Crown official dubbed "those pains & distempers that hang round this little crazy turf of earth." Covenanters simply called this period the Killing Time. In the twenty-two years between 1666 and 1688, some 60,000 Covenanters experienced persecution, and upward of 5,000 were killed or executed. The most feared and reviled persecutor of the Covenanters had been one himself. The Earl of Lauderdale, a nobleman who signed the covenant but abandoned it when it no longer served him, became Charles II's most trusted Scottish adviser and harshly implemented the king's policies against religious subversion. One of Lauderdale's most effective strategies was to increase persecution and then offer a general pardon to any minister willing to re-enter the state church. Offers of indulgence in 1669 and again in 1672 brought more than 100 ministers out of exile and effectively stemmed the tide of rebellion.[36]

The Killing Time effectively decapitated the Covenanter movement. Ministers, wearied by years on the run from the law, gladly received the benefits of state salaries and pardon. Conventicle-goers, meanwhile, were forced to fall back on the society meetings, where they could hold religious memorials to Holy Scotland without the benefit of clergy. Many of the most famous martyrs were not clergymen but commoners. Women played an especially prominent role in sustaining Covenanter resistance. In 1674, after a petition was "offered in a tumultuous way by some Women" for the right to hear field preachers, Lauderdale informed the king that he had them imprisoned for "presenting a most insolent and seditious petition."

When Michael Bruce was imprisoned for his antigovernment preaching, a group of conventicle-going women plotted his attempted rescue. They also assisted famed Covenanter preacher Donald Cargill when he was nearly trapped in Queensferry; at least one woman was arrested for aiding and abetting his escape. In Irongay, when a moderate minister was appointed to the kirk against the people's wishes, a group of women hurled stones at him with such accuracy that his installation service had to be held away from his new church. The public face of the movement tended to be female, as evidenced when a group of drunken royalists created and mocked a Covenanter in effigy. The dummy was "an old hag having a covenant in her hand."[37]

The few ordained religious leaders left in the movement did create one final resurgence in the late 1670s. One minister compared the movement to one of the twelve tribes of Israel, Naphtali, the most fiercely independent of the Jewish people. Covenanters' fierce independence could border on terrorism, as it did in 1679, when a handful of laymen stumbled upon the traveling Archbishop James Sharp. They murdered him on the spot. Expecting retribution, many began to organize the illegal weaponry they had been hiding from government officials. A month later even supporters were surprised when around eighty Covenanters beat back a royal force at Drumclog. Following their seemingly miraculous victory, the rebels made a declaration at Rutherglen in which they decried the renunciation of the covenants, government appointees in the kirks, and, for good measure, being forced to celebrate the king's birthday. By summer, an 8,000-man Covenanter army had mustered for battle against the Crown. Gathering at Bothwell Bridge, the ministers began a three-week theological debate regarding the exact doctrinal positions their rebellion should endorse. Commoners grew weary of waiting, and by the time the Duke of Monmouth's 10,000-man government army arrived, the Scots army had shrunk by half. The inevitable slaughter of the last Covenanter army was laid at the hands of theological bickering over minutiae; such wrangling became part and parcel of the Covenanter legacy.[38]

After the Battle of Bothwell Bridge, Covenanters were on the run from the law. What was left of leadership fell to two ministers: Donald Cargill and Richard Cameron. Cargill, old and wounded in the battle, was released on the assumption that he would die. Cameron was young and had missed the battle while studying theology in Holland. He was anxious for martyrdom in the cause of Holy Scotland. Cameron amassed a small band of cavalry and foot soldiers and proceeded to ride across Scotland, preaching against the government at conventicles. In 1680 Cameron got his wish when his tiny band was cornered at Airds Moss. Cargill was executed the following year.

Before their deaths, Cameron and Cargill created two of the most important documents of the entire movement. The Queensferry Paper and the Sanquhar Declaration were public declarations of independence from the Stuart monarchs of Scotland. "We do declare," stated Queensferry, "that we shall set up over ourselves and over what God shall give us power of, government and governors according to the Word of God." Similarly declaring independence, Sanquhar was signed by "the representatives of the true Presbyterian kirk and the covenanted Nation of Scotland," which evidently comprised twenty of Cameron's soldiers. Both Cameron's and Cargill's treatises taught that Scotland was bound by the Solemn League and Covenant to overthrow the Stuart monarchy and re-establish a Presbyterian Britain. After the deaths of their ministers, the remaining laypeople officially organized their praying societies into more organized cell groups to oversee worship and discipline. These remaining Covenanters were thus dubbed the Society People. As cause of their official breaking away from the corrupted Scottish kirks, they simply cited the Sanquhar Declaration. From this point forward, many simply referred to the few remaining Covenanters as "Cameronians," after Sanquhar's author.[39]

In 1685, every person south of the River Tay was gathered by town and forced to renounce the covenants in the Oath of Abjuration. Anyone refusing was shot on the spot or exiled to New Jersey. The purge effectively outed those Scots who preferred keeping their Covenanter sympathies private. Whereas they might not actively pursue revolutionary activity, many pew-sitting kirk members were not willing to reject outright the covenants of their fathers and their nation. Examples abounded. John Semple, who "never carried Arms, nor gave the least Disturbance to Government," but whose conscience would not allow him to attend the state church, was shot while climbing out his window to avoid capture. The particularly hated Earl of Claverhouse shot John Brown in front of his wife and children. All told around 100 executions occurred. The last victim was a sixteen-year-old boy named George Wood; shot in 1688, he was born thirty years after the Solemn League and Covenant was signed. One of the last outlaw ministers was Alexander Shields. He published a tract, *A Hind Let Loose*, that became a classic devotional text for Covenanters. Shields pointed to the variety of biblical passages in which tyrant rulers eventually received God's judgment of death. No matter how long they might suffer in exile, the movement would one day reclaim Scotland's, England's, and the world's thrones for Jesus. Until then, like wild deer, they would be spiritually free even as they were physically hunted.[40]

## *The Politics of Peace in Christian Scotland*

In 1688 everything changed again. The Glorious Revolution placed an avowed Protestant on the throne, and suddenly it was no longer dangerous to be a Scottish Covenanter. The 1689 Act of Toleration granted freedom of worship to all Protestant sects. The next year, Presbyterianism was restored in Scotland, and the Presbyterian Kirk became the Church by law established. The system of patronage, giving nobles the ability to appoint local kirk preachers, was abolished. The General Synod still sat beneath the king's authority, but beyond this events looked very much like total victory for Protestant Scotland.

Radical Covenanters, once the heart of a popular religious revolution against tyrannical government interference in local affairs, were now out of step with Scotland's prevailing social and political times. The overwhelming majority of Scottish laypeople found toleration quite pleasant. Meanwhile, at the top of society, increasingly popular Enlightenment teachings about rationality called religious extremism into question. Presbyterian leaders, newly re-established in a place of national prominence, inherited a church whose reputation was built upon violence, zealotry, and rebellion. Yet this was a generation longing for peace and moderation. Looking back on the past century, it appeared that Covenanters had decried state tyranny while operating as spiritual tyrants. Most Presbyterians now tried desperately to recast their own history as one that protected civil rights by reasonable dissent and eschewed religious fanaticism as the relic of a bygone age. The covenants were whitewashed into acts of national pride and steps against foreign enslavement rather than an explicit handing over of the nation to a Puritanical God. The few thousand remaining Society People languished in ideological exile. One bemoaned how times had changed, noting that if the Covenanter heroes of old were to return to early eighteenth-century Scotland, "they would be reckoned *Fools and Mad-men*."[41]

Zealotry still lay dormant in many kirks, however, and by the 1730s it manifested itself in the newest—and ultimately most vibrant—Covenanter sect. In 1712 the British government reinstituted patronage, the power of wealthy noblemen to choose local pastors. Two decades of frustration with noble meddling in kirk affairs, combined with growing fears that moderates were watering down Calvinist teachings, led to a 1733 schism in the national church. The movement, known as the Secession, was led by a host of popular preachers. The most prominent was Ebenezer Erskine. The Seceders effectively combined the old Covenanter sensibility, which Erskine called "the practices of Mr. Samuel Rutherford," with the new evangelical consensus that emphasized conversion of the soul. Seceders preached in the emerging mold of evangelicalism, speaking without notes to show their earnestness and endeavoring to effect personal conversions. They also sought to convert the state. In 1742 groups of Seceders were renewing the covenants in public ceremony, and Erskine himself refused to take the Oath of Abjuration because it violated the Solemn League and Covenant.[42]

In another respect, Seceders significantly modified the political nature of Covenanter religion. From 1743 the most stalwart traditionalists in the group explicitly stated that they were not bound by the civil parts of the Scottish covenants. It was difficult, they said, to "blend civil and ecclesiastical matters in the oath of God, in renewing the Covenants." The Seceders' religious denomination, the Associate Presbytery, condemned "the *dangerous extreme,* that some have gone into," of condemning the present government when it failed the covenant test. What most concerned Seceders, however, was that such condemnations happened "even though they allow us the free exercise of our religion, and are not manifestly unhinging the Liberties of the Kingdom." Seceder ministers were far more content with the Glorious Revolution settlement than other Covenanters such as the cell groups housing the Cameronians. Seceders did believe that magistrates *should* "have by the Word of God and our Covenants" a professedly Presbyterian stance, but they were not willing to kick the hornet's nest if the test was failed. "We shall not give up ourselves to a detestable Indifferencey and Neutrality in the Cause of God," they avowed, and they actively prayed for it to be so. Still, neither would they take for granted the active toleration of the state.[43]

Seceders were the new Covenanters, rebranded and redirected but still determined to live out the Good Old Cause in a new Britain. Many laypeople on the fringe listened to Seceder and Cameronian ministers indiscriminately, which caused no end of jealousy between sect leaders. Such Covenanter sensibility was quickly evident in 1747, when a debate arose between Seceder ministers about the Burgher oath. Required of newly installed local officials in Scottish towns, the oath obliged them to "profess the true religion presently professed within this realm and authorized by the law thereof." Because it went on to forswear any allegiance to "the Roman papistry," many Seceders believed that they could take the oath in good conscience. In essence, they gave the words a meaning akin to condemning Catholicism and favoring the ideal of Presbyterianism. This group became known as the Burghers. The more literal-minded among them, however, believed that the oath implied allegiance to the very church from which they had just seceded. They could not take the oath in good faith. These Seceders became known as the Anti-Burghers. The dispute highlighted other internal fault lines in the group, including those ministers prone to toleration and those holding more antistatist sentiments. The more fanatical Anti-Burghers went so far as to excommunicate the less zealous Ebenezer Erskine, the founder of their own movement. The entire episode illustrated how seriously Covenanters of all stripes took political theology. Furthermore, when Seceders moved into Ireland and the American colonies, where no Burgher oath existed, they retained the split on the theoretical basis of what someone *would* swear *if* elected *in another* country.[44]

## *Covenanter Ireland*

One of those countries was Ireland, and each of the varieties of Covenanters made its way there. Where English Puritans colonized Massachusetts, Scottish Presbyterians first settled in Ulster, Ireland's northeast corner just across the Irish Sea from Scotland. The sea, over which one can see the coast of one island standing on the other's shore, served as a Presbyterian highway throughout history. Beginning in 1610, the Stuarts used a massive influx of Scottish settlers to the region to reform the cultural makeup of Ireland in hopes of making the island both more profitable and less hostile to English interests. The Scots brought their kirks with them, and in 1638 and again in 1643, thousands of colonists stepped forward to sign the covenants. Throughout the Killing Time, renegade preachers passed back and forth between the two realms to lead large conventicles and hold communion. The murderers of Archbishop Sharp fled to Ireland, and Covenanter ministers often hid out in Ulster to avoid capture by Crown forces.[45]

In Ulster, religious zeal and political radicalism intertwined eagerly in the seventeenth and eighteenth centuries. The Irish majority was out of power in church and state, since a minority of English settlers dominated the state-established Church of Ireland. Across the island, the native Catholic majority resented the economic and religious policies that kept them down. In the North, there were more Presbyterians than members of the Irish state church. Their status as a tolerated regional majority bred frustration among Ulster colonists. Their ire focused on the Test Clause of the Acts of Supremacy and Uniformity. This required Presbyterians to take communion in a state church in order to receive certain legal privileges. As dissenters, no Irish Presbyterian could vote or be buried in official burial grounds. Since their marriages occurred outside of the approved church, their children were considered legal bastards. This kept property inheritance rights in constant jeopardy. Resentment against English law and church were more acute in Ireland than anywhere else in the Atlantic Basin. One Irish Presbyterian called the Irish Test Clause a Presbyterian "Badge of Slavery." Thus the Covenanter mantle in Ireland fit more comfortably across many types of Presbyterians, who felt themselves pressed beneath a tyrannical state power through religious means.[46]

Covenanters protested state power in Ireland at every turn. Disrupting funeral processions was one common means of protesting the state's religious oppression. These events were, in the words of one state-supported minister, "so well known, that I presume it may pass for a received Truth." These protests were held at funerals officiated by state-approved clergymen as a means to protest the shortcomings of religious politics in Ireland. If Presbyterians could not have a peaceful, state-approved funeral at the end of a lifetime protected by civil rights, neither would anyone else.[47]

Against such extreme backdrops, state clergymen found that it was politically effective to cast all Presbyterians as secret Covenanters bound on rebelling against the king and oppressing the people in the name of religion. If given power in Ireland, Presbyterian opponent William Tisdall warned, all "Crown'd Heads are rather Vassals and Subjects," and "all the Laws of the Nation which they shall judge in any way relating to the kirk (and what Law can they not?)" would be nullified. Identical accusations were made against Irish Seceders. A moderate Presbyterian warned his neighbors that Seceders were filled with "antichristian tyranny" and sought to bind "the consciences of the people by a *Solemn League and Covenant*" that they would cram "down the Throats of all men and women in the nation, under most unchristian pains and penalties." Once in power, critics predicted, Covenanters would become the most Catholic of Protestants, demanding total conformity from all people to doctrines they arbitrarily defined. The twin tyrannies of popery and Presbyterianism had "proved the Source of all our national Calamities," and it was best to leave such religious dogmatism in the seventeenth century, where it belonged.[48]

Irish Presbyterian leaders sought to distance themselves from this image of extremism. Still, either despite or because of their reputation for holding persecuting principles, Covenanter and Seceder elements grew throughout Ireland inside and outside of regular congregations. Many congregations simply spawned from overgrown in-house praying societies Covenanters continued to use. One historian identified Seceders as the growth sector of Irish Presbyterianism. The laity were drawn to earthy, passionate preaching that emphasized the old Presbyterian doctrines, condemned the evils of British government, and called the realm to repent and turn to God. These messages caused Irish Seceder congregations to grow at the rate of one new congregation a year between 1740 and 1780, making them easily the fastest-growing sect on either island.[49]

This explosive growth led to government suspicion that rebellious sentiment was again afoot among the Presbyterian fringe. In 1743 many Seceders reswore the covenants; soon after, local congregations began to regularly swear smaller, congregational versions of the old documents. When leading Seceder minister Thomas Clark began preaching that he was in agreement with "the old Covenanters," his enemies arranged to coerce him into an oath of allegiance. This required kissing the Bible, which was forbidden by strict Presbyterians, and Clark was forced to pay a stiff fine when he attempted to take the oath by simply lifting his hand. In 1754 Clark was tipped off that a local magistrate and government soldiers would be attending his Sunday sermon. Premeditatively provocative, Clark preached on the prophet Jeremiah's message to Israel: God was against the nation because it turned away from its covenant. Clark was immediately arrested for sedition. He continued to perform his ministerial duties from behind bars, including officiating illegal weddings through the jail window.[50]

Government officials were right to be worried. As the eighteenth century wore on, Covenanters and Seceders helped drive violent revolts against noble privilege, taxation, and government magistrates. The last major agrarian revolt in Scotland occurred in 1724, when the Hebronite Covenanters took an active part in a Leveler riot. Anti-enclosure demonstrations literally leveled fences to resist the enclosure of free lands, but in 1724, the Hebronite participants tore down their fences "in the name of the Covenants." Across Ireland, two violent Leveling movements called the Oakboys and the Steelboys included Covenanter agitators and organizers. The Oakboys began militant displays, often in the dead of night in order to remain anonymous, in the early 1760s. The Steelboys continued the tradition into the 1770s–80s. Radical Presbyterian participation was an open secret in Ulster communities. The Seceder ministers near Strabane were forced to publish an appeal to their own people to cease and desist because the violence was getting out of hand. "Under pretense of redressing grievances," Covenanter laypeople were burning down houses, destroying the crops, and even putting "harmless and inoffensive cattle to agonizing tortures." Worse than cattle torture, some were using murder and the threat of death to exact "unlawful oaths" from their victims. In some instances, vigilantes forced people to swear allegiance to the Solemn League and Covenant. An Anglican rector in County Tyrone believed that the Oakboys were "the spawn of Scottish covenanters," and other locals called Steelboys "members of the Holy league and Covenant, commonly denominated Covenanters." Although Covenanters were not alone in these activities, their imprint on these violent, antielitist movements was unmistakable.[51]

## *Covenanters and Slavery*

In both Scotland and Ireland, antislavery activism constituted another unmistakable aspect of the Presbyterian fringe. Opposition to slavery is generally viewed as a late eighteenth- and early nineteenth-century response to the growing horrors of the Atlantic slave trade and the unfair advantage the slave economy held against free white workers. But over a century before and for much different reasons, seventeenth-century Covenanters belied these paradigms. Covenanters of all stripes held unique and long-standing articulations of antislavery thought rooted in their logic and theories of Christian nationhood.[52]

The earliest antislavery Covenanter was Scottish theorist Samuel Rutherford. In *Lex, Rex,* Rutherford taught that "Slavery of servants to Lords or Masters, such as were of old amongst the Jews, is not natural, but against nature." Despite its presence in the biblical text, slavery for Rutherford was a *malum natura* that was only valid if it was a punishment for sin. The "buying and selling of men; which is a miserable consequence of sin," created "a sort of death, when men are put to the toiling pains of the *hireling,*" to "*hew wood, and draw* water continually." This was contrary to the nature of humanity. People were made in God's image and therefore "can no more by nature's law be sold and bought than a religious and sacred thing dedicated to God." Tying slavery to the state tyranny he discussed in his critiques of Charles I, Rutherford claimed that "Every man by nature is a freeman born, that is, by nature no man comes out of the womb under any civil subjection to King, Prince, or Judge to master, captain, conqueror, teacher." This was the heart of seventeenth-century Scottish radicalism. Both the individual and the state had the natural right to obey God. Neither the individual nor the state had the natural right to offend God. Both were free to do right. Neither was free to do wrong.[53]

This early birth and long incubation of Covenanter antislavery thought sprang from a different font than that of later activists. Though Covenanters were not Lockean liberals, their early articulations of Scottish radicalism's antislavery were grounded in natural law. They were not biblically literalistic and needed not be. Seventeenth-century paradigms had not yet encountered the commonsense literalism used by nineteenth-century pro-slavery advocates. But Covenanters had long experience with the literalism of figures such as James VI/I. Such conservatives used biblical texts to support the autocratic rule of kings, and Whigs across the British Isles refused to concede this point. Rutherford, like those who followed him, was antislavery because of his distinctive approaches to antityranny and religious liberty. Covenanters perceived their greatest threats in Catholicism's power over its member and the state's attempt to make "perpetual Slaves" to "our *English Pope*."[54]

The early slavery Covenanters opposed, however, was no metaphorical flourish. It was real oppression tied to their own experiences. Bond slaves from Scotland and Ireland populated the American plantation labor force. Yet to encounter monolithic chattel race slavery, Covenanter notions of bondage arose out of a compilation of forms of coerced labor and man stealing. In the mid–seventeenth century, North African raiders stole people from English towns, city streets were swept to export vagrants, defeated Scottish Royalists and Irish Catholics were deported, and London "spirit rings" stole thousands and shipped them—without indenture contracts—to Barbados and Virginia. In 1660, there were more bond slaves in the British New World than chattel slaves. This number soon included those on the Presbyterian fringe. Many survivors of the 1679 Covenanter debacle at Bothwell Bridge were exiled to the plantations of Barbados. In 1685 those refusing to take the Oath of Abjuration renouncing the covenants were shipped to New Jersey. Another group of Covenanter convicts outside Charlestown, South Carolina, were wiped out in an Indian raid. During the Killing Time, when most coerced expatriations occurred, Alexander Shields merged the language of religious tyranny and slavery in discussing the struggles of Scottish zealots. Covenanters were, as all people, "free born, and are not contented slaves, emancipated to a stupid subjection to tyrants' absoluteness." Their abhorrence of a very real and personal slavery was colored by their ongoing ideological conflict with an adversarial state.[55]

Antislavery language became an effective weapon in the Covenanters' rhetorical battle against the evils of Britain. In 1743, though state persecution had long-since subsided, the Scottish Society People formed a new Reformed Presbytery in Scotland and later approved their overarching principles in the 1761 *Act, Declaration and Testimony*. This missive chastised Britain's "constitution of government," which deprived "unoffending men of liberty and property." Slavery epitomized tyranny, and any state that enforced tyranny over its people was not a "moral institution, to be recognized as God's ordinance." Covenanters carried these antislavery sentiments with them as they emigrated from Scotland to Ireland and from Ireland to the American colonies. No doubt Irish Covenanters agreed when their American brethren cited slavery "introduced into the American provinces by the English government, and left as an unholy legacy to the United States" as further proof of Britain's sinful rejection of the covenants.[56]

## *Conclusions*

Future Covenanter generations never really got over the memory of Holy Scotland or Presbyterian Britain. Those exiled to the New World and those who emigrated willingly later carried a belief that not just Scotland or Britain but every nation was under obligation to forge a covenant with the Divine. As the Bible foretold in Revelation 1 and Daniel 7, Christ was the prince of the kings of the earth. One day all nations would bow before him, they foretold. The ideal church–state arrangement should separate the two halves of God's kingdom but never sever the two's connection since both would ultimately answer to Jesus Christ. The magistrate, always faithfully present in his pew on Sunday and sitting beneath the discipline of the kirk elders, would know and enforce the laws of God through the sword of the state, thus instituting the laws of heaven on earth.[57]

Covenanters took this ideological baggage with them across the Atlantic. It was different from that carried by other evangelicals and Scotch-Irish. Embedded in their weekly small groups and intertwined cell societies was a cultural sensibility bent on conversion not just of the people but of their laws, especially church establishment and slavery. There they sustained the memory of a Holy Scotland their forefathers once ruled and the dream of a Covenant Nation they might rule again. Wherever they went in the Atlantic world, Covenanters remained evangelical for the soul of the state.[58]

# 2

# *The Failure to Found a Christian Nation*

*They are Christian lips which plead that "Religion has nothing to do with politics."*

—The Rev. John Mason's warning on the presidential election of 1800

COVENANTERS FAILED TO convince Americans to found a Christian nation. It was not for lack of trying. Along the way they managed to confront and offend some of the most prominent Founders. Roger Williams first articulated a doctrine of separation of church and state in reaction to their Solemn League and Covenant. Revival preachers such as Gilbert Tennent warned Christians to avoid their political heresies. Benjamin Franklin profited from, George Washington sued, Thomas Jefferson reviled, and John Adams blamed his presidential loss on the Covenanters. Meanwhile, despite being one of North America's smallest religious sects, they found their way into every major revolt. American Covenanters were God's rebels—just as likely to be Patriots fighting Britain as they were to be Paxton Boys fighting Pennsylvania, Green Mountain Boys fighting New York, and Whiskey Rebels fighting the federal government. In many ways, the Covenanters were the most important religious sect in American history that no one remembers today.

Covenanters put the limits of Christian nationalism on display in early America. From their attempts to disavow George II in 1743 to their insistence that the US Constitution was a deal with the devil, they discovered and decried the boundaries between religion and government. Indeed, no group in early America came so close to the modern conservative evangelical vision of church and state as did the Covenanters. They demanded a Christian nation that acknowledged God's authority and Christ's sovereignty. They taught that Jefferson's wall of separation was misunderstood as a tool for insulating the state from Christian influence under the guise of protecting the church. They explained the nation's moral waywardness by way of its political turning away from the Bible. They pressed for reform. They championed a strong, pro-Christian state with power over people's personal lives. In short, Covenanters maintained those older European views of religion and the state that other Americans rejected.

When Covenanters condemned what their fellow citizens lauded, the frustrated reactions of neighbors and politicians clearly indicated what would and would not be acceptable interactions of Christianity and the state in Early America. By distancing themselves from church hierarchies, rebelling against a Christian monarch, and establishing a godless constitution, generations of Americans thoroughly rejected Old World solutions for their new nation. While Covenanters helped to clarify the United States' position on the wall of separation, they were forced to choose between theological consistency with political alienation or compromise with inclusion. In the end, America changed the Covenanters far more than they changed the republic. Even so, the Covenanters never stopped repeating their central critique of its founding.

## *Early Colonial Covenanters*

Roger Williams first spoke of a "separation of church and state" while in London. Parliament had just signed the Solemn League and Covenant to gain Scottish cooperation. Against that backdrop Williams published *The Bloody Tenet of Persecution for Cause of Conscience,* in which he decried the oppressive Presbyterian "bloody beast" that empowered the civil magistrate to be "the suppressor of schismatics and heretics." This persecution, he believed, lay at the heart of the Anglo-Scottish union. Detesting the Covenanters, Williams actively sought to keep Rhode Island free from "the New chaines of the presbyterian Tyrants." He made it his mission in life to resist persecutions by the "*Pope* and *Prelates,* and of the *Scotch Presbyterians,* who would fire all the world."[1]

Williams was not alone in his efforts or his sentiments. Cromwell sent the colonies their first Covenanters in 1651. These 150 political exiles, captives from battles at Worcester and Dunbar, settled in Massachusetts and coastal Maine. The Killing Time precipitated another wave of Covenanter exiles. Between 1684 and 1685, 112 treasonous Covenanters were sent as indentured servants to New Jersey. At the same time, efforts to settle a Covenanter colony in the Carolina backcountry commenced; Lord Shaftsbury went so far as to revise the Fundamental Constitutions of Carolina to offer religious independence in order to induce their immigration. This caused the King's Advocate to worry that "the Carolina project encourages much our fanaticks." That encouragement was short-lived. Only seventeen of the New Jersey exiles ever came to own land in the New World. The Carolinian Covenanters fared worse. Settled in land between Charles Town and Native Americans as a protective barrier against invasion, most were slaughtered by Spanish and Native forces shortly after their arrival.[2]

Thus dispersed, Covenanters mixed in with other Scots and English settlers in early America, with contingents within the confines of most colonial Presbyterian congregations. New Jersey Presbyterians at Basking Ridge went so far as to require signing the Covenant as a condition for membership. Farther south in Monmouth County, Walter Ker was one of several New Jersey exiles worshiping in a motley assortment of Calvinist settlers. Ker led the Scottish faction that eventually broke away from the congregation to form a more authentically Presbyterian body. They chose as their minister evangelical scion John Tennent. Similar instances occurred throughout the mainland colonies. Even as more distinctly Covenanter groups began to pour in, many Presbyterian congregations retained elements of the old fringe wing, which arose from time to time in moments of confrontation.[3]

After 1700, like most immigrants from the northern British Isles, Covenanters settled predominantly in Pennsylvania, with pockets in New York and the Carolina backcountry. They tended to settle later, in less fruitful lands, bringing fewer assets than other Scots. This was possibly an effect of resource-sapping decades of conflict with the British Crown. Although they held to the most quintessentially Scottish religion in the New World, Covenanters' rigid beliefs set them apart from other Scots more than drew them near. They were a people who seemed to struggle with time as they lived simultaneously in America and in the memory of a Holy Scotland their neighbors were keen to forget. Scottish ethnicity also counted for less than might be expected in part because so few Covenanters had ever been there. Far more came to the American colonies from Ireland than from Scotland, and many referred to Ireland as home. Less than 5 percent of Reformed Presbyterian (RP) ministers in early America were Scottish; the overwhelming majority of ministers came from Ireland. Although contemporaries did occasionally refer to them as Scotch-Irish, far more commonly they differentiated themselves from other Scotch-Irish immigrants by using religious labels. They considered themselves Strict Presbyterians, Covenanters, Cameronians, Society People, Seceders, and followers of the Good Old Cause.[4]

Remaining different came at a price. Much as they had in Ireland, most Society People and Seceders were forced to meet without ministers. Local elders divided families into cell groups that oversaw teaching, psalm singing, and personal morality. Here they kept alive their vision as a distinct people, telling and retelling the stories of Holy Scotland's triumph in the days of Rutherford, its tragic fall at the hands of Cromwell and the Stuarts, and the faithful martyrs such as Cargill and Cameron. Lay-led congregations continued on without the sacraments of baptism and communion, however, until traveling Covenanter ministers might itinerate through their area. When this happened, they immediately recreated the conventicle atmosphere of earlier times, holding outdoor worship and days-long festivities. Another, less popular option was to join ranks with other Presbyterians, choosing the least objectionable minister from the various factions. These marriages of necessity usually lasted until a group gained enough numerical strength to call a pastor more to their liking. One such group founded near York, South Carolina managed to stay together fourteen years before breaking apart. They called their congregation simply "Catholic." Yet in most places that ecumenical spirit had already died when the fires of revival struck in the 1730s.[5]

## *The Great Awakening and the First Declaration of Independence in America*

Benjamin Franklin disliked the religious fanatics of Pennsylvania's backcountry, joking with friends that they were "Piss-brute-tarians," but he was elated when the controversies they created were good for business. The revivals of the 1730s and 1740s, later dubbed the Great Awakening, brought unprecedented numbers into colonial churches; they also divided preacher against preacher and congregant against congregant. Evangelical Calvinists led by Gilbert Tennent joined with New Englanders such as Jonathan Edwards and the enigmatic Englishman George Whitefield to create an epic fervor for conversion. Their large gatherings and often emotional preaching styles set off traditionalists, who preferred their religion orderly and communal rather than vibrant and personal. For decades, in print and pulpit, this antirevivalist faction warred against evangelical ministers for audiences. In no group did division happen so forcefully as among Presbyterians. American Presbyterianism, now firmly planted in Pennsylvania and New Jersey, was rent in twain for seventeen years, between 1741 and 1758. Through it all, Franklin the Deist printed accounts of the controversies for revivalists and antirevivalists alike at a handsome profit.[6]

Covenanters were part of these controversies but fit cleanly into neither camp. Of all Franklin's pamphlet war printings, only one involved a declaration of independence from King George and a vow to fight political and religious heretics with sword and musket. Covenanters had populated the Pennsylvania backcountry, where one English missionary noted they "receive(d) their Sacrament with a gun charg'd and drawn sword" and "profess they'd fight for Christ against civil Magistrates." Disgruntled evangelical minister Alexander Craighead led this group. No one personified the Covenanter reputation as "sowers of sedition" in America so much as Craighead. His grandfather had been one of the Presbyterians ejected from the church by Charles I in 1661, was trapped briefly in the Siege of Derry, and vociferously attacked the Test Act of 1704. His father died (literally) in the pulpit. This admixture of Covenanting sensibility and evangelical zeal passed to Alexander, who traveled with George Whitefield on an American preaching tour in 1739 and helped instigate a revival in 1740. Continuing the Covenanter habit of preaching in other ministers' parishes, he became the principle cause of the 1741 rupture in American Presbyterianism. Opponents charged Craighead in church court with preaching in another minister's territory. Although church trials were supposed to be matters for ministers and elders, at Craighead's the crowd grew so large that it filled a tent outside the church house. From there, the laity, most of whom had sworn the Solemn League and Covenant, "railed" against the presbytery members who came to try the case. Along with the Tennent brothers, Samuel Blair, and other notable evangelical Presbyterians, the Irishman was labeled a "New Light," was expelled from Presbyterian jurisdiction, and helped form the breakaway Presbytery of New Brunswick.[7]

It quickly became apparent to Craighead that the other evangelicals would not subscribe, as he did, to the Solemn League and Covenant. He withdrew again and joined forces with the Pennsylvania Society People, who were growing in number and desperate for a pastor. Early the next year, a justice of the peace reported that Craighead was preaching sermons on the continuing validity of the Covenants to his congregation in Middle Octorara, in Lancaster County, Pennsylvania. He called for the laity to rise in action against the corruptions of church and state. "Some say," Craighead taught, that reformation of the state "should begin with Persons in great Power, or it won't do." But nothing could be further from God's plan. Such impurities as Britain possessed must be boiled out from below by the common people's religious fire. This was just what had happened in 1638 and 1643 when their forefathers of all classes stepped forward en masse to sign the Scottish nation over to God's authority.[8]

By 1743, Pennsylvania Covenanters asserted their independence from King George and declared war on the heretical British Empire. Thirty-three years before Jefferson put pen to paper to do the same, backcountry Covenanters listed their grievances with the British monarchy and intent to defend their freedom at all costs. Unlike in 1776, however, their proclamation hearkened backward rather than forward. On the 100th anniversary of the Solemn League and Covenant, Craighead's congregants renewed their spiritual and political allegiance to a true Christian state by connecting themselves to earlier rebellions for Christ's crown and covenant. They invoked previous declarations of disobedience such as Rutherglen, Sanquhar, and Queensferry. They praised the bright lights of Covenanter history such as Rutherford, George Gillespie, and the martyrs of Bothwell Bridge and Airds Moss. Like those who went before, they refused to bow to "the apostate, perjured and blood-guilty Condition of church and state."[9]

Declaring it their duty "to separate ourselves from the corrupt Constitution of both Church and State," the Middle Octorara Covenanters drew swords and declared "a defensive *War* against all Usurpers of the Royal Prerogative of the glorious Lamb of God." They felt themselves bound by the Law of God and the Law of Nature to "defend our religious Liberties wherewith Christ has made us free, and our Bodies and Goods" by any means necessary. With horror they recounted the illegitimate rulers of the past, including Charles I, Oliver Cromwell, Charles II, James II, and William and Mary. Now, they testified against George I and II for, among a host of other sins, "their being established Head of the Church of the Laws of *England*."[10]

Covenanters also declared their independence from American Presbyterianism. Craighead labeled their treatise *The Declaration, Protestation, and Testimony of a Suffering Remnant of the Anti-Popish,*

*Anti-Lutheran, Anti-Prelatick, Anti-Erastian, Anti-Latitudinarian, Anti-Sectarian, True Presbyterian Church of Christ in America.* While not the pithiest title, it nicely summarized the Covenanters' desire for battle with all comers and their claim to maintain the true version of Presbyterianism. They were especially irked that their demands for God's standards were met with charges of bigotry by the "pretended Presbyterians Ministers" in America. They wondered how enforcing God's political standards could be anything other than good law. After all, they pointed out, most people saw nothing wrong with the civil magistrate enforcing laws against thievery, sexual sin, cursing, and Sabbath-breaking. Laws restricting such freedoms were part of God's moral order. With "Errors and Immorality over-spread both Church and State," it was "the Duty of a Christianized people" to act to defend that order against the permissive moral decay of their contemporary world.[11]

Through the early 1740s, Franklin kept the public apprised of these developments by publishing news stories in his *Pennsylvania Gazette* and a series of pamphlets by Craighead and his detractors. The antigovernment machinations of the Presbyterian fringe drew quick responses, most notably from the Crown. The governor was understandably concerned. In the last hundred years, Presbyterians had played a leading role in three uprisings against English authority; he did not want to oversee a fourth in Pennsylvania. Sending an envoy to the Presbyterian Synod meeting in Philadelphia, he asked for an official response to the mutinous statement from Octorara. The synod stopped all other business and immediately denounced Craighead's teachings as "full of treason, sedition, and distraction" that "destroy the civil and religious rights of mankind." Craighead's former evangelical allies turned on him. Gilbert Tennent condemned the "sordid Meanness" and "Views of Bigotry" of the Middle Octorara Declaration. Another New Light minister, Samuel Blair, accused Craighead of boiling the whole *Westminster Confession of Faith* down to a few words in the twentieth and twenty-third chapters relating to the civil magistrate.[12]

Craighead eventually moved with segments of his congregation to Virginia, where in quick order he was accused of having "taught and maintained treasonable positions," escaped an arrest warrant issued by the royal lieutenant governor, was reabsorbed into the Presbyterian church, and swore an oath of loyalty to the king so that he could buy a farm. He then moved to Mecklenburg, North Carolina. His self-serving backsliding notwithstanding, Craighead never relinquished his radical inclinations. It was there, just before his death in 1766, that another minister noted that "they had a *Solemn League and Covenant* teacher settled among them; that they were in general greatly averse to the Church of England, and that they looked upon a law lately enacted in the province for the better establishment of the Church as oppressive as the Stamp Act, and were determined to prevent its taking place there."[13]

Historians have spilled much ink attempting to determine what impact, if any, the Great Awakening had upon the American Revolution. Some scholars have argued that American revivalists learned languages of liberty and forged networks of cooperation that carried into the conflict with Parliament. Other historians disagree, emphasizing the decidedly spiritual nature of the Great Awakening and equally secular nature of the Revolution. The fringe element of Presbyterianism has been largely absent from these debates. Many on the Presbyterian fringe diverged from the Great Awakening not over the work of the Holy Spirit on the soul but, rather, because the revivals failed to convert the state. For them, the revival period certainly helped dredge up dormant antagonism to the British Crown, but it did not create that angst. It is true that the Great Awakening pierced "the façade of civility and deference that governed provincial life to usher in a new age of contentiousness," yet that incivility had always been part of Covenanter spirituality. For several generations of Atlantic Presbyterians in seventeenth-century Scotland and eighteenth-century Ireland and America, their entire religious culture consisted of exercises in political resistance and agitation. Whatever impact the revivals had on the Revolution, the Covenanters needed no such awakening of their political spirits to confront royal power.[14]

## *Paxton Boys and Patriots*

Conflicts with British authority dominated colonial politics in the 1760s and 1770s. As officials in London sought to reassert control over distant populations, colonial resistance to any loss of autonomy and liberty intensified in kind. For Covenanters, the confrontation with Britain was seen through a denominational prism: England's political overreach stemmed from its systematic religious corruption of the true state–church arrangement. They believed that any government that put George III in the throne of Jesus was bound to err. When it inevitably did, resistance was part of right religion.

In the midst of these increasing antagonisms, a new Covenanter minister arrived in the colonies. Even in an age of remarkable ministers who traveled vast distances to preach to disparate peoples, Scotsman John Cuthbertson was unique. His ministry spanned the forty years after his 1751 arrival, and he traversed a remarkable 70,000 miles in his preaching tours through at least seven colonies. It was Cuthbertson who oversaw the scattered Societies and encouraged their faith in the Good Old Cause. Cuthbertson was also skilled at winning converts. Not long after he arrived, the Presbytery of New-Castle warned against the "Doctrine maintain'd by Mr. Cuthbertson" that "all civil government, is immediately derived from Christ as Mediator." Cuthbertson found that there were also occasional debates among Society members as to just how rigorously the Covenants should be applied in this faraway colonial setting. He noted in his extensive diary that he had "Conversed with 4 persons concerning Testimonies, Government" in late 1753. The following Sunday he made sure to teach "concerning So[lemn] League."[15]

Cuthbertson's flock was at their most disruptive a decade later when they helped organize and lead the Paxton Boys revolt, taking up arms and marching on the colonial capital. In 1763 Scotch-Irish settlers in central Pennsylvania, whose pent-up demand for Indian land was kept in check by policies from Philadelphia and London, responded to recent Indian attacks by decimating the Susquehannock Indians living in the village of Conestoga Manor. This small tribe lived under the protection of the Quaker lawmakers who dominated the colonial legislature; they were both peaceful and Christian. Afterward, an even larger colonial force turned east and marched on Philadelphia to demand more land and military protection for the backcountry. They dispersed only after Benjamin Franklin assured them that their demands would be heard by the legislature—and news arrived that British General Thomas Gage had dispatched troops ready to battle the settler army.[16]

Unknown until the twenty-first century, the central leadership of the Paxton uprising included Covenanter elder and cell group leader William Brown. Along with fellow backcountrymen William Smith and James Gibson, Brown led the armed party to meet with government delegates. There they drew up their grievances, but at the last minute Brown refused to sign the petition. He demanded that his name, listed first among the leaders, be scratched out because the petition referred to them as "his Majesty's faithful and loyal Subjects." As a Covenanter, Brown would be called nothing of the sort. In Scotland's Killing Time, government men shot his grandfather without trial in front of the man's wife and children for refusing to swear an oath of allegiance. Raised in the shadow of that memory, the grandson had almost certainly been with the Covenanters of Middle Octorara in drawing swords and declaring religious independence. Now, Brown embodied that Covenanter identity by simultaneously leading Pennsylvania's most aggressive agrarian revolt and being too religiously uncompromising to come to terms with an ungodly government.[17]

The majority of those participating in the massacre came from Presbyterian congregations in Derry and Paxtang, from which the revolt took its name. Yet Cuthbertson's Newcastle Covenanters also joined—and influenced—the revolt. The minister's generally apolitical diary noted the "great confusion" in which his people were embroiled. Detractors pointed out as well that the Paxton Boys' actions embodied Covenanter logic. Pennsylvania's Quakers believed that "not only Covenanters, but the whole Body of Presbyterians" were "actuated by the same rebellious Principles" that caused the Paxton insurrection. They accused Pennsylvania Presbyterians of revering "a Book called *Hind let loose*" (the Covenanters' beloved text of martyrdom), which was "almost as sacred among them as the Confession of Faith." As always, Covenanters' small numbers belied their great importance in antigovernment actions.[18]

Covenanters were primed for a fight, and colonial politics were increasingly providing opportunities. The Paxton revolt was simply the first in a series of confrontations between American settlers and the British Empire that led to the American Revolution. Covenanters participated gladly. In 1767, Covenanters held a Holy Fair that included several days of praying, teaching, examination of personal piety, and the sacrament of communion. Given the heightened anti-British fervor of the moment, throughout the week Cuthbertson preached on the political obligations of Presbyterians. His selected texts reminded them that it was Moses who gave the true law of God, a legal foundation that would stand the test of time. But for most Americans, the ongoing battle with Britain was based in Lockean logic, which asserted that natural rights were derived from a state of nature rather than directly from God himself. That night, Cuthbertson noted in his diary that he "quarreled concerning natural law" with some of those in attendance. The following morning he pronounced an extended dialogue on Rutherford's logic of rebellion, in which natural law was predicated upon obeying God's law perfectly. Echoing the Middle Octorara Declaration, Cuthbertson proclaimed George III an invalid king because he denied God's covenant, prophesying that God would "cut off all wicked doers from the city of the LORD." Such sentiments did not go unnoticed. As the Stamp Act crisis intensified, one stamp commissioner in Pennsylvania bemoaned that American Presbyterians were as "averse to Kings, as they were in the days of Cromwell." Some, he noted, had begun "to cry out, *No King but Jesus*."[19]

The Covenanters also took a prominent role in another hotbed of Revolutionary activity—the Carolinas. Rumblings against royal authority began in North Carolina in the 1760s. One of the first conflicts emerged out of the Rocky River and Sugaw Creek Presbyterian churches in Mecklenburg. There, settlers sat beneath the preaching of the notorious Alexander Craighead until his death in 1766, absorbing his admonitions against uncovenanted royal authority. In part, this convinced many settlers not to apply to the North Carolina governor for land patents. When royal governor Arthur Dobbs subsequently attempted to evict Craighead's flock in 1764, things turned ugly. Armed farmers ejected Crown agents. In 1766 North Carolina's new royal governor, William Tryon, tried to send an Anglican minister into Mecklenburg to establish state religion. He refused to go. The county was fraught, he said, with dangerous dissenters, "particularly with Covenanters, Seceders, Ananbapists, and New Lights." The cleric did not deem such "disagreeable relations" safe for a minister of the Church of England.[20]

In 1768, backcountry North Carolinians began petitioning the colonial government for redress of political grievances, especially corrupt local officials and excessive taxation. They took up arms under the name Regulators, with the rallying cry to fight for "King Jesus." At the Battle of Alamance in 1771, Governor Tryon, despite being outnumbered two to one, crushed the rebellion's 2,000-man force and ended the first stage of the American Revolution. Regulator leader Hermon Husband, once an Anglican who converted to New Light Presbyterianism, did not fight, because he had even more recently become a Quaker. Husband proudly noted that the Regulators, not unlike himself, were made up "Promiscuously of all Sects." Promiscuously enough, Craighead's former Mecklenburg parishioners did participate in the Regulator agitations. Though their Presbyterian ministers all promised aid to the governor in quelling the rebellion, many of Craighead's former pupils defied their authority by organizing the "Black Boys" in 1771. Mirroring the Irish Whiteboys movement, they covered their faces in soot and went out at night to blow up ammunition wagons used by Governor Tryon's militia forces.[21]

In the early 1770s, a new wave of Society People arrived in the Carolina backcountry and immediately dove into Revolutionary activity. In 1770, in Ireland's County Antrim, the Earl of Donegall raised the rent on his estates. The Rev. William Martin, Covenanter minister of the Ballymoney congregation, took to his pulpit and decried the rise in rents as oppressive. He declared his willingness to leave for the New World with all who would go. Martin responded to offers from South Carolina officials to defray the cost of passage for "every poor free protestant" who was willing to settle in the backcountry. Together with 467 families packed into five ships, he arrived in Charles Town in 1772. In pursuit of cheap land and religious comity, most moved to Chester District, South Carolina, where they settled alongside hard-line Presbyterians recently arrived from the Octorara congregation. There, they found an ecumenical gathering of all stripes of Irish Presbyterians worshiping at a church they called "Catholic" and overseen by Presbyterian New Light minister William Richardson. The arrival of Martin, coupled with the scandalous death of Richardson (rumors flew that his wife had murdered him), gave Covenanters all the excuse they needed to form their own congregation committed to more rigorous political piety.[22]

The South Carolina Society People led by Martin and the North Carolina Presbyterians previously led by Craighead took a leading role in agitating against British power from the backcountry. In North Carolina, news arrived that Parliament's Port Bill had closed Boston Harbor and declared a state of rebellion. When North Carolina leaders met in New Bern to send delegates to the Continental Congress, they also called for the establishment of local organizing committees in each county. In response to those instructions, leaders from Mecklenburg met on May 31, 1775. Unexpectedly, they went beyond their instructions. The meeting declared that "all Laws and Commissions confirmed by, or derived from the Authority of the King or Parliament, are annulled and vacated," that the state charters were temporarily suspended, and that the Continental Congress was now the supreme legislature of America. When the royal governor saw the published resolves, he sent them to his superiors in Britain, noting that they "surpass all the horrid and treasonable publications that the inflammatory spirits of this continent have yet produced." Even fellow Patriot leaders observed that the Mecklenburg resolves had gotten out ahead of all the other committees, including the Congress itself.[23]

After the Revolution, a local legend sprang up that the resolves had, in fact, been the first American declaration of independence. Based first on memory and then on subsequent forgeries, the fraudulent documents emerged featuring a list of signatories that read like a roll call of Craighead's former parishioners. In fact, this was probably the basis for the list. The circus that surrounded the debunking of the myth need not minimize the very real nature of Mecklenburg County's political extremism, which significantly outpaced the rest of colonial sentiment. Historian J. C. D. Clark has argued that the authentic Mecklenburg resolves from May 31, like the Octorara covenant thirty years prior, were "more reminiscent of the Scots Conventions charge in 1689 that James II had 'forfaulted' the Crown than of the language of Jefferson's Declaration of Independence." This undoubtedly is the case. As they encountered conflict with Britain, it was not unusual for Americans to look backward rather than forward to explain their moment. For Covenanter-leaning Presbyterians, this meant looking back to seventeenth-century Scotland.[24]

Covenanter laity and ministers were active on the Patriot side of the War for Independence, but no sooner had they risen up against the king than they faced their old dilemma anew. Should the newly independent thirteen states swear the covenants? In Pennsylvania especially, a debate over the applicability of a Scottish and British covenant to an American circumstance raged for some time among the faithful. The exigencies of war did not allow it to be resolved. Cuthbertson served in a militia company during the conflict. He and other Covenanters got around their moral dilemma when he "beswore fidelity to the state" and instead "swore all[egiance]. to John Pat[erson]," the militia company commander. He immediately proceeded to baptize Paterson's son, just as he baptized the Revolution with the spirit of the Scottish covenants.[25]

Seceder congregations evidenced early doubts about the morality of the fight, as well. Early in 1777, John Adams wrote to his wife, Abigail, that he worshiped with the "Scotch Seceders" of Philadelphia. He noted that, based on the sermon text and message, the minister was obviously "a warm American" despite hailing from Scotland and retaining his thick brogue. Adams noticed some reticence among the laity but felt confident that "the minister will in a short time bring his People in to his Way of thinking, or they will bring him, to theirs—or else there will be a Separation." A large part of the congregation's hesitancy probably centered on the issue of covenants, specifically aligning with an uncovenanted Pennsylvania. Adams went on to note that the Seceder Presbytery's recently called fast day was "as orthodox in Politicks as it is pious, and zealous in point of Religion." The future president caught the fractious nature of the Presbyterian fringe succinctly. The Covenanter sensibility inserted religious zealotry into all political considerations.[26]

In the Carolinas, a host of other Covenanter and Seceder communities joined the rebellion. William Martin's Chester followers took part in backcountry resistance to the forces of Lord Cornwallis. After the slaughter of captured colonists at the Battle of the Waxhaws, Martin preached a sermon that placed the British atrocities within the context of the British state's historic oppressions in Scotland and Ireland. He specifically invoked the memories of Airds Moss, Bothwell Bridge, and the terrible conditions in Scottish prisons. When he was finished, the church raised two companies that fought throughout the southern campaigns. British troops burned Martin's church as a sedition house and took him prisoner. Perhaps spuriously, local memory recorded his confrontational episode with Lord Cornwallis, in which he proclaimed that the Declaration of Independence was merely a reiteration of Covenanter principles of resistance to tyrannical governments.[27]

As Patriot troops marched north to Saratoga in 1777, a unit under Col. Fye Bayley tarried an extra day in Salem, N.Y. They desired to hear the preaching of seditious Seceder minister Thomas Clark. After his famous imprisonment in Ireland, Clark had emigrated with his congregation in 1764, taking their rebellious religious tendencies with them. Clark and his flock actually participated in two revolutions during the 1770s. The first was against Britain, and the second was against New York State, both of which refused to recognize Vermont's independence. Largely because of New York's refusal to relinquish land claims there, Vermont was denied statehood throughout the Revolutionary conflict. Among the earliest advocates for double independence were Alexander Harvey and James Whitelaw, the agents for the Covenanter and Seceder towns of Barnet and Ryegate. Before joining the movement, they sought Clark's counsel. When, in 1781, sixteen towns from northeastern New York State revolted to join Vermont, Clark's congregants joined the fight. Armed and allied with the Green Mountain Boys, these twice-rebellious settlers finally achieved statehood and entrance into the Union in 1791.[28]

Even Canada was not immune to Covenanter agitations. In Nova Scotia, Covenanter and Seceder strongholds around Picou, Amherst, and Jolicure peopled the makeshift Patriot force that attempted to take Fort Cumberland and join the American colonists in 1776. Though repulsed by royal troops, British Major General Massey noted that extremist Irish Presbyterians in Canada had joined the rebels "almost to a man." All across the Atlantic seaboard, Covenanters saw Patriot activity as akin to Covenanter militancy in Scotland—godly resistance against a covenant-breaking nation.[29]

## *Old Religion for a New Republic: The Associate Reformed Union*

During and immediately after the war, Americans conceptualized their religious organizations anew. Major revivals, in part spawned by the conflict, broke out between 1778 and 1782. Every major denomination rewrote its constitution to reflect a status independent of European bodies. Five new denominations came into existence, many of which created new faith traditions altogether different from those in the Old World. By 1815, nearly one-third of backcountry New Englanders belonged to such radical Revolutionary sects as the Shakers, Free Will Baptists, and Universalists.[30]

Likewise, the American Revolution created a watershed moment for American Covenanters. Many wondered how an ancient Scottish assembly could bind posterity when the sitting Parliament in London could not bind the colonists. Breaking free from the orbit of Britain, the various American Covenanter sects were simultaneously pulled together by the gravitational attraction of their shared sensibility and repelled from other New World Calvinists by their distinct political theology. Propelled by war, independence, and a political culture that increasingly emphasized government's inherent corruption, the kinetic energy of revolution demanded some disruption of the old views on the union of church and state. Each Covenanter group had always maintained the validity of national covenants with God, but they diverged sharply on the sacred community's role in effecting and enforcing that national standard. Now the problem was more acute, and it was one that faced each sect equally. How could Covenanters define their faith in relation to something other than Britain's moral failure?

Tentative meetings for an American Covenanter union began in Pennsylvania as early as 1777. Representatives appeared from the three strands of Covenanting groups: RPs, Burgher Seceders, and Anti-Burgher Seceders. After easily agreeing on every other theological issue, they inevitably ran up against the concept of a Christian magistrate. It took another five years and twenty joint negotiations between ministers and laypeople to arrive at a workable compromise.[31]

The original proposal veered toward older understandings, specifically an equation of natural law with biblical law and an insistence that, though "the true religion is not absolutely needful of magistracy," it could be "when it is made by the people a consideration of government." In other words, a Christian people would certainly want to choose a Christian government, and such a choice was at all times to be desired. That language pleased the RPs but not the Seceders. A subsequent, Seceder-driven amendment suggested that religion was indispensable to good government but not required for government to be obeyed. This language equally displeased the RPs. By the 1780s, compromise language was finally reached. Using Seceder thinking, they agreed that civil government came from God in his creation but not from Christ as mediator. Government, however, was still a sibling to the church and subservient to its interests. Furthermore, "magistrates among Christians ought to be regulated by the general directory of the Word." Religious tests could, and by implication should, be instituted by a Christian people as a prerequisite for office. This position set the stage for a 1782 joint meeting of all parties, which resulted in the formation of the Associate Reformed (AR) Synod.[32]

A compromise on what to do with the *Westminster Confession* itself took another seventeen years to work out. That time allowed an influx of younger blood into the ministerial ranks, infusing a Seceder interpretation into the final product. In 1799, ARs essentially rewrote three sections of the *Confession* dealing with the role of Christian civil magistrates. This sorely tested their consensus. Their most shocking decision was to eliminate language that empowered Christian magistrates to suppress "all blasphemies and heresies," call church meetings, and otherwise intervene to establish worship. They replaced the old language with an insistence that a Christian nation would choose a Christian magistrate and that such magistrates should promote the Christian religion even at the cost of curtailing the printing of dangerous or heretical views. In protest against such softening, three Irish-born immigrant ministers rejected the synod's authority and took five congregations with them.[33]

Most adherents were happy, however, because the AR compromise helped make Covenanter theology relevant to the political realities of post-Revolutionary America. During and after the war, everyday Americans were making and remaking new governments. By the turn of the century sixteen states were created, and no less than twenty-one constitutions had been written and approved by popular referendums. Nowhere was this process more active than in Pennsylvania, where most Covenanters lived. There, the initial 1776 constitution birthed by far the most democratic and unwieldy of the new governments, causing a new constitution to be created in 1790. The Covenanter union helped Americanize the old faith and freed adherents to participate in such projects of state creation; the AR union was a functional compromise between the various sects' understandings with one another and with the needs of a peculiar religion in an even more peculiar historical moment. The RP position that the state should be explicitly Christian remained dogma, while the Seceder belief that such obligations did not preclude political participation guided practice. What the nation should do, only God's people could make it do. Covenanters of all persuasions wanted a voice in that sanctifying process.[34]

Deeply embedded in the AR compromise was an unresolved tension. What should the church do if Christian magistrates were not elected? More pressingly for some, what should Christians do if Christian magistrates created unjust laws? As one AR minister in the South preached to his congregation, it was the duty of Christian citizens in a republic to elect men of piety first and look at the issues second. If the laws these men made were good, they should be obeyed. But it was also the duty of those believers to disobey any law that contravened the commands of God. This was especially true for his hearers as it regarded South Carolina's slavery laws.[35]

Though popular, the AR union never achieved universal acceptance. RP William Martin, who was currently suspended from the ministry for his drinking problems, joined Seceder ministers James Clarkson and William Marshall in dissent. Both groups retrenched to their old identities and appealed to Scotland for help. RP David Faris believed that "the enthusiasm of the Revolutionary War, and the active part taken by the Covenanters in the army, turned the heads of many" from the Good Old Cause. Those who refused to enter into the AR Church faced stiff public opposition. They were denounced "as *dangerous citizens, enemies* of their country, and finally as *anti-government* men." They took solace by comparing such charges to those their forefathers once received in Scotland.[36]

Where there had been hope for just one, there were now four Covenanter sects in America. The newly formed ARs and remaining RPs and two variants of Seceders all maintained some level of adherence to the Good Old Cause. It still remained clear that they had more in common with one another than with other Presbyterians. In 1785, the General Assembly of the Presbyterian Church began a wide effort to unite the strands of

American Calvinism under one ecumenical roof. The ARs entered into these talks, along with Congregationalists in New England and the Dutch Reformed Church. A plan of cooperation was formed late that year, but largely due to issues of doctrine regarding civil government and the practice of psalm singing, the ARs balked. The outlying hard-liners in the RP and Seceder congregations were uninterested in participating.[37]

## *Confronting Washington and His Constitution*

In the years after the Revolution, Covenanters expressed American politics in words of religion even as they experienced it through the lens of class—specifically the greater class status of others. Their ire fell even on George Washington, whom they cast in the role of godless oppressor rather than providential deliverer. In 1784, fresh off his victorious Revolutionary career, Washington asserted rights to some of the most fruitful land west of the Allegheny Mountains between Raccoon Creek and Millers Run. Ironically, his claim to the land was rooted not in his campaigns against the British Crown but in service to it; his French and Indian War participation secured land grants from the royal government. Time, distance, and revolution forced Washington to act as an absentee landlord. Muddying the waters was a competing claim made earlier than Washington's, signed between Indian trader George Croghan and the Native tribes. The American Revolution temporarily halted attempts to resolve the dispute. While Washington led the Continental Army, Croghan began offering highly advantageous terms to recent immigrants to settle transmontane Pennsylvania.[38]

After the war, the general arrived to press his claim but found it inhabited by Seceder Presbyterians from Ireland, formerly Steelboys. They had fled to America after another absentee landlord, Lord Donegall, began charging exorbitant fees to renew land leases. With the collapse of the linen industry in the 1770s and increasing food prices, the poorest 30,000 Irish Protestants fled the island for America in just five years. Among those were the Seceder families of James and Samuel McBride and John and David Reed. They responded to Croghan's call to take western lands, believing that his Indian treaty gave him clear title. One of their first acts was to form a church. Calling themselves the Chartiers congregation, they employed the only Covenanter minister of any stripe west of the Appalachians, built a sanctuary and gristmill, and settled thirteen separate farms. To this small Seceder community, these were their legally bought and vastly improved homes. To Washington they were squatters.[39]

The two sides met in September 1784. Seceder families were represented by their kirk elders; Washington represented himself. They gathered in the home of David Reed, and the negotiations were overseen by John Reed, one of the Seceders and a justice of the peace. Washington was frustrated from the start. He arrived late on Saturday. As he noted in his diary, the delegation refused to meet with him, it "Being Sunday, and the People living on my Land, *apparently* very religious." On Monday, negotiations broke down when the Seceders refused to lease the land and Washington refused to sell it. Then, "after hearing a great deal of their hardships, their Religious principles which had brought them together as a society of Ceceders and [their] unwillingness to separate or remove," Washington made one final offer to rent them the nearly 3,000 acres in dispute. He had not been listening. The settlers tried to explain to the world's most prominent revolutionary that, in Ireland, a faraway aristocrat who knew not their land or their religion had exploited them. They would not tolerate Washington playing that role anew.[40]

These accusations of oppression, Washington told his war companion Henry Knox, "set me at defiance." Local tradition maintained that Washington cursed and was subsequently fined by John Reed in his office as the town's justice of the peace. Negotiations from that point were futile. Washington left and took the Seceder immigrants to court. Washington's attorney believed that the settlers' legal case was strong. They had a clear chain of custody from an earlier treaty than Washington's, and they had vastly improved the land since their arrival. So, using the Virginian's powerful connections, the lawyer arranged to have the case transferred to the Pennsylvania Supreme Court, which impaneled a sympathetic jury and found in favor of Washington the following year. He then congratulated the general on his victory. "You have now *thirteen* Plantations—some of them well improved," and those who had improved them were "now reduced to indigence." Noting the Covenanter reputation for agrarian violence, he subtly suggested that Washington agree to let them stay on through the harvest season, "otherwise the fences & even the buildings will probably be burn'd or otherwise destroyed." The nation's foremost hero heeded the advice, and the families left after the next harvest. Washington, meanwhile, was at his Mt. Vernon estate overseeing meetings. Those collaborations proved to be a critical first step in creating a new constitution that would bypass the unwieldy Articles of Confederation. While continuing his part as a free nation's Cincinnatus, to frontier Seceders Washington had just played the role of an American Lord Donegall.[41]

Suspicion of Washington's bona fides as a Christian leader only worsened after the release of the new Constitution. After a summer of anticipation, many Christians who read the proposed document got quite a shock. What was in the Constitution was interesting and worthy of debate, but what was missing was far more controversial. God was nowhere to be found. This was especially unexpected, since the Articles of Confederation the new document was to replace at least honored "the Great Governor of the World" and the various state constitutions all acknowledged God in some explicit way. To make matters worse, the Constitution's one mention of religion was to disqualify it as a test of office. One dissenting delegate, Luther Martin, explained scornfully that the Almighty had been left out of the document because too many members found "belief in the existence of a Deity, and of a state of future rewards and punishments" to be "unfashionable." Martin complained that the religious test issue passed by an overwhelming majority and "without much debate." He protested that in any "Christian country it would be at least decent to hold out some distinction between the professors of Christianity and downright infidelity or paganism."[42]

The actual debates of the Philadelphia Convention bore witness to the religious apathy that so appalled Martin. By June 28, the delegates had been stuck for weeks on the particularly thorny issue of representation. Benjamin Franklin encouraged a turn to prayer since, he reminded them, "except the Lord build the House they labour in vain that built it." What followed was powerfully telling about the convention members' conception of church and state. After procedural haggling about the appropriateness of the motion, Hugh Williamson of North Carolina rose to speak against it. Williamson, a former Presbyterian ministerial candidate, pointed out that the motion was pointless since "the Convention had no funds." Civic prayer, from the Old World establishmentarian perspective, required payment of clergy by the government. By never setting aside funds for religious support, the delegates had in effect taken a position on the inappropriateness of involving the government in religious exercise. Franklin later recalled that he failed to receive the support of more than three or four delegates. The motion died without so much as a vote. No prayer was prayed.[43]

Thus, the loudest and most forceful calls for a Christian America in 1788 and 1789 were made against the Constitution, not in favor of it. Many believed that Article VI, which disallowed religious tests for officeholders, was especially dangerous since it would allow nonbelievers to hold power. In North Carolina's ratification debate, Anti-Federalists who spoke against the Constitution warned "that Jews, Mahometans [Muslims], pagans, &c., may be elected" to offices as high as the presidency. Another delegate worried that this was "an invitation for Jews and pagans of every kind to come among us" and that such immigration might "endanger the character of the United states." Backcountry evangelicals were disproportionately Anti-Federalists. They feared the loss of their religious liberties, but they also feared the means of that loss: centralized power, standing armies, and coercive state structures. Evangelical churches became fertile organizing grounds for Anti-Federalists where church elders gave speeches railing against the evils of centralized power in the proposed non-Christian union.[44]

Evangelical Anti-Federalists made multiple attempts to insert God into the Constitution. In Virginia, efforts in April and May 1788 both failed to modify Article VI to require tests of belief "in one true God, who is the rewarder of the good, and punisher of the evil." Meanwhile, a Connecticut delegate moved to change the language of the preamble; he proposed following "We the People" with a ninety-five-word statement declaring the nation's dependence upon God's "universal providence and the authority of His laws." The motion, and all like it, failed to pass. Soon after ratification, a group of Presbyterian ministers wrote to the new president lauding his election and extolling the freedom from religious tests. But they bemoaned the lack of "some Explicit acknowledgement of the *only true God and Jesus Christ who he hath sent* inserted some where in the *Magna Charta* of our country." They hoped that Washington would help "restore true virtue, and the religion of *Jesus* to their deserved throne in our land."[45]

That Covenanters were avowed Anti-Federalists came as no surprise. In Pennsylvania, it was AR assemblyman William Findley who led the movement to stall a ratification convention in 1787. When he and other ethnically aligned Scotch-Irish Presbyterians lost that vote, they organized a walkout to break the quorum and prevent the setting of a date. The tactic failed; missing assemblymen were chased through Philadelphia's streets and corralled back into their seats by a mob. Findley successfully hid in an attic. When the ratification meeting did occur, Findley actively spoke and wrote against the Constitution. Along with his political ally John Smilie, Findley concluded Pennsylvania's ratification debate with the seditious suggestion that passage of the Constitution might require armed resistance and a new, breakaway nation. He wrote under the pen name "Hampden," the prominent English Puritan leader of the English Civil War.[46]

The most virulent attacks on the godless Constitution came from those RPs who never entered the AR union. As one hard-line Covenanter minister told Findley, Britain had at least established a bad church. The federal government did worse. It "was rather our Gov't establishing all religions." RPs considered this all the more reason to remain outside the AR union, with its failed hope that an uncovenanted America would be better than a once-covenanted Britain. The newly reestablished Reformed Presbytery testified against "all such as deny, that civil government is God's institution and ordaining." According to them, "We the People" alone could not legitimately create a government. They certainly should not create one that contained no religious tests, even that "acknowledgement of the being of a God, is essential to the being and constitution of a lawful magistrate."[47]

In the eyes of many Covenanters, the individual states failed the test of faithfulness as brilliantly as the new federal government did. On the eve of the Revolution nine of the fourteen mainland British colonies maintained religious establishments. By the war's end, only South Carolina, Maryland, Massachusetts, Vermont, Connecticut, and New Hampshire continued to provide state support for religion. Vermont attracted Covenanter and Seceder immigrants in part because its 1783 constitution allowed for town-based provision for those ministers whom two-thirds of the community agreed to support. For Covenanters and Seceders, clustered around the Scots-settled towns of Ryegate and Barnet, this proved especially appealing. The Seceder church of Barnet, Vermont, was co-owned by the town and the Associate Presbytery. Civic prosecutions for moral sins continued in towns such as these long after such procedures died out in most of Vermont. Support for such religious restrictions soon began to wane throughout the nation, however, and Maryland disestablished in 1785, with South Carolina following in 1790. Disestablishment came later in New England, beginning with Vermont in 1807, continuing with Connecticut in 1818, and ending with Massachusetts in 1833. These states' nominal church establishments generally failed to gain the approval of even the most generous Covenanters, who felt that they gave too little support for too broad a Protestant faith.[48]

Covenanters feared the tyrannical effects of this ungodly republic of churchless states on their communities. Their fears were realized quickly.

In 1791, the new federal government implemented an excise tax on liquor at the point of production, rather than the point of sale. American Covenanters, like all Scotch-Irish, participated in a hard-drinking culture. John Cuthbertson constantly marked whiskey purchases in his diary, and both he and William Martin were suspended at times from the ministry for their excessive fondness for the bottle. More important than its use as libation, however, whiskey helped overcome the scarcity of hard money on the frontier—a scarcity made worse by eastern elites' attempts to limit paper money. Whiskey began serving as a medium of exchange. Because the drink was easily transported and sold, it became the favored use of excess wheat production grown by western farmers where Covenanter populations were densest. The tax was resented by western farmers, who agitated by organizing in democratic clubs, refusing to cooperate with the government, and preventing other locals from paying by organizing mobs. In 1794 a 7,000-man rebellious army marched on Pittsburgh, from whence they promptly scattered after receiving news of an even larger force led by President Washington himself. This remains the only instance of a sitting president assuming command of soldiers in the field. The effects of such actions were decisive.[49]

The Whiskey Rebellion crisis was lengthened, however, when federal officials demanded that former participants commit to oaths of allegiance to obtain pardon. These oaths included the pledge to "solemnly promise henceforth to submit to the laws of the United States." Oaths were sacred things to Covenanters. They were part of religious worship, promises to the divine, and therefore should be "taken with the same religious care and fear" as the Solemn League and Covenant itself. Congressman and AR William Findley tried desperately to explain to Washington and Congress that this was Covenanter country; insisting on solemnized oaths would only inflame local sentiment. His suspicions proved correct. The main gathering point of the Whiskey Rebels had been the Mingo Creek Presbyterian Church. Although the Mingo Creek congregation was mainstream Presbyterian, many members were Irish immigrants with Seceder backgrounds. Another seedbed of the rebellion had been the Covenanter stronghold at the Forks of the Yough, where one of the democratic society meetings at the center of local agitations was held. Local activists included the McBride family, whom Washington had thrown off his land a decade before. They had subsequently moved to the nearby township of Clinton, where they began anew the process of clearing lands, building homes and whiskey stills, and founding a Seceder church. Now,

Washington again headed west to invade the little spot of prosperity and peace they had labored to create. Federal troops arrested James McBride in November 1794, the day before seizing his brother Samuel's still and twenty-five gallons of whiskey. For a second time, these Seceder families were forced to bow to the overarching tyranny of Washington and his godless government.[50]

Since part of the reticence to embrace peace in western Pennsylvania stemmed from the government's insistence on swearing submission to the United States, US commissioners attempted to allay these concerns by removing the offensive word *solemnly*. The AR Synod also urged peaceful resolution to the Whiskey agitation, but some of its congregants were unmoved. Of the roughly thirty "unrepentant rebels" forced to stand trial for treason, at least one belonged to an AR congregation. Years later, RP minister James R. Willson remembered "the Excise Insurrection" as being repressed by "the terrors of the laws of the United States." Such were the sentiments of many Covenanters in the Early Republic.[51]

## *Covenanters and the Election of 1800*

If the Covenanters had no love for Washington, it was his fellow Virginian Thomas Jefferson who perfectly embodied their twin hatreds: slaveholding and godlessness. Jefferson's core constituencies in the 1800 presidential election were backcountry farmers and Anti-Federalists. Covenanters, despite their Anti-Federalist leanings and backcountry settlements, generally despised him. They complained that, in his *Notes on the State of Virginia*, Jefferson doubted biblical creation, suggested that immoral people could be good elected officials, and corrupted youth with secular reasoning. As one North Carolina RP summarized Covenanter sentiment later, Jefferson believed that "there never was a [flood of Noah]—that it was no injury to civil society whether we believed in one God or twenty Gods—that the languages of the Indians of North American are more ancient than the Mosaic account of the creation—that the classical writers of Pagan Greece and Rome are books more proper to put in the hands of youth than the holy scriptures." Such views did not endear Jefferson to those on the Presbyterian fringe.[52]

The election of 1800 remains one of America's most brutal public political campaigns. True to form, it was Calvinists at the fringe leading the assaults against Jefferson's religion. The chief instigators were Matthew Linn, a Dutch Reformed pastor in New York, and John Mason, pastor of the New York AR congregation. Linn asked Christian voters to consider whether choosing "an enemy of the religion of Christ, in a Christian nation, would be an awful symptom of the degeneracy of that nation" that constituted an act of "rebellion against God." His popular tract received a vehement reply from future senator and governor of New York DeWitt Clinton, who accused Linn of demanding that Jefferson subscribe to a particular creed "exacted from him by an unauthorized body of men," the clergy, "as a necessary passport for office." Such religious radicals, Clinton suggested, would institutionalize their religion over the American people.[53]

Mason rushed to Linn's defense, reiterating the anti-Jeffersonian screeds against godless politics. If they elected Jefferson, he warned, Americans "would declare, by a solemn national act, that there is no more religion in your collective character, than in your written Constitution." American Christians, Mason argued, were under a mistaken conviction that the church should not meddle in affairs of state. Too many people asked, "Why mingle religion with question of policy?" Jefferson himself provided the answer to this rhetorical question, Mason pointed out, when he argued that the belief or unbelief of a neighbor did him no personal harm and was therefore outside the bounds of government interference. If put into practice, the Virginian's famous assertion would restrict state governments from curtailing anti-Christian messages or heresies in the public square. A person could "trumpet Atheism from New Hampshire to Georgia" and, under Jefferson's leadership, never be stopped.[54]

Mason's larger condemnation was not of Jefferson but of Jeffersonian America. Religious toleration was becoming a cloak for atheism, and the Constitution's silence on God was ushering in an era of godlessness. It was not secularists, he observed, but "Christian lips which plead that Religion has nothing to do with politics." Such thinking, Mason argued, was as wrong as it was popular. The Scriptures commanded that believers should acknowledge God in all that they did, including their civic lives. "Yet religion has nothing to do with politics," most citizens were exclaiming. "Most astonishing!" yelled Mason, challenging American Christians to point to any other area of their lives where Christian theology did not matter. In business,

Covenanter sessions regulated against dishonesty and ill-gotten gain. In marriage, God's laws reigned supreme. Every aspect of life in Christian communities should be governed by Christian principles. What did it say about Americans, then, if their leaders were such infidels? Condensing Covenanter political theology, Mason argued that the civil magistrate was God's officer—protector of the Sabbath and supporter of the church. The federal Constitution had failed on these fronts and thus failed America's Christian people. It was up to people of faith to avert God's vengeance by electing Christian rulers and instituting Christian laws. To do otherwise would portend the coming judgment of God.[55]

If Covenanters disliked Jefferson, the Virginian returned the sentiment. He saw all Presbyterians as inveterate Covenanters. The mere fact that Pennsylvania, "the cradle of toleration and freedom," was experiencing "a threatening cloud of fanaticism" was shocking, he reported to Thomas Cooper: "This must be owing to the growth of Presbyterianism." True Presbyterians were "like Jesuits," Jefferson believed, and their "ambition and tyranny would tolerate no rival if they had power." History, specifically Scotland's from 1638 to 1662, had already proved Jefferson right.[56]

John Adams hated Covenanters as much as his opponent did. After losing the presidential election, Adams blamed his political fate on the same Covenanter imagery that Jefferson abhorred. Responding to critiques about Jefferson's lack of religion, Democratic-Republican newspapers had cast Adams as a domineering king in the making. They made much of the second president's issuance of a national day of fasting and the forthcoming Plan of Union between Adams's Congregationalists and American Presbyterians. By playing on Americans' fears of religious absolutists, he claimed, they "turned me out of office." There was, Adams argued, a "general suspicion prevailing that the Presbyterian Church was ambitious and aimed at an establishment as a national church," and he believed that he had been tarred with that brush. The Presbyterians themselves were accused of such machinations precisely because their opponents assumed that so many secretly maintained Covenanter sensibilities with designs on national dominance. Adams believed that the majority of Americans, terrified of Scotland's reputation for religious tyranny, would vote for "even atheists, rather than a Presbyterian President."[57]

## *Covenanters and Christian America*

Covenanters in early America were short on numbers, but they cast a long shadow over the church–state debates in the colonial and Revolutionary eras. They advocated explicitly Christian visions of political society precisely as generations of Americans began distancing themselves from religious authority. From Roger Williams's angst-ridden call for separating colonial church and state to their combative role in the new nation, Covenanters spurred Americans to protect themselves from religion in government. The nation's most famous Founders explicitly rejected such establishment of churches as counter to the experiment in new government that was the United States. Meanwhile, a generation of Covenanters reforged the Presbyterian fringe by organizing the AR Synod and repopulating the Seceder and RP churches with fresh immigrants from Scotland and Ireland. Despite internal varieties, they represented to other citizens a consistent, best-left-in-the-past hard line on public morality that led to a new popular moniker—"bigoted Scotchmen." The specter of Holy Scotland terrified Americans, who knew all too well what a Covenanter America would look like. Covenanter calls for a Christian America went unheeded, therefore, but not unheard. As the nation moved into the new century, the increasing reach of the federal government, the decadence of economic boom times, and the growing power of the southern states came to make Covenanter messages on sin and slavery seem increasingly relevant.[58]

# 3

# *Confronting the Godless Government*

*Atheists, Deists, Jews, Pagans and Profane men, of the most abandoned manners, are as eligible to hold office by the United States constitution as men fearing God.*

—JAMES RENWICK WILLSON, preaching before the New York State Legislature, 1832

COVENANTERS' INITIAL EFFORTS to clarify what was wrong with the Constitution were not well received. Covenanters reviled Founders such as Washington and Jefferson while Americans were busy learning to revere them; the reception to calls for national conversion was unsurprisingly cool when some on the Presbyterian fringe began to insist that these Revolutionary lights were dwelling in the everlasting fires of perdition. Slightly more effective were causes focused on creating a Christian people. For the first thirty years of the nineteenth century, Covenanters joined other religious Americans in a variety of efforts to sanctify culture with Christ. These included converting nonbelievers, warring with apostate Britain, and enforcing Sabbath laws. Though these activities put them in partnership with the emerging reformers of American society, Covenanters still failed to convince fellow moralists that the people's fallen ethics flowed from defects in the Constitution. This was hardly surprising, for as they preached conversion to the masses and rushed headlong to defend the United States in the War of 1812, Covenanters simultaneously taught that George Washington was dining in hell. This was not a message built for success in the dynamic and patriotic era of the early republic. Their limited successes and overwhelming failures caused new generations of Covenanters to seek out ways to make their religion relevant in a hostile climate. More importantly, Covenanters served as an unwelcome anchor on the emerging rhetoric for the Christian nationalism of figures such as Lyman Beecher and Ezra Stiles Ely. Suspicion of

Covenanter-styled intolerance tainted other calls for a Christian America and a Christian party in American politics.

## *Colliding with the Constitution*

Covenanters began to collide with the US Constitution in the Early Republic over the issue of oaths. Many hard-liners, imitating their Anti-Burgher ancestors, refused to swear an oath implying support of an ungodly government. This precluded them from taking oaths of citizenship and serving on juries. The position against serving on juries in the United States and swearing oaths in court was solidified in 1806 by an act of the Reformed Presbytery, although there was far from universal agreement on how such prohibitions applied. Division among Reformed Presbyterians (RPs) occurred in 1816 in the Chester and Fairfield districts of South Carolina over whether oaths to local governments fell beneath the federal prohibition. South Carolina's Associate Reformed Presbyterians (ARs) similarly struggled with the morality surrounding oaths of allegiance. South Carolina saw such contentiousness because it was a slave state, and Covenanter ministers reasoned that an oath to apply the state's laws was tantamount to upholding slavery. This refusal to participate brought the attention of the government. In 1823 the five-judge Constitutional Court of South Carolina ruled unanimously that York County Covenanters could not avoid serving on juries because of religious scruples with the state.[1]

As Americans came to increasingly celebrate the Constitution and idolize its authors, Covenanters were forced to clarify just what made the American Magna Carta so unacceptable. They hoped that the turn of the century would prove an auspicious moment for their message, as the election of Jefferson had already caused many Christian leaders to question the nation's faithfulness. Federalist ministers such as Charlestown's Jedidiah Morse and Yale president Timothy Dwight led outcries against the "national sin" of Jefferson's election. As states such as Vermont dropped their establishment clauses, other voices followed Morse's and Dwight's lead in decrying that "we have almost ceased to be a Christian nation."[2]

The Reformed Presbytery, its churches strengthened by immigration and its ministry repopulated by Scottish and Irish ministers, attempted to capitalize on Christians' angst by stating definitively the problems of godless government. The United States' open affronts to God's law, RPs warned, "perhaps exceed, anything that has ever been attempted in any country professing Christianity." During their 1795 annual meeting in North Carolina, RPs called for a day of public fasting over the nation's sins. Leaders were atheists. The Sabbath was more disregarded in America than in any Western country. Slavery continued strong. Even Catholic nations observed God's commandments more closely. All Americans shared in this shame, they insisted, as "Rulers seem to have no idea, nor ruled any desire, that civil power should be morally qualified." This mistake started with the Constitution. At Philadelphia, the nation's leaders made "poor improvement of the noble opportunity they enjoyed of setting up a good moral civil constitution." By 1807, the RPs codified religious dissent into their testimony and membership requirements. They stated in an official document that there were "moral evils essential to the constitution of the United States, which render it necessary to refuse allegiance to the whole system."[3]

Founding the nation on the authority of "We the People" represented, the RPs maintained, a flaw in Revolutionary logic: it removed Christ from his rightful place above the state. The US Constitution was a "manifest dethroning of the Lord and his Anointed from the government."[4] As mediator between God and all humankind, Jesus gave legitimacy to civil governments. Governments, in turn, acted to bring people to knowledge of God's goodness and law. Law, then, should be based on God's word even when that law seemed too harsh for liberal American sentiments. As one minister taught, "even the execution of fierce judgments is salutary, for when the judgment of God is in the earth, the inhabitants of the world will earn righteousness." Americans had forgone God's standards in favor of universal tolerance, which Covenanters found abhorrent and unscriptural.[5]

If God's way was moral tyranny, so be it. The logic was simple: either people were obligated to obey God, or they were not. If so, there was nothing like a right to defy God's commands. "This in modern style may be called persecution," they admitted: "So the government of God may be called tyranny. No matter." The American emphasis on freedom of religion, Covenanters insisted, simply created a breeding ground of heresy. As Vermont Covenanter Thomas Goodwillie explained, "Any kind of religion is better for a nation than atheism." Covenanters emphatically called for the establishment of a national religion, pointing to ancient Israel, where priests were supported through tithes collected by magistrates. In contrast, the federal government remained neutral on religion, while state constitutions were "nests for almost any uncleanness" whose effect was to "protect every enemy of God and his Christ."[6]

The Covenanter position was most thoroughly developed by Alexander McLeod, pastor of the New York RP Church. Well connected to the state's leading thinkers, McLeod impressed on delegates at the state's constitutional revision session of 1801 the need to acknowledge God's authority. Thus the New York constitution began: "We the people of State of New York, acknowledging with gratitude the grace and benevolence of God in permitting us to make choice of our form of government, do establish this constitution." Raised in a prominent Presbyterian family in Scotland and a later convert to Covenanting, McLeod possessed the intellectual refinement and well-heeled connections many of his peers lacked. He was thus perfectly suited to explain the distinctive nature of Covenanter thought in the Early Republic.[7]

Alexander McLeod carefully expounded on American Covenanter political theology in his 1804 pamphlet, *Messiah, Governor of the Nations of the Earth*, an exposition of the book of Revelation. McLeod situated Christians in a millennial present. The judgments of God in that mysterious book were less about the future than about the now—it was a prophecy for the nations to seek salvation or destruction. God's authority over the earth was given to Jesus, who ruled both Christian and pagan nations and directed them to his coming glory. According to McLeod, the United States should heed this warning by acknowledging Jesus as the governor of the nation and Christianity as the national religion.[8]

McLeod took direct aim at the widespread American consensus on the separation of church and state. American leaders "in press and pulpit" had set up the separation of church and state as the only sure means of protecting both. But such assertions, McLeod argued, mistook Jesus's teaching that his kingdom was not *of* this world to mean that it was not *in* the world. "To pretend ignorance" of the church, as the Constitution did, was "hypocrisy in the rulers of a land enjoying the light of the gospel." It was impossible, he asserted, to create laws for a Christian people as if Christianity did not exist. Even if it were attempted, avoiding submission to God was "direct rebellion against the authority of God." Furthermore, declaring neutrality on issues of morality was tantamount to siding with error. The US government gave as much support to "the Mahometan and the atheist" as it did to the religion of Jesus. To put Christianity in the same legal category as Islam and disbelief was to undermine God's dignity. No such nation could rightfully call itself Christian, regardless of what its people did on Sunday.[9]

On a more popular level, McLeod's good friend Samuel Wylie also explained Covenanter theology to churchgoing Americans. Wylie was an Irishman educated at the University of Glasgow. Forced to flee British officials for his antigovernment activity with the United Irishmen, he became an RP pastor and later a professor of Latin and Greek at the fledgling University of Pennsylvania. Wylie's educational achievements were on par with McLeod's, but he reached a broader—and often bawdier—audience in his two 1803 publications, *The Obligation of Covenants* and *The Two Sons of Oil.*

Wylie set out to explain to the common man how seventeenth-century Scottish covenants could apply to nineteenth-century Americans. Those covenants, he pointed out, had not been made to any particular government but, rather, to God himself *about* government. "His government," Wylie maintained, "cannot be dissolved." Since the obligation was to God himself, tolerance was of little value to Covenanters. Wylie admitted that the sacredness of individual conscience was "with the present generation, a very popular doctrine. . . . The man who denies it is accounted an enemy to society." Nonetheless, Covenanters maintained, "men have no right to worship God, any other way than he himself has prescribed, and that every deviation thereof, is a violation of his law, and rebellion against his sovereign majesty." Thus, in "things civil as well as religious," the only unerring rule was the word of God. The covenants were commitments to that unchanging rule.[10]

Wylie's *Two Sons of Oil* detailed Covenanter political theology, taking its title from a prophecy in Zechariah in which two anointed lampstands filled with oil were appointed to "stand by the Lord of the whole earth." These "sons of oil," as Wylie interpreted the vision, were the church and the state; they shone God's light through the spiritual and civic arenas. Wylie took pains to show how these two institutions were separate but mutually beneficial. The state could remove impediments to the spread of the Gospel and keep social chaos at bay. The church, meanwhile, had an ameliorating effect on the character of the people and thus encouraged order and national prosperity. Civil government, according to Wylie, sprang from neither a Hobbesian chaos of the fall nor a Lockean will of the people. Rather, government was the institution of God. Its goal, as the *Westminster Confession* taught the end of all creation to be, was the glory of God. A Christian government would acknowledge God, set up biblical laws, support and defend the church, and create a livable moral order for all. To any such government, Covenanters would gladly submit.[11]

Neither the leaders nor the framework of America made up a Christian government, Wylie explained; in fact, both had gone so far as to repudiate the very idea of a Christian America. The nation did not call on God in its founding documents, Deists and atheists could be president, blasphemy and heresy were protected "under the notion of liberty of conscience," slavery offended the God-given freedom of each person, and oaths of allegiance bound believers to support such immoralities. To make matters even more stark, just six years prior the Treaty of Tripoli explicitly "disclaimed the religion of Jesus" by declaring that "the government of the United States of America is not, in any sense, founded on the Christian religion." Three years after that, the nation elected Jefferson to the presidency, a decision Wylie believed called the Christianity not only of the government but of its people into question. Covenanters "cannot yield obedience, for conscience sake, to the present civil authority in North America," he explained, because it failed all the tests of Christian nationhood.[12]

Covenanter neighborhoods flirted with political anarchism after reading Wylie's writings, at least according to reports from backcountry judges. A group of Covenanters informed one passer-through that they could murder him with impunity since the US government, because it lacked Christian authority, held no jurisdiction over them. Reports surfaced that Covenanter laity, gaining an increasing reputation as antislavery men, taught that slaves murdering masters was warranted by God's laws. For many Society People, rejection of the federal government came in tandem with the institution of God's martial law in their towns.[13]

Not all Covenanters held to the extremes of the RPs. ARs continued to argue that the church could Christianize the state from within, through evangelization and church discipline. This was an increasingly popular argument across the religious spectrum during and after the Second Great Awakening. Thus raised to right religion, a generation of the godly would "control all that is tender and sacred in the interest of church and state." ARs also taught that people had the rights to personal and political freedom so long as they openly submitted to the restraint of righteous laws. Yet the case for moderate Covenanter beliefs can be overstated. At both the lay and ministerial levels, the borders between sects remained porous, and many ARs continued to be stringently orthodox on church–state relations. On the whole, though, ARs were more flexible in this regard.[14]

Increasingly, less rigid Covenanters even came to accept the logic of a federalist argument: the secular national compact was a marriage of convenience among several Christian states. That South Carolina's Anglicanism would not meld well with Pennsylvania's Quakerism required a studied neutrality from their contract. This was all the more manifest as attempts to unite American Calvinism, including backcountry Presbyterians and New England Congregationalists, foundered on the shoals of such technicalities as mixed communion and psalm singing. If denominations could not successfully merge their common faiths, how could states?[15]

The most ardent supporter of accepting the flawed Constitution on this basis was, ironically, AR congressman William Findley. Findley was the archetype for the Americanization of Covenanters during the Early Republic. His transformation tracked closely the transition many experienced across the Atlantic. In Ireland, he was an obedient Covenanter, reading Alexander Shields and traveling to hear Seceder sermons. Immigrating to Pennsylvania, he joined the very society that drew swords to renew their antigovernment protests in Middle Octorara. Yet, over time, and especially in the conflict with Britain, Findley came to see himself as an American and to apply his faith to his more immediate circumstances. Tempering his Anti-Federalist passions after ratification, he was elected to Congress seven times between 1803 and 1817. It was in this capacity that AR ministers and laity begged him to refute the anarchist appeal of Wylie's *Two Sons of Oil*.[16]

Findley published his 1811 *Observations on "The Two Sons of Oil"* in response to the ongoing popularity of Wylie's Covenanter tract. Findley cast Wylie and his ilk as Scotland's "bigoted popish missionaries," who would demand that others' consciences and lives conform to their authorized understanding of God. According to Findley, it was mostly recent Covenanter immigrants who pushed these beliefs, since those who had lived through the Revolution understood the dramatically different circumstances of American and European political life. Truly American Covenanters had already joined the AR fold.[17]

Findley compared Wylie with Islamic extremism. His theology was grounded in a misunderstanding of the difference between moral precepts, which were universal, and moral laws, which applied to the places and times God gave them. Wylie's ideology could "receive the right hand of fellowship from the Mahometan camp" since both agreed in "propagating and enforcing religion, by the sword of the civil magistrate." Wylie was wrong not only in theory but in practice as well. Findley's decades of experience confirmed for him that anyone acquainted with real politics would understand that giving religious authority to civil leaders could only lead to "the union of church and state, or, in other words, tyranny over both the souls and bodies of men."[18]

*Observations* zealously defended the liberty of conscience that Wylie and McLeod attacked. At the heart of the conflict, Findley insisted, was disagreement over whether citizens must worship God according to their own consciences or the Covenanters'. The standard of Pennsylvania was that each person was free to worship God as he or she understood to be right. Findley believed that this was the essence of Christian forbearance and thus more biblical than Wylie's own strict moralism.[19]

Yet Findley and Wylie agreed on one vital point: the United States was not a Christian nation. Although he attributed the Treaty of Tripoli's disavowal of Christianity to the negotiating official, naval officer Richard O'Brien, Findley believed that Wylie's larger point was correct. The United States was not predicated on Christianity in any way. The federal government itself was a compact among sovereign states, each of which approached religion differently. Thus, it could not in any effective manner take a position on religion even if it tried.[20]

Findley's critiques went further. He argued that American Covenanters had possessed misgivings about the Solemn League and Covenant for some time. As the conflict with Britain had escalated, he remembered, many RPs began conversations about the appropriateness of applying political terms of communion on churches in a distant land. Even long-serving minister John Cuthbertson had privately spoken with Findley about the issue and signed on to the idea that the political implications of the documents should be removed as a term of communion. Findley and others now worried that the hard-liners had made an idol of the historic documents by placing them on par with the Old Testament covenants. God instituted each of those Scriptural commands. But in 1638 and 1643, who spoke for God? These events were political documents, he insisted, created by committees of politicians for particular moments and places. The United States could not possibly be equated to those nations. There was no American Solemn League to reject, no king sitting on Christ's throne, no tithes to an apostate church, and no system of patronage appointing pastors against the people's will.[21]

Findley's writing and personal authority helped bridge the gap between Americanization and Covenanting. His ameliorating message influenced communities as far away as the Carolinas. Irish and Scottish immigrants were flocking into AR churches, which, because of their political theology, psalm singing, and Old World church discipline, were the congregations that most closely replicated the hard-line Presbyterianism they had left behind. As recent arrivals completed the five-year waiting period for their naturalization oaths, one pastor wrote Findley, they worried that the US Constitution "contains things they believe to be immoral." Disestablished churches, the toleration of heretics, and the absence of religious tests caused even the less stringent among them to distrust the American government.[22]

As Findley explained in *Observations* and through personal correspondence with AR pastors, the states, like so many families gathered in a community, had originally possessed their own religious cultures: Congregationalist New Englanders, Episcopal Southerners, and the more broad Trinitarianism of the middle states. After some time passed, however, it was "believed that real Religion such as discovers itself by its fruits prevailed not where the state was left connected with the Church." Thus most states had abandoned or were soon inevitably going to abandon these connections. Yet it remained the decision of each state to create its own religious criteria or not, and the restriction against religious tests for federal office was intended to prevent Pennsylvania's rather liberal religious standards for federal officials from being undermined by South Carolina's more rigorous ones. For Findley, the religious oaths test was federalism, pure and simple.[23]

Disestablishment did not unseat God from the throne of government so much as it dethroned fallible men from ruling the church, Findley insisted. "We have no Theocracy now nor any reason to expect one," he explained, and most who were acclimated to America's religious pluralism knew to be thankful. Complaints about the lack of religious tests coupled with nervousness that there was no guaranteed toleration by the government demonstrated that these immigrants were still operating on an Old World mentality. "A religious test is the child of religious establishment," he explained in a letter, "and can never take place but where man or human authority sets itself in the temple of God, interposes between God and the conscience." Such people "may profess to have the Bible in their hands, yet they tell the people that though this Book is the word of God you must receive it in the sense I affix to it." New immigrants were not to assume that the federal government was "like the consolidated Gov'ts of Europe." With no established church, there was no need for toleration.[24]

Not everyone subscribed to the AR latitude on church and state. RP James Renwick Willson attacked Findley's argument that the Constitution was nothing more than a glorified treaty among autonomous states. This was foolish, Willson claimed, because it implied that the United States was not a nation—which it obviously was. Moreover, the states obviously were not. "No one ever says the nation of Pennsylvania," he scoffed, or "the nation of New York." Findley "might as well plead, that because the [biblical] twelve tribes were confederated together under one government, they were on that account" not obligated to act as God's chosen nation.[25] At least according to Covenanter theories that nations were defined by their documents, Willson had a point.

## *The War of 1812*

In 1812, the intertwined issues of oaths, constitutions, and loyalty ceased to be theoretical. War with Britain, which many at the time viewed as a second war for independence, gave the Presbyterian fringe a chance to prove their civic trustworthiness to a skeptical American public. Their perceived loyalty to Scotland, unwillingness to swear oaths of allegiance, participation in the Whiskey Rebellion, and regular habit of publicly condemning the Constitution cast them in the role of potential subversives. Here, then, was a chance to justify the worthiness of both themselves and their message to a skeptical American audience.

South Carolina RP Hugh Henry, who had fled Ireland after assaulting a British solider, served in the war until it was discovered that he had never taken the oath of naturalization because of his religious views. He was released on grounds of being a legal alien. With Covenanter laypeople across the nation facing Henry's loyalty dilemma, the RP clergy sprang into action. Meeting in Pittsburgh in August 1812, the RP Synod appointed a committee to reassess the denomination's hard-line prohibition against government involvement and reassure neighbors of their American commitments. The committee returned with a declaration that the denomination approved "of the republican form of the civil order of the United States" and that they "prefer this nation and its government, to any other nation and government." The body pledged to support US independence and to protect it from "all foreign aggression, and domestic factions." Thus, they sought to assure the nation that they disclaimed any allegiance to any foreign empire. American RPs emphasized that their public critiques were driven from a belief in the "duty of all nations, formally to recognize the sovereignty of Messiah" and to construct governments from such Christian principles. Going further, they created an oath of loyalty that hard-line Covenanters could take in good conscience. The oath read "I, A.B., do solemnly declare, in the name of the Most High God the searcher of hearts, that I abjure all foreign allegiance whatsoever, and hold that these states, the United States are, and ought to be, sovereign and independent of all other nations and governments, and that I will promote the best interest of the empire, maintain its independence, preserve its peace, and *support the integrity* of the Union, to the best of my power." Bypassing the Constitution altogether, the oath solidified loyalty to the ideal of American independence and antagonism to its enemies. The nation should not be independent of God, but it should definitely be independent of covenant-breaking Britain.[26]

Alexander McLeod also produced a ringing endorsement of activism in the war that went through multiple editions during the conflict. McLeod's tract began with a refutation of the idea that ministers should have no place in political debate. It was impossible, he argued, to segregate the Bible from politics, despite the emerging American consensus to try: "The objection proceeds upon the principle, that the gospel doctrine, the Christian religion, is to be perpetually separated from the polity of nations." But Covenanters "go upon the directly opposite principle," he explained, "that civil rule should be regulated by the maxims of Christian law." The Christian should derive his or her politics from the Bible.[27]

McLeod next judged the competing national governments, British and American, against one another on the weight of their respective national sins. Repeating a common refrain, McLeod admitted that Americans' sins were obvious and important: they were silent on God and did not overturn the slavery in their midst. But these were sins of neglect. Britain, meanwhile, had rejected its covenant with God outright after 1643 and brought slavery to America's shores. These were sins of action.[28]

Yet McLeod's critique went deeper and displayed the profound ways American Covenanter thought was slowly making its peace with American democracy. Scottish Covenanters, McLeod reminded readers, were the original Whigs. They held the great political insight now embodied in the United States—"that representative democracy is the ordinance of God." All other details of government must be subsumed beneath this truth: "Divide power as you will—make the arm of authority weak or strong, as suits your purpose; call your chief magistrate King, Consul,

Emperor, President, Governor, or whatever you please, form your legislative councils of one or of many chambers; let your courts, your judges, your officers of law, be many or few; but maintain the principle of representation inviolate." According to McLeod, representative government was supported by the trifecta of authority: common sense, experience, and Scripture.[29]

Britain was a guilt-saddled nation, from the Covenanter perspective. The British had forced war on the Americans by enslaving American sailors. This was a singular symptom of Britain's larger moral decay. Erastian ecclesiology placed the state over the church, taking the crown off Christ's head and placing it on the king's. They were murderous in India and oppressive in Ireland and denied the fundamental freedoms of conscience to Presbyterians across the realm. In the end, McLeod assured readers, Covenanters could bear arms in the conflict not so much for the American state as against the British Empire.[30]

Thomas Jefferson was less fond of McLeod's argument than was the reading public. Jefferson accused McLeod of violating America's consensus on separating church and state. The minister was in "breach of contract," he told an acquaintance, for preaching beyond his bounds of knowledge. "Religion," Jefferson opined, "is a separate department" from that "of Mathematics, of Natural Philosophy, of Chemistry, of Medicine, of Law, of History, of Government." McLeod had no more right to speak on government than to give "a discourse on the Copernican system." After stewing on the matter, Jefferson never mailed his letter, lest the "honor and charity of a Macleod" be harmed or, worse, the clergy of Massachusetts use the letter against the former president and his political allies.[31]

A decade afterward, many Covenanters saw the War of 1812 as the shining moment that sanctified their role as "the Christian patriot party." One remembered it as a day of gloom when, with the capital in flames and many American clergymen doubting the conflict's morality, Covenanters ably maintained their critique of godless government while defending their homeland against invasion. This resistance was tied to their historical memory of "twenty-eight years [of] persecution of the Covenanters, after the restoration of Charles II," when views of liberty were inculcated into the community's sensibility. Now, having built patriotic capital out of their ongoing conflicts with the British Crown, they intended to spend it on an effort to reform the twin evils of American government.[32]

Covenanters' perception that their wartime service gave them political capital was a prominent feature of their public interactions in the following decades. In 1819, Rocky Creek RPs informed the government of South Carolina that they viewed "the constitution of this State, in many respects excellent, destitute of this principle and sanctioning without regard to the law of the God of heaven." The state had repealed its religious tests for political office. South Carolina, in its boundless toleration, "Authorizes men to profess & practice whatever religion they choose without regarding the conformity to the will of God." It also preserved slavery. After expounding on the litany of sins of the state of South Carolina, they promptly requested special privileges. Citing their widespread service in the American Revolution and War of 1812 as justification, they asked for relief from penalties for nonservice on juries. Surely, they argued, "It cannot certainly be an unpardonable offence against the State of South Carolina" for such honorable people "to believe that its constitutions & laws ought to be ruled by the Bible." Also citing their loyalty in the War of 1812, in 1833 the Covenanters of Vermont petitioned for the right to legally hold their land without being naturalized citizens: "When America was struggling a second time for free trade and sailors rights, for their independence on the ocean as well as the continent," they reminded legislators, there were no groups more committed "with the tongue, the pen, and the sword." Although Covenanters of all stripes held high hopes that their military service would land them a wider audience, they were sorely disappointed. Most Americans continued to look askance at their political faith, calling it un-American bigotry.[33]

## *The Damned Founders*

After the 1810s, Covenanters advanced an even less effective strategy for attracting Americans' attention to the cause of a Christian nation—desecrating the Founding Fathers. When Thomas Jefferson and John Adams passed away on the same Fourth of July in 1826, the nation was in the middle of celebrating its fiftieth anniversary of freedom. The news of their timely, near-simultaneous deaths elicited outpourings of adulation for the two presidents. But the Covenanters were not ones to laud the Founding Fathers. In the pages of the *Evangelical Witness,* RPs interpreted the moment as proof that "the wages of sin is death." Adams, a Socian, and Jefferson, a Deist, were not to be lauded, they warned. The writers urged Christians to "enter into solemn protest" against the canonization of "ungodly men." The piece closed with the biblical warning that without holiness, no man could hope to see the Lord.[34]

Accusations of the Founding Fathers' eternal damnation did not go over well in the Early Republic. In 1832, James Renwick Willson preached the Covenanter political creed before the New York State Legislature in Albany. His topic, the ungodliness of American government and its creators, was not what the legislature had anticipated when sending him the invitation. "There were infidels in the [Constitutional] convention," he insisted, including Benjamin Franklin and pretty much everyone else of note. Willson preached to the stunned crowd that there was more evidence that the atheist Rousseau was fond of Christ than there was that General Washington, who was on top of it all a slaveholder, ever followed Jesus. Among the famed first president's Cabinet officers, "vital godliness would have been mocked as fanaticism." Jefferson's religious views were notorious. John Adams, though he occasionally mentioned Jesus, turned to Unitarianism while in office and thus rejected the Messiah's Godhead. James Monroe "lived and died like a second rate Athenian Philosopher." Taken together, these men had created a government in which "Atheists, Deists, Jews, Pagans and Profane men, of the most abandoned manners, are as eligible to office by the United States constitution as men fearing God and hating covetousness." Willson asked how such a legacy could possibly be conceived as being anything other than an anti-Christian national government. Such sentiments were censured by the legislature. The "Rev. James R. Willson of this city," the assembly resolved, "has wantonly assailed the good name of the revered Washington, and insulted the memory of the illustrious Jefferson." Such accusations were not taken lightly.[35]

As it turned out, informing the public that Washington, Jefferson, and Hamilton were currently burning in everlasting perdition led to massive unpopularity. Willson was spat upon in the streets and burned in effigy. In Revolutionary fashion, a mob descended on his house to burn it down, but he had absconded. Locals called his speech a "religio politico sermon . . . worthy of the proscriptions and exclusions of a dark and bigot age." As historian James Kabala has pointed out, Willson's strident Covenanter message forced the New York State Legislature into some soul-searching regarding its practice of intermingling clergy with politics. This crisis led state leaders to reject the Old World consensus of union of church and state outright and drop the practice of invited sermons.[36]

Though the event was notorious, such sentiments were not the isolated teachings of a raving madman as much as the thoughtful Covenanter critique of the failure of America's leaders to constitute a Christian nation. Thomas Goodwillie preached a similar, though far more tactful, message to the Vermont legislature. He warned that "an unrighteous constitution is a sin and reproach," set up "in opposition to divine government." He implored them to consider that "there ought at least to be public profession of a belief in one Supreme Being, to whom all men are amenable, and in a future state of retribution." Messages such as these were ill received by an American nation proud of its Revolutionary heritage and sure of its increasingly Christian population's ability to separate out issues of faith and policy for themselves.[37]

## *The Great Awakening at the Post Office*

The prospect that fellow citizens might hearken to Covenanter calls for repentance began to look up, however, as religious revivals swept the nation. In the early years of the nineteenth century, Covenanter opinion of American religiosity was low. As one AR wrote about visiting the infidel capital of South Carolina: "Nine tenths of the inhabitants are destitute of the form of religion and are mockers of morality." The other tenth were, to his chagrin, Methodists. All that changed very quickly, in large part because of Methodists, Baptists, and evangelical Presbyterians. This Second Great Awakening revitalized church membership through emotional preaching, singing, and calls for conversion that simultaneously hearkened back to the Holy Fair services of the past and challenged conventional standards by encouraging unprecedented numbers of people to make individual choices to follow God. Preachers interwove the democratic American ethos into calls for every believer to decide their salvation for themselves.[38]

Though revivals may, or may not, convert the soul, they failed to convert the state. This was the central (though not the only) Covenanter critique of the Second Great Awakening, which they saw as part and parcel of the revivals' rejection of Calvinist orthodoxy. Though they rejoiced at the "wonderful regenerations and amendment of life," they were worried that the revival services might be "desperate acts of Satan to introduce wild, enthusiastic fire in place of the regular operations of the Holy Ghost in the conversion and sanctification of men." In part, this sentiment grew out of Covenanter opposition to the singing of hymns, which were the revivals' primary worship music. Revivalists replaced the exclusive singing of the Psalms, which Covenanters across the spectrum maintained was the only biblically approved way to worship God in song, with hymns. Main-line Presbyterian Adam Rankin was so put off by revival hymn singing that he got himself suspended from the ministry and later joined the ARs. These critiques ran much deeper, however, than song preference. By rejecting the Bible's book of praise in favor of the inventions of men, the revivals re-enacted America's perennial sin: they placed man as the authority for worship instead of God. Five Seceder ministers published a pamphlet opposing the revivals in 1804. The awakenings failed to promote "a covenanted work of reformation," they complained. ARs in the South agreed, calling excessive emotion and focus on individualism "the fruitful mother of doctrinal error and heresies of every form and hue." Education of the person, community, and nation was a necessary part of real religion. Anything less was grossly insufficient.[39]

The most notable instance of antievangelicalism arose in the heresy cases of Seceder father and son Thomas and Alexander Campbell. The elder Campbell was chastised in Ireland for taking part in the overly ecumenical Evangelical Society of Ulster. As in America, the Irish Anti-Burgher synod worried that the rising tide of evangelism reformed the soul but not the state. Upon his immigration to America, Campbell's enthusiastic support of revival and his rejection of the confessional tradition again led to his censure. Thomas Campbell and his son left Seceder authority to spawn what would become known as the Restoration movement. They maintained the Covenanter emphasis on reverting to biblical mandates but rejected the acceptance of confessional doctrine as a means to that end. These new evangelicals broke the ties to old identities. As one revivalist preacher told his audience, when God judged between souls at the end of time, the question "will not be, Were you a Presbyterian–A Seceder–a Covenanter–A Baptist–or a Methodist"? Those who embraced the new developments in religion, like the Campbell family, were forced to leave the old tradition altogether and identify as something broader than Covenanters.[40]

For those on the fringe, the most nefarious result of the Second Great Awakening's conversion of souls but not states was that it convinced too many Christians that their religion had no political importance. They were correct. Especially in the slaveholding South, revival preachers avoided political topics as overly divisive. Baptists and Methodists, whose early radical leanings on moral issues such as slavery had kept them on the sidelines of religious influence, exploded on the scene as they simultaneously quieted their social and political critiques. Covenanters complained that these "bigots to liberality" were so "fierce for moderation" that they voided any importance of the Gospel beyond that to the individual's eternal soul. The social and political applications of the Gospel for a Christian nation were, Covenanters feared, lost in a message that worried only about the afterlife.[41]

Despite the many drawbacks Covenanters saw in the Second Great Awakening, they also welcomed what it could mean for a revival of Christian America. With conversions springing out everywhere, the ground had never been more fertile for the Covenanter argument that the Bible was the supreme law of the land. If Americans writ large became a churchgoing, God-honoring people, there was yet hope that they might be able to convert the nation. After decades of revival, America was being remade in an evangelical image. Many churchgoers began to believe that God's millennial reign was at hand, and what better place to start the end of days than the United States? One prophet of the Second Coming proclaimed that the nation's destiny was to usher in the reign of Christ's peace because the American republic, so peculiarly like heaven, was a land of "liberty, equality, unity, and peace." Efforts began in earnest to reform the American people of such vices as drinking, horse racing, and sexual promiscuity. Voices urging the American government to enforce Christian morality gained strength. Covenanters saw the awakening as their first real opportunity to Christianize the government. "Suppose it should last," one wrote in 1823. Wasn't there good reason "to suppose the Bible [will] influence politics? Or that legislators, will be obliged by public sentiment to regard its dictates and be governed by its statutes"? They began to refer to their beliefs as "the public cause of God." In 1827, RPs changed the title of their denominational publication from the *Evangelical Witness* to the *Christian Statesman*. Using the rebranded message, they hoped to start a movement for the confession of national sins and reform the government one voting believer at a time.[42]

Covenanters' first attempt to woo new allies from the expanding evangelical population into conflict with the godless federal government involved the Post Office. The conflict over Sunday mail delivery was the first time religion and politics truly collided in American national politics. The issue at hand was the use of federal facilities on Sundays. Most local postmasters were also the local merchants who sold liquor by the glass; this led to the opening of all stores on the Sabbath, since in effect it required competitors to remain open. All this mailing, drinking, and shopping violated local ordinances in highly religious towns, as well as biblical proscriptions against work and frivolity on the Sabbath. Supporters of these local religious restrictions who stood against federal authority were called Sabbatarians. This fight to protect Christian morals and local laws against faraway heretics and their federal powers set the stage for Ezra Stiles Ely's 1828 call for "a Christian party in politics." Ely believed that every citizen should be a believer, only devout believers should be elected leaders, and those who denied the Truth should be ousted from office. Ely, not coincidentally a Presbyterian minister, was an outspoken advocate of the nonpreferentialist position, which argued that Christianity was an existing part of American common law and most states' constitutional law. The First Amendment, therefore, left America's Christian people as it found them and simply refused to play favorites among Christian sects. Presbyterian-turned-Episcopal Jasper Adams of Charleston argued that the Constitution charted a "middle course" between the religious establishment of Europe and the "infidel" position of Jeffersonian Deists and French Revolutionaries. The premier Christian America advocate of the Early Republic, Connecticut clergyman Lyman Beecher, issued calls to "constitute a sort of moral militia" that could repel any secularizing federal assault on religion in local governments. Ely, Adams, Beecher, and others' controversial advocacy for a Christian nation galvanized Jacksonian opposition to church–state collusion. Opponents such as the Rev. William Morse decried Sabbatarians as "theological tyrants" who sought "to extend their influence by seeking alliance with the civil power." The Post Office showdown between supporters of Christian local law and secular federal authority was a high-profile political fight in the Early Republic.[43]

According to federal officials, the mail was an issue of national security and commercial success that was especially vital in wartime. Judges ruling on related cases agreed, calling the issue one of necessity for national defense and interstate commerce and thus beyond the scope of local power to restrict. In 1810, Congress upped the ante of this church–state issue when it passed a law requiring all postmasters to open their offices on any day of the week a patron requested and to sort the mail on the day it arrived. This included Sunday. Now, a federal government that once seemed distant and unobtrusive was overruling the Sabbath laws of every local town and city in the United States. Presbyterian and Congregationalist ministers set out to mobilize a petition campaign to get Congress to overturn the federal statute and protect the local moral order. Main-line Presbyterians in Washington, Pennsylvania, went so far as to put the local postmaster on trial for sin when he obeyed orders to open the mail on Sundays. In the crosshairs for his role in violating church teachings as an arm of the state, he was expelled from fellowship.[44]

The federal government now ordered and enforced the desecration of the Sabbath for all Americans to see. The Covenanter critique of the state thus attained its first true entry point with other Protestants. Unlike most evangelicals involved in the debate, however, for Covenanters the Sabbatarian movement was not the product of the piety reforms that grew from the Second Great Awakening. The fight was an extension of their view on the appropriate admixture of church and state. In Vermont, future governor John Mattocks spent a night in jail when he dared to travel through a Covenanter town on the Sabbath. In the Covenanter towns such as Barnet and Ryegate that became the heart of Vermont's Sabbatarian movement, congregants signed petitions demanding that the state observe the Sabbath strictly years before the issue became a national one.[45]

Covenanters served as the shock troops of Sabbatarianism once the movement gained steam in the 1820s and 1830s. They enjoyed styling themselves "soldiers for Jesus" in his war to regain the crown of authority over the state. At a national level, Ely and RP minister James Renwick Willson shared ideas about the applications of theology to politics in personal correspondence. Local auxiliaries of the General Union for Promoting the Observance of the Christian Sabbath were populated with AR, RP, and Seceder ministers. Such organizations in some areas were a de facto alliance of Covenanter peoples. The Pittsburgh auxiliary and its later incarnations were overwhelmingly filled with ministers and laypeople from local Covenanter churches. Their involvement and emphasis made sense given their long focus on the failures of American government. A group of Seceder ministers noted that violations of the Sabbath were to be expected in a non-Christian nation. Since Americans had "not been duly concerned to acknowledge the Lord in setting up our civil rulers," it should be no surprise when such leaders "added to the causes of his wrath" by "making impious laws." ARs in South Carolina also blamed the godlessness of American government, evidenced recently by the "Congress of the United States in more than one instance holding their sessions until near day-light on Sabbath morning." For several decades, Covenanters held out hope that their agitations were gaining ground on the irreverent political leaders who insulated the state from the church's influence.[46]

In the end, however, Sabbatarianism was fiercely and successfully resisted. Those who favored Sunday mail decried "the Christian party's plan" to overthrow the secular Constitution. In 1829, the US Senate commissioned a report that concluded Congress was "a civil institution, wholly destitute of religious authority," and therefore could not inject religiously motivated changes into the postal service. The authors of the report were not avowed Deists. They were both evangelical Baptists: Senator (and future vice president) Richard Johnson of Kentucky and minister (and former Senate chaplain) Obadiah Brown. Christians, they argued, observed the Sabbath on Sunday but were divided over how exactly to honor it. Jews celebrated the Sabbath from Friday to Saturday nights. Whose Sabbath would the government choose, and how? "The Jewish government was a theocracy," they posited, but the American Constitution set up "a civil, and not a religious institution." The Founders had wisely withheld from the federal government the power "to determine what are the laws of God." Jacksonian Democrats roundly condemned Sabbatarians as religious meddlers offering the "first salvo of a campaign to reunite church and state." Andrew Jackson himself considered resisting Sabbatarianism one of his presidency's great achievements. Most Baptists, as part of their long-standing resistance of church–state communion, rejected an active role in Sabbatarian agitation.[47]

The failure of the Sabbath movement, RPs claimed, proved that American politicians believed that "the law of God does not bind the government of the United States." Sabbatarianism, unsuccessful though it was, became a proving ground for evangelical action in politics. Early political agitators began mastering the techniques of political mobilization such as petition drives and mailing lists. Many leaders, especially Covenanters, became prominent in the next wave of Christian politics, which formed the abolitionist movement.[48]

## *Covenanters in an Un-Christian Land*

Their inability to puncture the wall separating church from state left an enduring mark on each group at the Presbyterian fringe. All Covenanters struggled to reconcile themselves as distinct people within the nation. No group wrestled more than the RPs. There were shifts in rhetoric beginning in the 1820s that displayed the emergence of more pro-engagement views regarding the relationship between children of the Scottish covenants and the American government. These rumblings eventually split the RPs apart in 1833.

In 1827, the RP Synod of North America wrote to the RPs in Ireland proposing a universal Atlantic Covenant that could apply to all Covenanters in all types of political situations. "There is danger," they explained, of "our existing uselessly and ignobly" in this strange land with its secular government. American RPs struggled to modify their message in ways that would not be wholly lost on an American population that was obsessed with change and ignored tradition. "There is a perpetual fluctuation in the population," they explained in a letter to their Irish brethren: "A spirit of enterprise impels to frequent change of both employment and residence among our people." This people on the move required a fresh approach to the old religion. Little came of this effort at a united Atlantic Presbyterian fringe because the members themselves were sorely divided on the particulars.[49]

Perhaps no one moved American Covenanters more to change message than the Scottish fiction writer Sir Walter Scott. RPs were distraught that his wildly popular writings of historical fiction, set in Scotland and romanticizing the past, cast Covenanters in the roles of "fanaticism and sedition." Slowly, some adherents began wrestling with their outsider status and attempting to restyle their message to fit mainstream American morality. Many, most notably *Two Sons of Oil* author Samuel Wylie, began to gravitate to the old Seceder position that even ungodly rulers could be theoretically legitimate in God's eyes. The Bible was replete with such examples, beside which it was simply unfathomable that every civil government in the world was invalid. Some RPs began arguing that using the franchise would allow the election of godly officials; these would, in turn, Christianize the nation, if only by degrees. Wylie acknowledged that, with years of hindsight, "no Government on earth has had a fairer claim to recognition, as the ordinance of God, than that of these United States." It was flawed but fixable. Hard-liners shot back that voting for a godly person to take an oath to a godless government was to demand that the person violate moral principles on your behalf.[50]

The die for division was cast in 1831, when at a meeting of the RP synod Wylie and others presented a theological statement justifying political participation. The two sides now acquired the traditional labels of evangelical division: New Lights, who sought to engage the political world, and Old Lights, who remained distant. With the proposal debated and rejected, Wylie and his New School allies went on a publishing offensive. In 1832, they published their opinions in *A Pastoral Address* and *The Moral Character of Civil Government in Four Letters*. These polemics sealed their fate; many prominent ministers were charged with heresy, refused to defend themselves, and were tried in absentia. The 1833 synod faced the singular problem of deciding how to constitute a meeting in which the duly elected moderator had been suspended from ministry. The ensuing split created yet another fissure in the Presbyterian fringe. Congregations split in two as internal divisions became apparent, often between immigrant and American-born factions. In Bloomington, Indiana, the RP congregation was evenly divided, with family members on both sides of the issue. The session proved evenly divided as well, before the pastor cast the tie-breaking vote favoring strict construction.[51]

The New Lights, or Engagers, hinged their hopes for national reform on an emerging plan for amending the Constitution. They still believed in the necessity of Christian America. It was the duty of believers, therefore, to reform government. They believed that the Old Light, hard-liner position inadvertently created a de facto and "detestable neutrality in the cause of God." There was still "a way left open, constitutionally, to employ all moral means to obtain a remedying of defects." It was now incumbent on Covenanters to be active reformers in favor of amending the Constitution to acknowledge God and end slavery. New Light RPs still preached a political gospel. Though the national person was damnably sinful, it could still be saved by repentance via the votes of three-fourths of the states.[52]

Discussions about mounting a crusade to amend the Constitution to recognize God first began among RPs in the 1820s. Initial efforts centered on explaining the biblical logic of their position to other Christians affected by the Second Great Awakening. The nation, like Israel in the book of Judges, was a land where every person did what was right in his or her own eyes. In America, "the will of the majority, whether agreeable to the word of God or not," was believed to be the supreme standard. Americans loved to speak about their rights. These sacred rights were not the things God commanded in his word but whatever the will and whimsy of individual opinion might dictate. Like Old Testament Israel, the nation needed a more explicit dependence on God.[53]

Efforts at constitutional reform began in earnest with the publication of "The Travels of Titus." Titus was a fictionalized Covenanter layman who traversed the nation confounded by the paradox of ungodly politics celebrated by Christian people. Titus arrived in Washington, D.C., and, like Luther in Rome, surveyed with wide-eyed dismay the Whore of Babylon. American politicians were embarrassed to be thought too religious. They profaned the Sabbath with political activities, afterward carousing with their mistresses at drinking parties. They drank too much, danced too well, and prayed too little. Buildings in the capital city were designed in the pagan Greek or Roman styles, repudiating plainness and celebrating grandeur. The courts of European monarchy were recreated off the Potomac. Religion was a political tool, to be used to sway good people to vote for bad men. The Covenanter pilgrim was puzzled when Americans claimed that "because they are elected by what you call a Christian nation," the government must reflect its people. It was, at least, "very strange, that religious men should choose such representatives."[54] When the traveler asked a fictional US senator if he were not obligated to legislate for the glory of God or bound by the teachings of the Bible, the senator replied quizzically, "What has God, or the Bible to do with Congress?"[55]

Titus's travel narrative suggested that the solution must be to change the Constitution itself. "Alter the Constitution!" one surprised character howled. It seemed preposterous. His companion replied that constitutional amendments, especially in the states, were quite common and not at all shocking. "It is the magnitude of the subject and its being so foreign to all our common habits of political speculation" that must be overcome by the audience. Titus even pointed to some promising signs of church–state cooperation. Congress voted to fund missionaries to Indian tribes, and in its cooperation with local ministers founded nearby Columbian College (now George Washington University) for educating missionaries. Though some saw this as evidence of a Christian nation at work, Covenanters pointed to both these actions in a very different light. They saw evidence that "ambitious men would attempt to make religion an engine to promote their own views of self aggrandizement." Congress had meddled in religion without being in any way religious. Presidents Monroe and John Quincy Adams, they claimed, only used the college to woo the emerging behemoth of Baptist voters.[56]

Being known first and foremost as the religious group who hated George Washington's memory was not a workable reputation for people intent on changing the nation's mind about God and government. Many Engagers thus employed a swift course correction from their old tendency to defile the memory of revered American political leaders. In particular, there was a new imperative to sanctify the memory of Washington.

Samuel Wylie began insisting that Washington most likely had been a devout, if private, man of faith. Wylie also reversed his position on the damning of the American people, conceding that the overall Christian character of the population should count for something when evaluating America's civil religion. The Constitution vested sovereignty not with the state but with the people. The people spent the first decades of the republic actively setting up and supporting religion. The people were, in a highly inventive sense, a collective Christian sovereign. Provisions against the establishment of religions were provisions against the actions of the *state* but not provisions against the activities of the sovereign American people. In America, "We the People" had established a government in 1787 and established Christianity in the endless series of churches that formed each town's skyline. The repackaged Covenanter message put less emphasis on the anti-Christian founding and more on asking what harm could come from acknowledging a union that already existed.[57]

In 1843, a decade after the RP split, efforts began to create another grand American Covenanter union. Ongoing meetings, called the Convention of Reformed Churches, brought together representatives of the Engager-leaning General Synod of the RPs, the AR Synod of the West, the AR Synod of New York, and the Seceders. Reports indicated that the delegates continuously stumbled on two issues, "the subjects of *Slavery* and *a testimony*" regarding the role of civil governments. An 1844 meeting in Alleghany, Pennsylvania, centered on the chapters of the *Westminster Confession* relating to the civil magistrate's role in the life of the church. Seceders noted their openness to some alterations, and the AR General Synod of the West approved a union on those terms as well. Terms of union were agreed upon by 1845. By 1847 the union of all the Presbyterian fringe bodies broke down. Seceders and northern ARs were able to come together in 1858 to form the United Presbyterian Church of North America (UP) but were unable to convince the rest to join. Despite centuries of passed time and having achieved unanimity regarding psalmody, communion, personal and corporate covenanting, and every other doctrinal issue, the one insurmountable hurdle continued to be the fine print of a Christian civil magistrate.[58]

It was the unique Covenanter experience in America to wrestle for an Old World church–state ideal in a new nation that so popularly separated the two, and each sect found its own way to explain its views to itself and the world. Traditionalist RPs retrenched and demanded that America conform to its covenant obligation, sworn generations before, to acknowledge Christ's headship over all nations. New Light RPs and Seceders of all stripes lived awkwardly between the general acceptance of that ancestral perspective and the acknowledgment that they lived in a different time and place. No groups typified this Old Word–New World tension more than the ARs and UPs. They cheerfully greeted the American republicanism that freed the church from state strictures. Yet, with such scruples removed, they were forced to articulate why they could not find unity with other American Presbyterians. In part, they clung to Old World practices, most notably the Psalms, to make distinct their experience from their neighbors. This was a true distinction but insufficient. ARs and UPs also maintained very real differences of political theology from other American Presbyterians. They still held that "neglecting to call upon God constitutes a heathenish nation," regardless of its outward signs of Christianity. Despite continued organizational divisions, the groups on the Presbyterian fringe had more in common with one another than they had with other Presbyterians or Protestants in America. Each maintained the obligation of the state to conform to the church in some way. Their pulpits and periodicals taught that, through its failure to acknowledge God, there was something amiss with the federal government. Where they disagreed was how to go about changing it. It seemed to those on the fringe that it would take a great reckoning for the nation to come to grips with its un-Christian ways. That reckoning lay ahead with the nation's other great sin: slavery.[59]

# 4

# *Slavery and the Sin of Secular America*

*I know that your mind is deeply exercised in behalf of the slave, but I would suggest to you another feature of the "irrepressible conflict" on which you may not have bestowed so much thought: God's controversy with this nation for dishonor done to his name. This nation, in its Constitution, makes no submission to the King of Kings.*

—A. M. MILLIGAN TO JOHN BROWN, who was awaiting execution in Virginia, 1859

NOT ONLY DID the Constitution ignore Jesus, but it protected slavery. Human bondage was, therefore, a church–state issue of the highest order. Only a Christianity with the weight of a Christian government behind it could force slaveholders to let God's people go. This was something American Christianity was unable to accomplish because of disestablishment. The American experiment that moral disputes could be resolved by freeing Christianity from state involvement was tested by slavery and found wanting. American Christians proved incapable of resolving large-scale social dilemmas without the state's interference, and that interference took the form of war. Covenanters saw the debate over slavery as their long-sought entrée into the nation's dialogue on God and government, possibly because it was now clear that the American way was not working. As they thrust their abolitionist vision upon the nation, they challenged the racism of Andrew Jackson, preceded William Lloyd Garrison's radical antislavery activism by decades, and ran the Underground Railroad's most active stations. They challenged institutional bondage in John C. Calhoun's hometown, comforted John Brown in prison, and personally pressed their case for amending the Constitution to bring God in and send slavery out to President Lincoln himself. All of this fueled the Covenanters' ultimate argument: America's slavery problem stemmed from the nation's failure to be a truly Christian nation.[1]

In making that case, Covenanters mounted a witness against the sin of slavery unlike any other in both North and South. First, their antislavery ideals antedated even the Quaker abolitionist movement; Covenanters were some of the first people in Britain or America to take a public stand against the institution. Second, they created a unique biblical interpretation that did what neither abolitionists in the North nor pro-slavery Christians in the South were able to accomplish: they reconciled biblical literalism, with its clear sanction of slavery, and abolitionism, with its emphasis on human liberty in a state of nature. Third, Covenanters in the South tested the limits of pro-slavery hegemony by publicly lauding the American Colonization Society (ACS) as the nation's best hope to end slavery. Ironically, for a people so steeped in religious radicalism, southern Covenanters became some of the leading moderate voices in states such as South Carolina that tolerated few dissenting voices. Finally, Covenanters gave a clear and unambiguous interpretation of the cause of the Civil War. Before, during, and after the conflict, and in both the United States and the Confederacy, Covenanters testified that the war was God's conflict with America for the sin of slavery.[2]

## *Early Antislavery*

The first radical thing Covenanters did to slavery was calling it a sin. Most early antislavery advocates came to slavery-as-sin language in the mid- to late eighteenth century. For the Presbyterian fringe, antislavery hearkened back to the teachings of Samuel Rutherford in Scotland. Thus their logic was more seventeenth century than nineteenth, seamlessly moving between slavery's perceived threats to human liberty and the tyranny of the Catholic Antichrist. One publication decried "man stealing, man selling, and thus like, the mother of harlots, the Roman Catholic Church," which like "slave ships traffic in the souls and bodies of men." During the colonial era, when Reformed Presbyterians (RPs) were still organizationally an arm of the Scottish Presbytery, they held to the 1761 *Act, Declaration and Testimony*'s stance that the British government was invalid in part because it condoned slavery and participated in the slave trade.[3]

American Covenanters' earliest antagonism to the institution emerged in the South. In 1795, South Carolina RPs decried that state's "abominable species of murder, even enslaving thousands of fellow creatures for life and their posterity without end." Of all the sins that flowed from the Constitution's failure to honor God, this was the greatest: slavery treated people as animals. In 1798, these Covenanters met in the Rocky Creek district of South Carolina. Their meeting's minutes bewailed the already growing force of slavery in the southern backcountry. "Oh, America," they prayed, "what hast thou to account for both to God and man on the head of Slavery alone!" Surely the time was soon approaching when God would arise and answer the "cries of the oppressed."[4]

From the perspective of dismayed southern Covenanters, slavery had shown up in the southern backcountry after they moved in. Predominately arriving just after the Revolution, they founded towns of small farmers in tight-knit, ethnic enclaves removed from the slavery of coastal plantations. Quickly thereafter, the economic logic of slavery overran their homes. From 1790 to 1826, the greatest wealth accumulation in the nation occurred in the backcountry South, not on the coast. Small family farms proved no match for the overwhelming production capacity of cotton plantations and their unfree laborers. Most southern Presbyterians quickly capitulated to, and still others yearned for, the logic of the age: slavery was the path to commercial success in the modern economy. As slavery expanded, it became increasingly difficult to hold radical opinions on the subject. At Kings Mountain in the Carolinas, a minister named Banks preached for two years to the Associate Reformed (AR) congregation called Bethany. The session book recorded that "his abolition sentiment made his stay uncomfortable," so he moved north. In 1790 Thomas McLurkin, a Presbyterian layman, married Elizabeth Smith, an RP. In order to join the RP congregation near Rocky Creek in Chester District, McLurkin dutifully freed his four slaves. This did not sit well with local Presbyterians, who arranged to have McLurkin called for jury duty four consecutive times. Unable to serve because of his Covenanter religion, he was forced to pay a fine each time.[5]

Meanwhile in the North, an RP congregation in New York City was discovered to have slaveholders in 1800. In a unanimous vote, the synod demanded that the offending members immediately emancipate their slaves or face excommunication. The New Yorkers complied. The synod then sent two young ministers on an antislavery preaching tour of the American South to reinforce that human bondage was a sin and would not be tolerated. Along the way they joined forces with Seceder David Hume and an AR minister named Craig. After traversing through Kentucky, Tennessee, and Virginia, they arrived in the Carolinas. There, they were shocked "with what alacrity those concerned came forward and complied with the decree." They estimated 3,000 guineas' worth of slaves were freed from RP congregations. Only one slaveholder, from North Carolina, refused. He was subsequently excommunicated.[6]

One of the ministers on that tour was Samuel Wylie, who later authored the controversial Covenanter tract *The Two Sons of Oil*. Applying Scottish Covenanter doctrine to American circumstances, Wylie went so far as to suggest that the killing of masters by their slaves in Haiti was justifiable. Simply put, God's moral law was higher than sinfully corrupted governments. He argued that "the practice of slave-holding, is flatly repugnant" to God and against the Bible's explicit commands. It could, therefore, legitimately be resisted. Covenanter laypeople were known to repeat that refrain in conversation and apply it to American contexts.[7]

The anarchist strain in the document caused AR congressman William Findley to publish his retort to Wylie; yet even Findley proved to be in remarkable accord with Wylie on the issue of slavery. He labeled slavery a "mighty political evil" and acknowledged that there was something in the nature of Atlantic slavery that was far worse than that of the ancient world. Findley was more optimistic than Wylie. He believed that Christianity was having an ameliorating effect on global slavery, which would soon enter a new era of Christian-inspired abolitionism. He even argued that the United States had done more to end slavery than any nation in history, since over half of the original thirteen states had abolished the institution in some fashion by the early nineteenth century. As a congressman and state assemblyman, Findley maintained a consistently antislavery voting record in his Revolutionary and Early Republic political career. For all their differences, Wylie, the radical RP, and Findley, the Americanized AR moderate, both displayed the antislavery strain at work across the Presbyterian fringe.[8]

After the RPs declared slavery a sin in 1800, the other sects also expressed antislavery positions. In 1804 ministers and elders of the AR Synod of the Carolinas asked the General Synod to consider a petition against slavery. This exclusively southern body also protested when the state of South Carolina considered reopening the Atlantic slave trade. Seceders followed suit, officially condemning slavery's sinfulness in 1811. Most Covenanting people in the South also held firm to such teachings. Their efforts met with much local animosity and very little success. In South Carolina, when several judges ruled against Covenanters' right to abstain from jury duty, they included a jab at the fringe's tendency to rail against slavery and fuel insurrectionary sentiment among slaves. No matter what their differences of doctrine, all true religions must acknowledge "that man is bound to do his duty in whatever situation he may be placed by God," the court opined. The judges demanded that "the covenanter will then, in common with all good men and Christians, obey the powers that be" under the same "principle, which reconciles even the slave to his master." Southern neighbors might tolerate the Covenanters' religious oddities, but they could not bear their antislavery heresy.[9]

Soon, Covenanters began leaving the South in droves. In Kentucky, Seceder ministers Robert Armstrong and Andrew Fulton joined the entire Associate Synod in condemning slavery. This presaged an 1815 exodus of antislavery Seceders into Ohio. In 1828 South Carolina's Rocky Creek congregation moved en masse to Xenia, Ohio, because of the slave issue. Such moves were not isolated. The nuclei for many RP, Seceder, AR, and United Presbyterian congregations in the Midwest came from southern exiles. Ongoing tensions, especially between these Midwestern groups and the more moderate presbytery of the Carolinas, culminated in the 1831 excommunication of all Seceder slaveholders. The Seceder congregations of the Carolinas declared themselves independent of the synod, and most of the ministers were expelled or fled north. The AR story in the South was nearly the same tale of conflict and outmigration. In 1827, the AR Synod of the West refused to unite with the AR Synod of the South in large part because of differences over slavery. The members of those northern churches had fled from Abbeville and Chester districts in South Carolina to avoid living in a slave society. They resented their old neighbors' unwillingness to take the same radical steps.[10]

One of the last to flee Chester was RP James Faris. A schoolteacher, Faris purchased a slave he subsequently attempted to free. He was barred from doing so by South Carolina law. After unsuccessfully attempting a reversal of the statute, Faris expatriated to Philadelphia and freed the slave in 1825. In 1857 a speaker at the Covenanter meetinghouse in Chester District explained that the reason only a handful of RPs survived in the South was their "peculiar principle" that criticized both state and slavery. Such messages were doubly unpopular to southern audiences.[11]

## The Bible and Slavery in America

The Covenanters accomplished something unique among American Christians on the topic of slavery: they managed to be antislavery biblical literalists. This was a unique position in the nineteenth century. American Protestants knew that the Bible contained slavery and that the book never condemned the institution of human bondage in clear language. Explaining what this meant broke down into several broad interpretive strands. Radical abolitionists such as William Lloyd Garrison conceded that the Bible accepted slavery but argued that commonsense ethical imperatives overruled the ancient text. Opposite the abolitionists stood pro-slavery orthodox literalists, such as South Carolina Presbyterian James Henley Thornwell. Thornwell argued that since the Bible, the ultimate authority for religious life, accepted slavery, every Christian must concede the institution's morality. Two middle-ground positions attempted to embrace a discomfort with slavery without jettisoning the Bible's authority completely. The first argued that the spirit of the Bible's overall teaching was one of expanding liberty. The biblical passages correctly described their ancient age but were inapplicable to the freedom-loving present. A less popular approach attempted to parse the difference between the Hebrew and Greek words for "servant" and the modern slave. Such nuanced arguments largely failed to supersede the far more simple and popular arguments at the extremes. The pro-slavery argument held a decided advantage among churchgoers because it successfully married simplicity with biblical authority. Those in doubt needed only to read their Bibles for themselves; the self-evident presence of slavery would carry the day. If slavery was wrong, the Bible itself was suspect. Arguments of these kinds rose to prominence in the 1830s–60s.[12]

Because Covenanter antislavery arguments predated these dichotomous American solutions, they were able to accomplish a mental task that eluded two generations of the nation's most articulate Christian voices. They simply rejected the dilemma altogether. Rather than accepting that antislavery challenged the biblical text, American Covenanters combined Rutherford's natural law logic with a proposal that pro-slavery Christianity failed to be sufficiently biblically literal. This was most artfully stated by Alexander McLeod in his 1802 tract, *Negro Slavery Unjustifiable*. While McLeod embraced the biblical literalism that became the hallmark of southern pro-slavery arguments in the nineteenth century, he turned that hermeneutic on its head. Instead of occupying the high ground on biblical slavery, he claimed, pro-slavery Christians actually were not literal enough.

McLeod based his opposition on Exodus 21:16: "He that stealeth a man, and selleth him, or if he be found in his hand, he shall surely be put to death." Man-stealing was a direct violation of biblical law. The argument from man-stealing was long in the arsenal of antislavery teachings, however, and pro-slavery Southerners created a rather substantive defense against it. Slaveholders claimed that inheriting slaves was not the same as stealing them, that most American slaves were not stolen but born into slavery, and that the Bible tacitly approved of certain people, such as the Canaanites, being enslaved for life.[13]

McLeod used biblical literalism to combat his opponents' first two arguments. Inherited stolen property carried biblical curses that fell generation upon generation. If any group believed in descending obligation, surely it was those who lived in the shadows of the 1638 and 1643 Scottish covenants. But by questioning the concept of biblically condoned lifelong slavery, McLeod set a precedent that southern Covenanters would follow for years to come. He disagreed by agreeing. Yes, indeed, the Bible condoned slavery; but the only way that Southerners could rightly keep their slaves was by proving that the biblical mandate for slavery applied to them. "You cannot argue conclusively, in defense of negro slavery," McLeod wrote, "from the practice of the ancient Hebrews, unless you can prove 1st. That the slavery into which they were permitted to reduce their fellow creatures was similar to that in which the negroes are held, and 2dly. That you have, the same permission which they had, extended to you. If proof fails in *either* of these, the objection is invalid." In order for a literal reading of the text to support southern slavery, slaveholders had to prove both that they were the direct genetic descendants of the people of Israel and that each individual slave they held was a direct descendant of the people of Canaan. Barring such proof, slaveholders literally failed the biblical test.[14]

Covenanter political theology was distinctive in America. They therefore needed their own testimony against slavery in the United States, and McLeod gave them one. All RP churches were encouraged to keep a copy of McLeod's works in their church libraries. Eleven editions of *Negro Slavery Unjustifiable* had been produced by the time of the Civil War.[15]

Covenanter ministers leaned on the logic of Rutherford and McLeod to be simultaneously orthodox and antislavery in an American context that increasingly equated orthodoxy with pro-slavery Christianity. For most Southerners, pro-slavery Christianity and biblical literalism were seen as intertwined views of the world by the 1830s. The *Evangelical Guardian*, a Midwestern Seceder paper founded by former Southerners, acknowledged as much when it claimed that many people saw "orthodoxy and pro-slavery sentiments united." Yet, the editor insisted, the ties between literalism and pro-slavery did not hold. Those Americans on the Presbyterian fringe characterized pro-slavery arguments as "a pretext for abusing orthodoxy." One Seceder, an exile from the South living in the Midwest, provocatively turned the demand for rigid biblical literalism on its head, using it to condemn the masters rather than support modern slavery. "Whatever resemblance there may be supposed to exist between Abraham's slaves and American slaves, there would not be found much between their respective masters and mistresses," he opined. Abraham could "run and fetch a calf from the herd," and Sarah knew how to "make ready and knead meal." Southern masters and mistresses, on the other hand, could barely fend for themselves because their dependence on slaves made them both physically and morally degenerate.[16]

Slavery in the Bible was not the only point of contention between Covenanter and mainstream American intellectual culture; there was also the creation of Adam and Eve. Decades before Charles Darwin published a word, increasing numbers of American thinkers began rejecting the biblical creation accounts in favor of polygenesis theories that explained humanity's racial distinctions by positing a variety of human origin points on various continents. Covenanters roundly rejected such racial theories of creation because they contradicted the literal Bible and undermined Covenanter political theology. "The Africans are men," James R. Willson insisted: "Before God and the Universe, their right to protection by every legal barrier, is as good as that of any British subject, or any American citizen ever was." In an article in their denominational paper, South Carolina ARs insisted that "the European, the Indian, and the African have the same common origin" and because of their shared humanity, they deserved equal treatment. One Covenanter in Charlotte, North Carolina, compared the open discrimination of Jews in Europe with the denial of "the citizenship of the Africans among us." Both were rooted in unchristian racial pride. RPs believed that racial hatred was at the root of President Jackson's Indian removal policies and petitioned him to reconsider his actions. Jackson replied that he admired "the zeal which animates your board on behalf of the Indians" but met their request with an unreserved no. Such racial policies, the Covenanters felt, were an assault against the Creation narrative of the book of Genesis. As one minister preached, even emancipation was insufficient until the "repeal of every enactment which is based upon a distinction of color" was done away with in American law.[17]

Biblically literalistic antislavery and racial egalitarianism set Covenanters apart in America's slavery debates. In New York on the eve of the Civil War, Covenanter teacher J. R. W. Sloane summarized several generations of antislavery biblical literalism. Sloane was perplexed that most Christian abolitionists, when pressed, resorted to "whining about the ameliorating influences of the Gospel" instead of to "an appeal to the Bible argument." Sloane donned the Covenanter mantle. He was "no heathen philosopher," groping for "the light of nature" or the "corrupt and fickle tribunal of human reason. I plant myself upon the Inspired Word." As such, he argued that American slavery failed the biblical test, text by text. The Hebrew experience of servitude was dramatically different from the American institution of slavery. The Old Testament lacked "any permission for the sale of one person to another" and prohibited man-stealing. The Fugitive Slave Act was both unconstitutional and unbiblical, since Deuteronomy 23:15 forbade people to deliver "unto his master the servant which is escaped from his master unto thee." The year of Jubilee did not exist in southern slavery; nor did slave owners obey Exodus 22:21's prohibition on oppressing racial strangers (based on the fact that the Hebrews were once "strangers in the land of Egypt"). Saint Paul told Timothy that the moral law itself was made to restrain "menstealers." In Jesus's first sermon, he declared that he was sent to "preach deliverance to the captives" and "set at liberty them that are bruised." Mocking southern apologists such as "Poor Dr. Thornwell of South Carolina" and "the bellicose Dr. Palmer of New Orleans," Covenanters scoffed at the idea that American slavery had a biblical basis. "American slavery," Sloane insisted, "could not live a day" under a literal biblical formula.[18]

## *Abolition versus Colonization*

Ten years before William Lloyd Garrison created the American Anti-slavery Society, Covenanters worried "that no liberal, sincere, and efficient plan [was] proposed and urged by any distinguished statesman for emancipation." The increasing popularity of antislavery sentiment in the North made the issue the most compelling Covenanter political critique of the new nation. Fringe Presbyterians legitimately claimed that they had anticipated the nation's moral problem before their neighbors. They complained that Americans did not recognize slavery as a crime against human nature, were insensible to its cruelty, and were unmotivated to reform it.[19]

Garrisonian abolitionists, including early on a young former slave named Fredrick Douglass, preached a message of prophetic nonparticipation in politics. They called the nation to repentance rather than attempting to change its laws in Congress. This was an attractive message to those possessed of a Covenanter sensibility. Garrison's fuzzy interpretation of scriptural authority, however, did not sit well with anyone on the Presbyterian fringe. Many hard-liners would not join the traditional abolitionist groups such as the American Anti-slavery Society because they feared that this would constitute immoral association with unorthodox people. Nonetheless, many Seceder, AR, and some RP churchgoers did actively work for the cause, including forming local abolitionist societies. Even breakaway sects, such as that of former Anti-Burgher Seceder "The Prophet Mathias" in 1830s New York, gravitated toward antislavery. Mathias continued to read Alexander McLeod's work long after abandoning his Seceder membership; his most famous disciple was the freed slave-turned-abolitionist Sojourner Truth. Another former Seceder, Alexander Campbell, founded the Disciples of Christ, which was initially an antislavery denomination.[20]

Covenanter ministers were vocal opponents of slavery in the public sphere. In 1827, RP Thomas Goodwillie preached an antistatist message before the Vermont legislature, demanding that Vermonters repent of their state's sins, especially having "a tenth part of our population groaning under the iron rod of slavery." James R. Willson's infamous sermon to New York's legislature condemned the constitutional protection of the slave trade until 1808, which made the traffic in effect "a national slave trade."[21]

In western Pennsylvania in 1838, AR minister Samuel Taggart preached and published an immediatist sermon entitled "The Power for & Against Oppressors." Taggart's message was closely aligned with McLeod's logic; he rooted his argument in the *longue durée* of Covenanter historical memory. Like McLeod, Taggart argued that pro-slavery biblical literalists failed their own test. "The right (to use men as property) must either be derived from God himself or else is assumed without any authority from the Creator," he insisted. Try as one might, the Christian would find "no such right given to the white man over the black, or to the black over the white" in the Bible. Addressing the southern argument that slavery was a human institution supported by the Bible, the Pennsylvania pastor echoed McLeod's belief that "unless it can be shewn that they practiced slavery in the same manner as [the Israelites], which we believe cannot be done," then the argument was invalid. To buttress his argument, Taggart quoted the Scottish Seceder poet Thomas Pollok. Covenanters sought only "to set the sin-bound prisoner free."[22]

How to go about setting the prisoner free remained a thorny question. Covenanters of all stripes roundly condemned slavery and called for abolition. Many embraced calls for immediate emancipation and participated in subversive activities such as the Underground Railroad. The railroad was less an organization than a collective experience, emerging as fugitive slaves crossed over from the most dangerous portion of their treks into the only slightly safer northern states. Sympathetic whites who encountered runaways directed them to the nearest antislavery towns and groups they knew or escorted them to safer hideaways. Because of their well-known views on slavery, Covenanter churches were interspersed within this informal network of underground stations. This was especially important in communities such as Randolph County, Illinois, where an RP congregation called Bethel became a first stop for slaves crossing the Mississippi River.[23]

In his 1898 study of the Underground Railroad, based on extensive interviews with railroad participants, William Siebert argued that communities of Quakers and Covenanters "became well known centers of underground activity" and that two Midwestern sects, the Wesleyan Methodists and the Covenanters, had reputations for interracial religious fellowship that assured fugitives of equal treatment as fellow Christians. Multiple Covenanter families appear in Siebert's compilation of underground participants. They populated the underground stations in towns such as Princeton, Indiana; Utica, Ohio; and Oakdale, Illinois. In a 1948 study, David Wilcox examined the antislavery RPs of the Midwest and found extensive overlap between known lines of the railroad and pockets of RP settlement. Wilcox found that the historical memory of RPs was laden with stories of slaves hidden in family homes and on church balconies.[24]

What set Covenanters apart from other stations was the use of force. Unlike the pacifist Quakers, the Covenanters held no reservations about employing firearms in a righteous cause. Midwestern whites interviewed after the war remembered that few fugitives were ever forcibly taken from under "the aegis of the Hayes and Moores and Todds and Mclurkins and Hoods and Sloanes and Milligans of that region"—all prominent Covenanter and Seceder families. One center for railroad activity was Geneva College in Northwood, Ohio. Covenanter college students connected their family farms into a network of safe harbors throughout Ohio, including a cave on RP Isaac Patterson's property where fugitive slaves were kept and fed for two- to three-week periods until the search parties were safely gone. In one instance, armed students posing as a "hunting party" organized two wagons to transport runaways from the caves ninety miles overland and helped procure their further passage to Canada.[25]

Immediate abolition was especially popular among Covenanters in the Midwest, many of whom had immigrated out of the South. Others on the East Coast, however, gravitated away from a staunchly immediatist position, instead leaning toward gradualism. McLeod, the intellectual voice of American Covenanter antislavery, led the way. He typified the move from radicalism to moderation by becoming an early and strong advocate of the ACS's vision to send freed slaves as missionaries to Africa. Samuel Wylie believed that not since "the discovery of America, and the Reformation by Luther" had there been an idea "more pregnant with more important consequences." In 1828, the Reformed Synod officially approved support for the ACS and recommended that its congregations support the organization financially. It included a resolution that emancipation "be accompanied in all cases, not contrary to the will of the emancipated, with a removal from the United States, to such place or places as the emancipated shall choose." Covenanters across the North viewed colonization as a viable means to abolition and for resolving the race issue in America.[26]

Many Covenanters clung to the belief that the ACS originated from within their own religious tradition. Wylie codified this creation narrative in his biography of Alexander McLeod, substantiating it by including letters from RP ministers in the book's appendices. According to tradition, McLeod had taken part in the discussions about organizing the ACS and argued for seeking out the support of President James Monroe and Congressman Henry Clay. At McLeod's funeral, it was stated that he had handed the plan for the ACS to Presbyterian academician Robert Findley, who then took it to the capital city. At least four Covenanter ministers informed Wylie that they had always believed this to be the case. One recalled McLeod's claim that the plan for the society "was penned in my study."[27]

It was important to many Americans on the Presbyterian fringe to maintain their radical credentials among their Atlantic brethren. McLeod's own rock-solid antislavery reputation helped make that case. Colonization, they insisted, was means to abolitionist ends. American delegates to the Synod of the RP Church of Ireland in the early nineteenth century assured their abolitionist brethren that "many efforts are a making to lessen [slavery's] baneful influence " primarily through the arm of "that truly laudable institution, the American Colonization Society." The delegates believed the ACS's early work to be "happy presages of a total emancipation, one day to be enjoyed" by all of the "oppressed sons of Africa."[28]

Covenanter defense of colonization did not go uncontested, and support for immediate emancipation remained strong. In the North, the RP Synod reversed position in 1836 in favor of immediate abolition. In 1838, a Covenanter served as president of the Union Antislavery Society of Philadelphia. Ministers such as N. R. Johnston in Vermont befriended William Lloyd Garrison. Garrison spoke fondly of the RPs as having the perfect example of abolitionist principles: to hold "No Union with Slaveholders, either religious or politically." In the 1820s, James Renwick Willson became editor of an abolitionist periodical, while Irish-born Covenanter John Black published a tellingly entitled tract, *The Bible against Slavery*, in 1839. Black argued against slavery using McLeod's literal logic: the church should admit neither man stealers nor horse thieves into its ranks. Another Covenanter saw racism as endemic to the colonization enterprise. Americans, he argued, "despise the colored man at home" but adored him in Liberia. In Africa, that man was "Mr.," or even "his excellency," but should that same man remain in the United States, the nation of his birth, "he is a 'nigger' and not to be walked with, nor ate with, nor sat with, even in church!" As late as the 1850s, however, many Covenanter laypeople and ministers, by now avowedly immediatist and opposed to the colonization scheme, still fondly recalled McLeod's role in founding the ACS. RP and ardent abolitionist minister J. R. W. Sloane publicly praised "that *amiable* and eminently *pious* institution, the American Colonization Society," in 1859. Whatever course it later took, Covenanters proudly claimed that the organization had been a kind of practical abolitionist society at its inception.[29]

## How to Be Antislavery in South Carolina

The issue of pragmatics was especially acute for antislavery people living in the pro-slavery South. Abolitionist Presbyterians in the South muted their beliefs after the initial fervor of the American Revolution. In 1787, Presbyterian Henry Pattillo of North Carolina was teaching that blacks and whites were equal and that abolition was a certainty; but in later years, he was hesitant to preach on the topic since "it offended some & pleased none." Abolitionist James Gilleland could only obtain ordination in South Carolina after promising never to preach on the topic, a promise he could not keep. After failing to keep his opinions quiet, he was forced to flee to Ohio. In Alamance, North Carolina, Eli Caruthers kept his antislavery views private until the outbreak of the Civil War; when he spoke out, he was subsequently sacked by the church session. Covenanters found antislavery in the South equally difficult.[30]

More Covenanters lived in South Carolina than in any other southern state—and ironically, it was the most pro-slavery of the pro-slavery states. It was a state with no political left, run largely by a hegemonic slaveholding oligarchy whose only struggles were with the poorer backcountry residents. Even these upstate citizens were generally amenable to laws that made it more difficult to manumit slaves, restricted the movements of free blacks, and outlawed teaching slaves to read. Given these circumstances, antislavery activism by AR and RP South Carolinians was far more radical than it might now appear. Their activities included agitation for the manumission of slaves, fundraising for the ACS, illegally teaching slaves to read, and advocacy for the legality of slave marriages.[31]

John C. Calhoun was the pro-slavery giant in the US Senate. He was on his way to becoming vice president when a Covenanter disrupted the local politics of his hometown. Calhoun was the primary patron of Pendleton Academy, an upstate institution that hired RP James Faris to be its new principal. Faris subsequently purchased a twenty-seven-year-old slave named Isaac for the express purpose of setting him free; this was meant as an object lesson in America's need for repentance. The lesson fell flat with neighbors, and he was forced to petition the Assembly of the State of South Carolina. Arguing that "every man is born free," Faris, "in agreeableness to this principle of natural and republican equity," sought to free Isaac. But the bulk of his petition dealt not with the slave but with slavery itself. This offending institution, whose assaults on freedom and family Faris enumerated, "[called] loudly for a remedy." The burden of providing that remedy lay on the state assemblymen, in order that "the vengeance of a righteous Providence may be averted from our guilty land." Faris was sacked and sent on his way, but this would not be the last time Calhoun's home territory was agitated by Covenanter antislavery.[32]

Raising the hue and cry against the sins of slavery could easily lead to exile from—and, not uncommonly, death in—South Carolina. Thus, southern Covenanters who did not participate in the mass exodus northward were especially prone to support the ACS plan; it was the only viable antislavery activity their southern neighbors would tolerate. One group of adherents just across the North Carolina border acknowledged that slavery was "both a moral and political evil, as it exists in our country." Yet, they believed, "until a revolution takes place in the public mind" of fellow Southerners, "every attempt towards emancipation must prove abortive." Covenanters in RP congregations in South Carolina advised the synod that regulating the treatment of slaves was best left to the southern congregations rather than to synod legislation, because "the power of the State is employed to prevent emancipation." In their tricky local circumstances, the memorialists promised to "act on the true moral intent of the avowed principles and laws of the Reformed Presbyterian Church." Hugh McMillan, who abandoned his labors in the South and moved to the Midwest, remembered the dilemma posed by preaching against slavery in South Carolina. "What shall I say to the slaveholder?" he asked. "If I say emancipate, he replies, it is impossible; I cannot free the slave here; and I cannot remove him out of the State" because of state law. McMillan was especially proud of the connections between colonization and abolition. "I was cheered to see that while the hand of slavery was closing the door of emancipation, the hand of Providence was opening it," he remembered.[33]

What Southerner Covenanters saw, and what they feared their non-southern brethren did not understand, was that even colonization represented a radical position in the Deep South. In September 1830, the ACS newspaper *African Repository and Colonization Journal* ran an article called "Colonization in South Carolina," penned by an AR minister. It depicted a hostile arena for colonization's aims, characterized by "censure and calumny, and abuse." South Carolinians could not be reasoned with, as logical "arguments are often powerless." Main-line Presbyterians whose farmland buttressed the land of an AR community in Abbeville District dismissed a pastor in 1838 simply because they suspected his pro-slavery advocacy of being insufficiently rigid. A Greenville man was beaten in 1851 merely because he was a member of the ACS, and the 1840s and 1850s saw at least eight convictions for abolitionist crimes across the state. Supporting colonization was made even more difficult by the South's taboo on preaching on political topics, especially on preaching against slavery. Southern Presbyterianism's most respected divine, James Henley Thornwell, proudly removed from his church the "angry disputes of the forum" and bragged that he "never introduced secular politics into the instructions of the pulpit." This pulpit gag rule stifled even the most careful of calls for rethinking the biblical morality of slavery.[34]

It was a bold challenge to the cultural norms, then, when South Carolina Covenanters disproportionately supported the ACS. Of the upcountry colonization donors, 63 percent were ARs. By the final decade of the antebellum era, the numbers were striking. Between 1850 and 1861, 88 percent of the money raised for the cause in upstate South Carolina came from identifiably AR sources, even though they never made up more than 1 or 2 percent of the state's population. This starkly contrasted with the Covenanting people of Vermont, who had only four people active in the ACS—representing only 3 percent of that state's membership rolls.[35]

The most open and avowed advocate of colonization in South Carolina was AR minister William Hemphill of Abbeville. Raised in Chester District, where McLeod and Wylie ended their antislavery preaching tour, and educated alongside Samuel Taggart in western Pennsylvania by antislavery Covenanter ministers, Hemphill was the son of an Irish RP. He lived most of his life as a pastor and educator in Abbeville District, South Carolina. He told his Carolina congregation in 1837 that the "accursed traffic in human flesh" had "long desolated that gloomy continent." The sin of the slave trade "brought a curse upon the world" that would never recede until the "jubilee of freedom" was "sounded there and everywhere." In 1852, he predicted that slaves would occupy higher places in heaven than their white masters. Those who had been "forbidden to read the word of God and who receive very little spiritual instruction" would "rise at the judgment day to condemn their superiors," he preached. Such words were rare in South Carolina's stifling racial climate.[36]

For Hemphill, colonization offered a moral way out of a tricky dilemma: how to live out the Old World faith in a New World dominated by slavery. As a Southerner, he could—and did—denounce northern abolitionists for "meddling with matters that by no means concern[ed] them." As a person of the Covenanting tradition, he in the same breath decried "the Riots that have taken place in the North," initiated by those trying to shut down abolitionist meetings and presses. He compared abolitionists with Paul in Ephesus and pro-slavery rioters with the mob that attempted "to put down Paul's preaching of the gospel message." Hemphill told a crowd of southern slaveholders in 1840, "If any nation on earth ought to feel interested in any scheme that would better the condition of Africa, it is the people of this nation." Americans had "long had in possession her sons + her daughters + have grown rich as a people by the process of the proceeds of their industry." Moreover, colonization could form a bridge between the moral correctness of the abolitionists and the social conservatism of slave owners. "This emancipation," he insisted, "would be far different" from that advocated by abolitionists and feared by slaveholders.[37]

Covenanter critiques of slavery and support for colonization were unconventional in the South. The Covenanters' literacy work among slaves was downright illegal. South Carolina passed laws against teaching slaves to read in 1740, 1800, and 1834. In 1801, Chester District ARs, under the leadership of William Hemphill's Irish father, John Hemphill, had argued that the antiliteracy law "infringes upon religious right." In 1828, the AR Synod of the South, the only group to protest South Carolina's literacy laws, proclaimed that these bans represented "serious infringement on the rights of conscience." A generation after their first appeal, the Chester congregation asserted that the 1834 literacy prohibition "invades the *rights of conscience,* and in so doing is unconstitutional." Many of their number felt "compelled from a sense of duty to violate the laws of the land." Subsequently, main-line Presbyterians from Abbeville District complained that local ARs were keeping "Sunday Schools in which a number of negroes are taught to read." Chester and Abbeville ARs responded to their neighbors' complaints with still further petitions to the legislature, claiming that "the law cannot be enforced." Even more unique, these petitions argued for slaves' rights under the "8th Article of the [state] Constitution," which mandated that "the free exercise of religious profession and worship without any examination or preferences, forever hereafter, be allowed within this state to all mankind." Surely, the petitioners reasoned, "our servants are part of mankind." As members of mixed-race religious communities, the AR petitioners were advocating not just for white rights but for black rights as well. The state could not interfere with rightly practiced religion, and when it tried the church trumped the state. This was the central tenet of all Covenanter teachings.[38]

The Covenanters' condemnation of both literacy laws and the abuses of slavery in South Carolina was intimately interwoven with their more overarching religious concerns. Cell group devotionals were the heartbeat of Covenanter piety dating back to seventeenth-century Scotland, and they viewed literacy as instrumental to those religious meetings. Black attendance in AR churches was high in the South, and membership was open to both slave and free applicants. In South Carolina, the black attendees made up nearly one-quarter of congregants. In Alabama and Mississippi, the proportions were almost equal. Not until 1850 did AR congregations begin segregating white and black applicants during communion, and church discipline was meted out with remarkable parity.[39]

Protecting the slaves' rights to read was vicariously a protection of Covenanter church autonomy. Even as southern ARs slowly drifted into a position of studied neutrality on slavery, they retained a fierce devotion to the idea that they advocated for civil and religious liberties. The state had no right to interfere with Covenanter religious devotionals that taught whites and blacks the tenets of Calvinist orthodoxy and Covenanter political theology. Moreover, by instructing slaveholders to "establish catechetical exercises on his premises" for blacks and whites alike, the Covenanters performatively recalled their legacy of outlaw conventicle piety. In an 1847 editorial, the South Carolina ARs stated boldly: "If the institution of slavery be so corrupt and brittle a thing as to be endangered" by making slaves "acquainted with the Scriptures . . . then let slavery go to the winds." Challenging the apolitical Presbyterianism of Thornwell and others, they argued, "If to sustain and perpetuate the relation between master and servant it is necessary to keep the Bible out of the hands of the latter, and to hold him in spiritual darkness—then that relation must be radically wrong and utterly indefensible."[40]

In 1845, South Carolina's political leaders gathered in Charleston to talk about slave religion. Current senator Daniel Huger and former secretary of war Joel Poinsett joined future Confederate treasury secretary Christopher G. Memminger and "Father of the Secession" Robert Barnwell Rhett. The South's religious leaders were there, too. Bishop William Capers had recently helped found the Methodist Episcopal Church, South, and the Reverend Richard Fuller arrived fresh off the train from the first meeting of the Southern Baptist Convention. Both of these new denominations had formed in defense of pro-slavery Christianity. A preeminent missionary to slaves, Presbyterian missionary Charles Colcock Jones, also attended. Jones had long ago abandoned his efforts to teach slaves to read out of deference to paternalistic masters. Few churches sought to catechize slaves, and those that did emphasized oral rather than written learning. For example, John Douglas, the Presbyterian minister from

Chester District, noted that about 100 blacks (eighteen of them members) attended his two congregations; however, his churches had not "introduced any system of catechetical instruction for the children and youth." Instead, "a gallery, or a quarter of the [worship] house [was] appropriated to them in all our churches." To explain the lack of black-focused evangelism, Douglas pointed out that there were no ministers working directly with the slaves in his area. Such statements were the norm.[41]

The next report, also from Chester District, came from Irish immigrant and AR pastor Warren Flenniken. His testimony was decidedly different from Douglas's. "There are about 213 negroes belonging to the people of my charge," he said, referring to his sect as "Seceders." Twenty-three of those African Americans were church members. Then, in his much more telling point, he claimed that "22 of this number (23) can read and probably two-thirds of the whole number (213) can spell and begin to try to read." He informed the stunned Charleston crowd that all of these slaves were catechized through writing exercises every Sunday during the intervals between worship services. AR elders did the teaching, using the *Westminster Shorter and Larger Catechisms*. Flenniken claimed that he interviewed slaves on his family visits and found that "almost every family catechizes them with the white children." Furthermore, the level of family devotional interaction went beyond weekly recitations. "Generally servants are required, and always permitted, to be present at family prayers," he said. Family devotionals were integrated and, most important, fostered literacy. Spoken in a state where teaching slaves to read violated the law and in the city that remained the hotbed for agitation in favor of that law's enforcement, Flenniken's claims amounted to a proclamation that ARs were in willful violation of state mandates and southern social mores. Such actions could not have been more counterculture in antebellum South Carolina, when most evangelicals were desperately trying to retain the good graces of slaveholders. These lawbreakers were not being good southern evangelicals. They were trying to be honest Covenanters.[42]

Literacy efforts did win some converts from beyond the AR fold, though these were isolated cases. In 1844, a South Carolina lawyer educated by the ARs at their college in Due West gave a lecture to the Abbeville Bible Society on the Christian duty to place a Bible in the hands of every slave and teach them to read it. Also in Abbeville, Presbyterian plantation owner A. E. Lesly noted in an 1859 diary entry that his slave, Henry, had commenced study in writing under the tutelage of an AR minister. These efforts made little headway against pro-slavery sentiment, however. Just two years later, Abbeville became the first town in the state to vote in favor of seceding from the Union.[43]

Covenanters also combated the evils of the godless southern slave state by trying to reform marriage laws. In 1845, Hemphill proposed a resolution that would require AR slave masters to restrict cohabitation among unmarried slaves and encourage marriages sanctioned under church law. Thus, masters would be restricted from separating slave spouses from one another under penalty of church censure. The resolution was moved to committee and passed the following year, stating that it was "the duty of all persons holding servants not to separate them when married to such a distance from each other as virtually to dissolve the marriage relation." If the husband and wife belonged to different masters and a sale by one of the masters was pending, it was "the duty of such church-members to adopt all fair, reasonable and honest measures to prevent the separation." Baptists in the South had similar discussions, but ARs alone attempted to make such actions binding on masters.[44]

Other, less systematic actions were taken by southern ARs and RPs against slavery. In 1845, the AR *Christian Magazine of the South* published a condemnation of the current slave trade, done in the name of Christian governments of Europe, with "all the injury done by slave-ships approaching a heathen coast under the abused flag of a Christian nation, to seize and fetter its unoffending inhabitants, and bear them away to helpless bondage." The magazine also reprinted a letter from the Presbyterians of Ireland calling for universal abolition, an action violating Southerners' tacit agreement to keep discussions that might inflame local sentiment out of local print. As late as the mid-1840s, ARs in the South were celebrating the writings of northern Covenanter Alexander McLeod, including his *Negro Slavery Unjustifiable*. These were bold moves in a state increasingly dominated by slaveholding political elites who tolerated little dissent about the peculiar institution.[45]

The AR response to the Nullification crisis of the early 1830s was also distinct. Ironically, ARs, whose tradition was so rich in radicalism, took on the role of southern moderates in the political conflict between state and national power. In 1828 and 1832, new and unpopular federal tariffs set South Carolinians aflame, giving rise to the idea that their state could nullify federal authority. Thinly veiled behind southern defiance were fears that if the national government could impose unwanted tariffs on the slaveholding South, forcible abolition might follow. Before it was over, President Andrew Jackson was authorized to use military force against the state's government, South Carolinian John C. Calhoun resigned as vice president and authored a thorough intellectual defense of states' rights, and the stage was set for the generations-long conflict between South and North. The Nullification theory espoused by Calhoun and his political allies, although reviled by most in the nation, was wildly popular in South Carolina.[46]

The crisis put Carolina's Covenanters in an awkward position. Should they stand up against the godless federal government or against the humanity-enslaving and rebellious state of South Carolina? Generally, they bucked local sentiment and opposed nullification. ARs referred to Nullifiers as "the violent party" and reported attempts by Nullifiers to suppress their right to vote for Unionist candidates. When one wayward son of the Chester AR church visited his friends, the lady of the house cleaned his clothing in the hopes that she could "steam the nullification out of him." Antinullification sentiments were not universal, however, and the conflict brought strife to congregations that church elders had to resolve using old-fashioned, Scottish-style church discipline. Just after South Carolina repealed the Nullification ordinance in 1833, William James Strong complained that David McCalla and three other church members "violently assault[ed] him & [beat] him with a stick." The session investigation found that "McCalla & Strong differed on politicks," and the elders chastised both men for fighting. The struggle of those at the fringe to remain a distinct people became a daily battle for those in the South. Being antislavery in the South, and especially in South Carolina, dwindled RP congregations into oblivion. The experience slowly eroded the radicalism of other Covenanters into a shadow of their eighteenth-century ancestors' faith. Still, the shadow remained far longer and stronger than that of any other sect in the South.[47]

## *Antislavery within the Fringe*

Just as it shook southern congregations, abolitionism was also a fertile fighting ground between the various sects on the Presbyterian fringe. Adherence to abolitionism served as a barometer of Covenanter authenticity. Some viewed antislavery as an extension of their own struggle against Britain, pointing out that "many of the persecuted covenanters were conveyed across the sea and sold as slaves to the colonial planters." Slaves, then, were fellow brethren enslaved by an evil, powerful, and God-defying government. What to do about this was a less settled matter, however.

Various groups claimed the Covenanter mantle, as debates raged between those who claimed to be the most true to the Good Old Cause and those who argued that principle without pragmatism was doomed to fail.[48]

Increasingly, the immediatism/gradualism distinction was becoming an internal dividing line among Covenanters. RPs were the most consistent immediatists, and ARs were the most gradualist. Though there were some interdenominational divides, the biggest divides were geographically rooted within each sect. The most dogmatically abolitionist ARs, RPs, and Seceders were found among the Midwestern exiles now residing in Ohio, Indiana, and Illinois. The people who remained in the South, and therefore lived surrounded by the conundrum, were more apt to gravitate toward gradualist approaches such as colonization. Somewhat more divided were East Coast churches in Pennsylvania and New York, although their abolitionism was, on the whole, more consistent than their gradualism.[49]

RPs, in by far the most hard-line denomination, divided on the moderation problem along geographical lines. In Charlotte, North Carolina, one Society member cautioned his northern brethren to tone down their antislavery articles in denominational publications because "too much vehemence manifested on the subject of slavery" made relationships with their neighbors difficult and rendered local activism unproductive. "We see the disease," he assured his northern brethren, but finding a remedy was made harder by antagonizing slaveholders. This call for pragmatism played a role in the 1833 schism in the RP Church. The Southerners requested that the excommunication of slaveholders be at the discretion of individual church sessions, which could take into account those local circumstances, where "the power of the state is employed to prevent emancipation." Engagers were sympathetic to these requests and admitted that it was "much easier to expose [slavery's] evils, than suggest or execute a feasible plan for its extinction." Engager hopes increasingly—and ironically—began to hinge on the US Constitution itself. The provision allowing Congress to act against the Atlantic slave trade after 1807 had indeed led to the trade being outlawed. And, as the Nullification crisis demonstrated, even powerful slaveholders could not stop the federal government from forcing its laws on unwilling states. Perhaps, they reasoned, activist Christian influence in Washington, D.C., would convince the federal government to impose abolition on the South.[50]

This logic was anathema to Old Light RPs, who continued to maintain that they could not in good conscience engage with a wicked government.

If obedience was mandatory even to wicked powers, then slaves had no right to seek their freedom. This struck hard-liners as absurd. "Jesus Christ had not robbed him of the very elements of manhood," one minister asserted. The right to choose liberty or death, so sacred in America and to Covenanters writ large, could not be denied to slaves. If resistance was justified, then, justified by what? Resistance, therefore, was justified by "the unrighteousness of the ruler or the institution of rule itself." To abandon such a position on disobedience, they felt, opened the door for confusion on the slave issue.[51]

The struggle among ARs was even more pronounced, since a greater percentage of that denomination was located in the southern states. Many of the internal debates between AR ministers began while they were in college. Most were trained in Pennsylvania schools such as the neighboring Jefferson and Washington colleges, both established with the help of Seceder ministers. There, southern ARs, such as colonization supporter William Hemphill, studied alongside northern AR abolitionists, such as Samuel Taggart. The peculiar institution was a constant topic of debate in the various campus literary societies, and these debates continued to rage in the unofficial correspondence between ministers throughout their careers. Hemphill freely lectured Taggart on the "dangers of immediacy," while Taggart scoffed at his old friend's accusation that "the abolitionists have caused the Legislature of [South Carolina] to throw a serious obstacle in the way of teaching the black." One AR minister admitted that his fellow Southerners "cannot or will not view the subject in the same light which it is viewed in the North and West." Both sides were talking past one another in an effort to prove that they were either more authentic or more reasonable than the other.[52]

In denominational publications, Midwestern ARs accused their southern brethren of being "magnetized by southern principles," in effect turning their moral compass's true and principled north into a corrupted south. Letting slavery be, they avowed, was akin to standing still in a moral race: "We think a stationary church is, something like a stationary Christian, in a somewhat precarious position."[53] Southerners, meanwhile, accused northern ARs of the "use of Abolitionist drugs," which caused their moral zeal to overheat. Their publications genuinely congratulated the Northerners for refusing to hold slaves and barring slaveholders from church membership. Yet they also defensively insisted that they had never once passed resolutions approving of slavery and pointed to their efforts against slave literacy bans as evidence that they disapproved of legislation that treated one group of humanity differently than another. Their protest was not against antislavery actions but, rather, immediatist abolitionists, they insisted. They cautioned that loud ultimatums for slavery's immediate end were spurring their slaveholding neighbors to increasingly desperate measures. "History will record that a fanatic North," AR planter George Pressly noted in his daybook, "is the cause of occasion of the dismemberment of this Union."[54]

Southern ARs were more deeply ingrained into the slave economy than they liked to admit, however. They consistently refused to make slaveholding grounds for excommunication and struck an awkward internal peace between their slaveholding and antislavery members and ministers. When the southern Seceders were ejected by their northern brethren over a debate about slavery's sinfulness, they easily merged with the AR Synod of the South in 1844. Some ARs owned slaves, and a few participated directly in the plantation economy. Somewhat less clear is how ARs treated their slaves. Most members certainly internalized the mainstream southern ideals of white paternalism, in which the masters' love for their slaves as "family" existed in tandem with cruel, often inhumane discipline to keep their workforce in line. Somewhat more controversially, AR documents record the regular hiring out of slaves for wages. This in and of itself was not uncommon; however, these records seem to indicate that the wages were paid directly to the slaves themselves, rather than to their masters. For instance, in 1855 in Abbeville, South Carolina, three slaves named Washington, Ned, and Caesar were hired for thirty-three days of work. Washington received $1.25 per day; Ned, $0.75; and Caesar, around $0.70. Another AR slave, carpenter George Grier, was hired out to a Presbyterian planter. When he was overheard preaching an antislavery sermon infused with Covenanter theology, the resulting controversy (in which local ARs supported his message) indicated that he lived a semi-independent life under the protection of his master. After the Civil War, AR slaves were also able to purchase delinquent plantation houses with their antebellum savings. Whether these examples represent anomalies or unclear bookkeeping or hint at efforts by ARs to keep black church members legally protected but functionally free can only be speculated.[55]

The people who made up the Covenanter movement were not monolithic, and there were outliers who rejected the overwhelmingly antislavery consensus. Most of these people left the denominational confines altogether. Early Covenanters were antislavery but had few qualms about bound indentured servitude. John Cuthbertson, the only Covenanter minister in the colonies at the time, had a young woman named Margaret Bell "bound with me 2 years and 5 [months]." But outright slave ownership and avowedly pro-slavery arguments were always considered a bridge too far. William Martin was expelled from the RPs because he owned and sold a single slave. Alexander Craighead owned several slaves late in life, but this was after he had abandoned his official correspondence with the RPs of Scotland and rejoined the mainstream Presbyterians. Some southern Covenanters similarly rejected their old radicalism. Though his grandfather had been an antigovernment conventicler "who followed field meetings" in Scotland, Robert Witherspoon distanced himself from his Covenanter roots to avoid the taint of the RP antislavery tradition. He left his Irish Knockbracken home for Williamsburg, South Carolina; became a slaveholder; and refused to enter into fellowship with the Society People.[56]

No Covenanter rejected the old faith more visibly than Senator John Hemphill of Texas. The son and namesake of an RP pastor who had entered the ministry soon after the AR union in 1782, he was the sharpest mind in a family richly blessed with mental acuity. His father was a leading southern Covenanter in the Early Republic, and his brother William led the church's ACS and slave literacy campaigns. John Hemphill went to college, entered the newspaper business, and studied law, despite his father's wish that he enter the ministry. The young lawyer rejected his father's piety with a vengeance. He survived multiple stabbings and duels, killed at least one Indian, and fervently supported nullification and slavery. His knife fight with a Unionist-leaning opponent in the 1830s precipitated a riot in Sumter, South Carolina, that filled the streets. His political rise came after he immigrated to the new nation of Texas, where he became the chief justice of the Texas Supreme Court and was twice considered for the presidency. In 1859, he took Texan hero Sam Houston's seat in the US Senate, where he spoke out strongly for the southern right to secede. Elected as a senator in the Confederacy, he helped write the Confederate Constitution and died in office in Richmond in 1862.[57]

But even in his rejection of the family faith, all was not as it seemed with John Hemphill. Though he renounced Covenanter doctrine, Hemphill could never completely shake off his heritage. Hemphill's judicial rulings on issues of race displayed a surprising racial parity. His was one of only two southern courts to rule that blacks, whether slave or free, held common law rights. He overruled Texas laws that prohibited manumission and that required free blacks to leave the state or re-enter slavery. His racial egalitarianism may have been rooted very close to home. Hemphill, who never married, was in love with his black mistress, Sabina, with whom he had two daughters. As the Civil War approached and he left to write the Confederate Constitution, he sent his girls away to attend the fledgling Wilberforce University. Wilberforce was an abolitionist institution in Ohio named for Britain's most famous emancipator.[58]

## *Covenanters, Conflict, and Civil War*

As the national tensions intensified in the 1840s and 1850s, Covenanters in the North took increasingly radical positions, while southern ARs awkwardly continued to seek a middle ground between their religious traditions and contemporary circumstances. As southern politicians pushed the United States into war with Mexico in 1846, the RP Synod declared the conflict "an unjust and bloody war against a neighboring republic." Worse, it had "the evident intention of enlarging the slaveholding power of the United States." Meanwhile, the ARs in the South, where the war was far more popular, called the nation to repentance. They countered wartime enlistment advertisements with calls to defend "the throne of the Prince of Peace" instead of the honor of the United States.[59]

In the buildup to crisis that led to the Compromise of 1850, the RP Synod pointed not so subtly to slaveholding senators such as John C. Calhoun and lamented that "the manstealer is exalted to the high place of power." Woe unto the nation, they cried, that it was guided by such leaders. That same year, at the University of Illinois, D. S. Faris wrote an undergraduate paper on the evils of slavery, declaring in magniloquent republican fashion that the "arbitrary, villainous law, the Fugitive Slave Act," was "unspeakably more insulting and violating to the conscience of freemen than any act of the British Parliament." In 1851, the RP Synod agreed, stating that the law was "essentially tyrannical." It was now the church's prophetic duty to teach Americans that "magistrates in Christian lands should yield to the authority of God's law, and that any law that is in opposition to the precepts of the Bible does not bind the conscience, and ought to be resisted." Covenanter writers labeled the 1857 *Dred Scot* Supreme Court decision, which ruled that slavery trumped the laws of free states, had "reached a deeper depth of iniquity" than the nation had ever seen before. The ruling was deemed "far worse than the Constitution itself—bad as that is."[60]

Covenanters interpreted the crises of slavery throughout the 1850s as further evidence of the guilt of the US Constitution and God's coming judgment on the unchristian nation. That document's "pro-slavery clauses," especially the three-fifths clause, undercut the twin foundations of right government: "the fear of God and regard for human rights." So long as the Constitution stood, freedom could not truly exist anywhere in America. Hope remained, however. If the free states would break fellowship with the South and acknowledge God's headship, "the slaves would see to the rest." Covenanters saw violent conflict as all but inevitable and hoped that God would use war as a crucible to grind a sinful secular state into a truly Christian American nation.[61]

On the eve of the Civil War, Covenanter political preaching took on increasing relevance. It also came under immense scrutiny, from both within and without Covenanter denominations. "The Bible is a great political work," RP J. R. W. Sloane proclaimed in 1859. He urged his fellow ministers to engage in "Political preaching," which would require "rebuking great national and political sins. . . . This kind of preaching is not only legitimate, but the very kind which, in this age—when national iniquity is coming in like a flood—is especially demanded." Never before had the nation sat at the precipice of a war, ready to fight over what was or was not sinful. This was a moment fertile for receiving the long-ignored Covenanter witness.[62]

Slavery caused the Civil War—on this all Covenanters agreed. In 1859, abolitionist John Brown ushered in what northern Covenanters saw as the first glimmer of light in national darkness when he attempted to raise a slave army in the heart of Virginia. Covenanters were eager supporters of Brown. RP A. M. Milligan wrote to the would-be revolutionary, now awaiting execution in jail, extolling him as "a martyr to civil liberty." After an extensive outpouring of Scriptural encouragement, Milligan asked Brown a peculiar question. Had he made his raid into Virginia simply on behalf of the slave, or was it also "for Christ's sake, as well as for the cause of his oppressed people"? Milligan and his flock urged Brown to be a witness of "God's controversy with this nation for dishonor it does to his majesty. This nation, in its Constitution, makes no submission to the King of Kings." Brown replied warmly to "my Covenanter friend" and noted that Milligan was one of the few people "whose judgment so nearly coincide[s] with my own." Publishing it just two months after Brown's execution, the *Reformed Presbyterian* used the letter to demand that "the evils in the Constitution be removed" and that it be amended to "exemplify the scriptural institution of civil government." Northern Covenanters eagerly anticipated the unraveling of the Union and the national cleansing they hoped would follow the ejection of the sinful South.[63]

Below the Mason–Dixon line, Covenanters were of a different mind than both their northern brethren and their southern neighbors. As a traveler through upstate South Carolina's heavily AR Chester District reported, "Disunion [was] a no go in this district, at least owning Seceders." Southern ARs initially supported the Republican Party. But after the 1860 election, they began fearing that it was too quickly drifting into the arms of ultra-abolitionists; the radicals would light a spark in the dry tinder that was the southern political environment, rife as it was with conspiracy theories of northern plans to free the slaves. When war came, both sides of the Covenanter family felt that it fulfilled their long-standing prophecies. For Southerners, it was the inevitable result of not listening to their calls for moderation and pragmatism on the slave question. For Northerners, it portended God's conflict with the ungodly nation.[64]

Fighting the war again caused division between the engager and hard-liner impulses within the movement. RPs especially believed that the Civil War endangered their peculiar political testimony. For hard-liners, the unbroken witness of centuries of political dissonance was imperiled by the allure of patriotic service. For Engagers, by far the majority across all sects, the danger was equally real. After centuries of testimony against the sinfulness of slavery, failing to show up for the fight seemed something akin to political cowardice hiding behind religious skirts. To sidestep issues of conscience, the RP Synod approved an alternative enlistment oath in which people could swear fealty to the country itself instead of to the (sinful) Constitution. Thus freed from their overly rigid nonparticipation requirements, Covenanters joined the Union Army and fought in the earliest campaigns all the way through Sherman's march. Geneva College, an RP institution, saw most of its students leave in order to fight. Two of the sixty-seven students who served the North rose to become generals. Twelve were killed. Covenanters had long predicted this crisis; they were excited that they could now help resolve it.[65]

Only the most dedicated hard-liner elements within the Reformed Presbytery resisted enlistment efforts. This Old Light remnant believed that "putting down a slave holder's conspiracy and freeing the slave to preserve a nation in rebellion against the Lord" was "doing the work of the Lord deceitfully." A minority report from the RP Synod of Iowa protested an 1861 synod decision to allow enlistment despite denominational qualms over the Constitution. They could not be bound "to take up arms in this war for the maintenance of the Union and Constitution," because it was "still immoral, unscriptural and slaveholding." In 1862, the Synod of Alleghany also modified its engagement by approving general support for the war effort *against* the slaveholding Confederacy but not *for* the Union itself. Even this extreme minority of Covenanters, however, dove headlong into what they saw as a moral war against an ungodly oppressor. During and after the conflict, several went as missionaries to freedmen and freedwomen in Arkansas, Florida, South Carolina, and Washington, D.C. A short-lived mission to Mississippi was destroyed by white terrorists. As with AR in the Carolina backcountry, the heart and soul of the northern Covenanter mission to freedpeople was literacy education and the catechisms. The pinnacle of their work was when they recruited free blacks to Geneva College.[66]

Southern Covenanters watched with horror as the war forced them to choose between their old religious identities and their emerging place as loyal southern moderates. The first meeting to vote for secession in South Carolina occurred in Abbeville District, the home of the very colonizationist ARs who for decades had urged antislavery on unwilling neighbors and gradualism on their northern brethren. At the Abbeville Courthouse meeting, AR E. L. Patton counseled caution—but he was shouted down by the crowd. Thus began Patton's and other Covenanters' transitions into new roles as "reluctant Confederates." This evolution from sectarian outliers into mainstream Southerners is interestingly documented in a single diary entry from Virginia AR minister John H. Simpson on May 10, 1861. "Great changes take place in one year," he noted. That same day one year earlier he "was in Chicago at the Convention which nominated the vile Abe Lincoln for President of the U.S.A. But thanks to God not of the South. Read Bible." Southern Republicans were already a rare breed by 1860. By 1861, even those southern Covenanters willing to reside far outside of the mainstream had integrated into the southern cause. Most never looked back. At the AR college and seminary in Due West, South Carolina, nearly the entire student body enlisted in the Confederate Army.[67]

The only thing that unified all Covenanters through the Civil War was a belief that slavery caused the conflict. Even Southerners agreed. "Slavery is the chief cause of this war," one South Carolina AR wrote in an editorial, and he doubted whether "God would allow such a dreadful war as that which now rages, and is falling with such ruinous effect on the South, on account of slavery, if the institution was perfectly free from defects."

After the Confederate loss at Antietam, Abbeville District ARs were certain that God had not smiled on the southern cause: for decades, southern slaveholders had assaulted God's holy institution of marriage. "There is no law," one pointed out, "as far as known to us, in any of the slave-holding states to protect the marriage relation of slaves, and any master through the promptings of interest, may separate his servants who claim to be husbands and wives and sunder the marriage connection." Such a sinful invasion into the family was the tyranny of master over slave. "We have not a doubt," Covenanters opined, "that this state of things is one reason why the terrible judgments of heaven are upon us, and these judgments will continue until the evils complained of are remedied." God's judgment extended to all unrighteous acts of government from Scotland to Ireland and from America to the Confederacy. Having lived through the intertwined politics of states rights, nullification, and slavery, the ARs in South Carolina were convinced that the Civil War was a conflict first and foremost about slavery. "The perpetuity and extension of the institution of slavery," William Hemphill stated in 1862, "was the principle thing which led to the war." It was "not at all probable that God would allow so great a calamity" on account of the sin of slavery "and then leave it just as it stood before the war." By 1864 they were more sure than ever that the sin of slavery had brought about southern destruction as powerfully as the Union Army. "If slavery is the cause of the war there must be some radical defect in the system," one South Carolinian Covenanter wrote, "or God would not, on account of the system, bring such a terrible judgment on the South, in fact the whole country."[68]

Northern Covenanters referred to the conflict not as the Civil War but as the "slaveholders rebellion" or that "iniquitous war now raging, *in the interest of slavery*." Covenanters were just as certain of this as they were of their belief that the nation was not Christian. For them, the two tragedies were one. Historians of the Civil War generally resist the urge to cast the conflict as inevitable. They emphasize the contingencies of human choices rather than some deterministic force rooted in a peculiarly American dilemma only solvable by division and conflict. The Covenanters had no such qualms. For them, the Civil War was the inevitable result of a Constitution with religious defects. One RP reflected that secession was rooted in Americans' belief that the Constitution was "only a compact between sovereign and independent States . . . from which any of the parties can withdraw at pleasure." He speculated that a Christian government "might have restrained the Southern States from their folly and madness, and saved the nation," since southern Christians would not want to rebel against God himself.[69]

Slavery was simply the nation's back-breaking straw of godlessness, according to the Covenanter ministers. "That slavery is the immediate or proximate cause of the war, can hardly be doubted by any whose eyes are open," RP James Wallace told his audience at a political rally; and that "God intends to destroy slavery by this war, is almost equally certain." J. R. W. Sloane looked out upon the Jefferson College graduates of 1862 and assured them that they were living through "a grand historical epoch, like the period of the Reformation, the English, French, or American Revolution." Americans could not exit out the door they had entered; they must arrive at the war's end as a different people. The immediate political question was slavery, but for Covenanters this led to another, more pressing matter that the war must forever decide: "Are we not a Christian nation? And are we not nevertheless in the furnace of war, heated in God's wrath seven times hotter than is wont? I answer, in sorrow, *No*. We are not in any true sense a Christian nation."[70]

The United States could be a Christian nation, though. This was the message a delegation of Covenanters brought to President Lincoln in the White House in 1862. The War between the States mirrored God's conflict with the nation, and God had a plan. The American Revolution had created an independent America, but now the Civil War could create a Christian America.

# 5

# *Rejecting a Christian Nation*

*We the People of the United States, humbly acknowledging Almighty God as the source of all authority and power in civil government, the Lord Jesus Christ as Governor among the nations, in order to constitute a Christian government, to form a more perfect Union. . . .*

—Constitutional preamble as proposed by the National Reform Association, 1874

THE COVENANTERS NEARLY put Jesus into the Constitution. In the process, they helped a new American liberalism find its voice and set the bounds for acceptable religious reform in American politics. During and after the Civil War, members of Covenanter denominations mounted a high-profile campaign to amend the Constitution's preamble to establish an explicitly Christian government. Finally, if only for a brief moment, the nation was listening. By the time their campaign was over, the Covenanters had presented their case in the presence of, and in some cases convinced, leaders such as President Abraham Lincoln, Senator Charles Sumner, US Supreme Court Justice William Strong, and prominent evangelist Charles Grandison Finney. One of their supporters, Associate Justice David Brewer, successfully declared the nation Christian in *Holy Trinity v. United States*. Yet, in their vehement and successful counterattack, America's secular Left coined the term *liberal* for themselves. Through political rallies, reform organizations, petition drives, press offensives, a Pulitzer Prize, and strategic partnerships with other evangelical reformers, Covenanters gained new currency for their ideas in postbellum America. Ultimately, they exhausted that credit in a failed bet that Americans wanted a Christian nation.

The postwar experience again took northern and southern Covenanters in different directions. In the North, adherents retained a distinctive voice of political dissent even as they increasingly interacted with the nexus of moral reformers attempting to regulate Americans' personal lives. In the South, bereft of the slavery issue and with only their psalm singing to set themselves apart, Associate Reformed Presbyterians (ARs) quickly absorbed southern racial conservatism until there was little distinct left about their religion. In both regions, Covenanter groups struggled to enforce their vision of Christian government on unwilling neighbors. In the North this involved lectures and lobbying; in the South it eventually involved leaving the Covenanter legacy behind.

## *President Lincoln and the God Amendment*

When Abraham Lincoln sat down with his Cabinet in December 1864, he made a shocking proposal for his upcoming State of the Union. He had drafted language recommending that Congress amend the Constitution to recognize God's authority over the nation. After his Cabinet members universally condemned the proposal, which Secretary of the Navy Gideon Welles noted had been urged on the president "by certain religionists," Lincoln agreed to lay it aside.[1]

These "religionists" were Covenanter ministers, who had launched a petition campaign aimed at amending the Constitution to make the United States a Christian nation. Two years earlier, in late 1862, J. R. W. Sloane and A. M. Milligan had met with the president, bringing with them two appeals for constitutional changes: one to end slavery forever, the other to submit the nation to God. The president's recently announced Emancipation Proclamation, which freed only those slaves living in Confederate territories, had given Covenanters the hope that the once improbable was now possible. Since the nation's founding, those on the Presbyterian fringe had consistently witnessed against the Constitution's protection of slavery and for the inclusion of God. Once thought impossible, the first of those reforms was now within reach. Covenanters believed that there would never be a better time to achieve the second.

For over an hour, the two hard-liner Reformed Presbyterians (RPs) pleaded with the president for their twin causes. Calling themselves abolitionists "of the most radical school," they demanded that he go beyond freeing Confederate slaves and grant "immediate, unconditional and universal emancipation." More fundamentally, they asked him to use the crucible of war to correct the mistake of the Founders. Lincoln had the opportunity to make the United States "an example of a Christian state governed, not by mere political expediency, but acting under a sense of accountability to God," a nation that based its laws on obedience to the "immutable morality" of the Bible. The president, who had a line of angry and impatient callers waiting in the hallway, politely took their written petition, placed it on his personal desk, and thanked them for their time. Then, to everyone's surprise, he sat back down, stretched out his long frame, and began to wax philosophic on the nature of God and government in a civil war. Using words he would echo in his Second Inaugural Address, the president noted that while northern Christians considered the war God's judgment for the sin of slavery, Southerners considered it a punishment for interfering with a biblical institution. While he had always considered slavery an evil, he felt that it was only fair to recognize "that men were preaching and praying on both sides of the controversy." Besides, Lincoln said with a keen sense of the exigencies of war, the conflict was the punishment of providence for both sides, and the result might be different from what he or his petitioners hoped. The Covenanter ministers, undaunted, urged the president to see the conflict through their theological lens: God was scorned at the nation's founding, and his children were enslaved in his name. Surely, just as it was for the ancient Egyptians and the enslaved Israelites, violent judgment and divine deliverance was only a matter of time. The *New-York Daily Tribune* reported that the president listened attentively to a second Covenanter presentation in 1864. He promised to take the matter under serious consideration "and give it such attention as his duty [to] our Maker and our country seemed to demand."[2]

Lincoln evidenced great shrewdness in wielding the political power of religion. From his earliest days in politics, the young lawyer waged war for the moral high ground among the predominantly churchgoing voters of Illinois. As a young man, he rejected the extreme Calvinism of his Baptist upbringing in favor of the deistical skepticism of a precocious young mind. This heterodoxy proved politically perilous; he lost his first bid for a congressional nomination amid accusations that Christians could not in good conscience vote for him. From that experience, and from his active participation in grassroots political organizing, Lincoln came to respect the ability of church networks to mobilize votes on moral issues. Thereafter, he used religion to great effect in his political career, casting his campaign platforms in stark moral terms, calling more thanksgiving and fast days than any previous president, and meeting constantly with visiting clergy. This approach paid dividends. When Lincoln won re-election in an electoral landslide, it was in large part due to the overwhelming support of northern clergy who baptized the Union, the war, and the president with religious meaning.[3]

Yet Lincoln paid more than lip service to religion. Notoriously guarded about his personal faith before his election, once in office, the sixteenth president both privately and publicly wrestled with the relationship between the divine and the human more than any other president before or since. The dismemberment of the nation in 1861, the subsequent battlefield losses, the death of his beloved son Willie in early 1862, and his decision to tie the Battle of Antietam to emancipation later that year all awakened out of his lifelong fatalism the sense that a providential God works out his ends in the affairs of men. When Lincoln stretched out in his chair and waxed theological on the dangers inherent in presuming to know the mind of God, he was revealing to Covenanters his ongoing private struggle. Sometime during this period, the president scribbled his now-famous "Meditation on the Divine Will." In it, he first worked out the idea that God had a plan and that in the struggle between Union and Confederacy, "both *may* be, and one *must* be, wrong," since "God can not be *for* and *against* the same thing at the same time." If the North fought to preserve the old Union while the South fought to protect the slaveholding states, God's purpose might be a new Union purified from the sin of slavery. Two years later, these ideas also reappeared in Lincoln's Second Inaugural Address.[4]

With his re-election secured, and despite the doubtful political utility of such a move, Lincoln suggested to his Cabinet the idea of inserting God in the Constitution. In contemplating a religious amendment, Lincoln brought to bear his conflicted sense about God and America. The nation was at war both with itself and with divine providence. Only a higher purpose could redeem the series of failures that had brought about and perpetuated the violence. But Lincoln the philosopher was also Lincoln the lawyer; he recognized the validity of his Cabinet's concern. A Pandora's box of divisive constitutional issues would be opened by such a move. This legal logic was lost on American Covenanters, who were disappointed in Lincoln's failure to follow up on his earlier positive remarks and were unaware of his brief flirtation with inserting a much-reduced version of their plan into his 1865 State of the Union.

Like other radical abolitionists who helped propel Lincoln into the White House, the Covenanters now sought to move from the fringe to the forefront of American political life. Before the century was over, one of the nation's smallest fringe religious sects spawned a large, mainstream effort to amend the Constitution and create a Christian America. The politics of the 1860s gave Covenanters legitimate hope that the nation could and would change its Constitution to rid itself of unchristian legacies. Total emancipation had finally been achieved in the 1865 Fourteenth Amendment. If slavery could be eradicated from the nation's Magna Carta, why not political atheism? The Covenanters called for an end to slavery long before it was politically popular or plausible. They now sought to re-enact the abolitionist movement and baptize a God amendment with legitimacy. They reached out to "all evangelical denominations," asking them to take part in a "concert of action by pulpit and the press and by memorials" to raise awareness and bring political pressure to bear. Their White House audience marked the beginning of Covenanters's national political relevance, and they were determined it would not be its apex.[5]

For several years prior to the Lincoln meetings, the idea of a Christian amendment to the Constitution had gained traction among Covenanters of various denominations. They set out to upend the cultural complacency they found endemic among American Christians comfortable with "the entire divorce between religion and government which exists in the United States." In 1856, Erasmus D. MacMaster, Covenanter and first president of Miami College of Ohio, worried that the nation might need "some future Gibbon" to "sit amidst the ruins of the Capitol, and project the plan of the History of the Decline and Fall of the American Empire." MacMaster believed that such eulogies would be unnecessary if just two reforms were implemented: acknowledgment of God in the Constitution and the eradication of slavery. "The State," he told his students, was "instituted by God, as the Creator and Ruler of the world." Nations were, in a sense, individual people themselves. Thus, nations, like people, must confess their sins and look to the saving power of God.[6]

In 1859, the RPs called explicitly for a constitutional amendment. They enjoined Congress to "acknowledge the authority of Jehovah and his Son, Mediator," as well as to "effect the deliverance of the millions of human beings in bondage under its constitution." After drafting proposed language for the memorial, the Covenanters distributed copies to local congregations and solicited signatures. In a singular departure from their long tradition of separation, they also suggested participating in this effort with non-Covenanters.[7]

Calls for a Christian America fell on deaf ears until the Civil War prompted seismic shifts in thinking about the nature of government. As with so many things, the Civil War proved a turning point nationally for the overt Christianization of the federal government. Between 1861 and 1865, Congress called for fast days, began employing mass numbers of chaplains in the military, and placed "In God We Trust" on its money. Responding first to the war and then to the postbellum experiences of Reconstruction, economic collapse, and Catholic immigration, American evangelicals and establishment Protestants began to see their government as a tool for asserting hegemony over American culture. For the first time, American Christianity seemed open to exploring new and more permeable boundaries between church and state.[8]

The Civil War profoundly changed the relationship of Covenanters to the nation firmly to the advantage of the group's Engager strands. One-half of America's great offense to God was undone. The nation was entering a new era. "The coming age" was the "place and time in which the great problem of the proper relation of the Church of Christ to civil government is to find its true and final solution," the Rev. Sloane preached to the RP Synod. The Covenanters must take an active role in leading the nation from its deistical past into its Christian future.[9]

Hoping that a nation in crisis might now listen to its prophetic calls, the RP-affiliated Lakes Presbytery published an 1861 resolution informing the United States that the war was "God's controversy with this nation for their rejection of his name and authority." They called for an amendment by which the Constitution would "acknowledge God, submit to the authority of his Son, embrace Christianity, and secure universal liberty." Until the middle of the war, however, these efforts remained isolated to hard-liner Covenanters.[10]

News accounts of the conference with Lincoln breathed sudden and dramatic life into a previously internal debate among members of the Presbyterian fringe. Calls went out from a small cadre of Covenanter ministers for a meeting to debate the need to reform the Constitution itself. In early 1863, a "Convention for Prayer and Christian Conference" was held in Hamilton, Ohio, and then again in Xenia. United Presbyterian (UP) ministers dominated the meeting, as well as Engager and hard-liner RPs. A variety of local evangelical Methodists and Baptists also attended. The Covenanters used their abolitionism and Underground Railroad bona fides to pitch the idea of introducing an acknowledgment of God's authority and Jesus's magistracy into the Constitution. Attendees argued that the nation's sin was more than simple neglect of God's authority; it was outright idolatry. The Constitution founded the nation on the authority of "We the People," effectively placing humanity in the role of God. This drew general agreement, but the particular language used by the hard-liner RPs seemed too theologically restrictive to some attendees, and a message was finally agreed upon that all deemed sufficiently broad to encompass American Christians. A proposal was made to amend the Constitution to follow the words "We the People of the United States of America" with "recognizing the being and attributes of Almighty God, the Divine authority of the Holy Scriptures, the law of God as the paramount rule, and Jesus the Messiah, the Savior, Lord of all." Then, the proposal said, the Constitution could continue with "in Order to form a more perfect Union."[11]

Initially, the reception by nearby Ohio evangelicals was cool. Abolition was a known quantity, but most people gladly accepted the separation of church and state. Additionally, non-Covenanter attendees worried that the amendment introduced "denominational peculiarities of a distinctive nature" they deemed disruptive. In the wake of the meeting, Methodist newspapers displayed particular outrage at the idea of an amendment. Efforts—largely based out of UP circles in western Pennsylvania and funded by a wealthy RP merchant named John Alexander—to organize more meetings continued, however. Calls went out to evangelical ministers to support a movement to insert Jesus into and delete slavery from the Constitution. In an attempt to increase attendance and tap into patriotic energy, the next meeting was set for July 4, 1863, in the Covenanter heartland of Pennsylvania.[12]

On that surprisingly eventful Fourth of July, General Robert E. Lee's defeated Army of Northern Virginia began the long march south from Gettysburg. That same day and in that same state, a small band of Covenanter ministers gathered for their long-awaited "national" meeting. The Covenanters were nearly as disappointed in their results as Lee was in his. The northern invasion coupled with widespread Methodist disavowal of their ambitions thwarted their hopes for a larger and more ecumenical gathering. Covenanters such as RP Thomas Sproull had not helped the cause. Sproull had recently argued, in classically Rutherfordian fashion, that the proposed amendment could not violate individual rights since there were "no rights that stand in the way of honoring Christ." The moment to export Covenanter ideals of church and state into wider American Christian dialogue was quickly passing. Disappointment with the 1863 Pennsylvania meeting took the shape of a mass appeal to all evangelical Christians. The assembly eschewed their earlier hard-line antagonisms. They claimed that the American government had, by implication, recognized God's authority and Christianity when it passed the Judiciary Act of 1789. That act required that all oaths in the judicial branch be concluded with "so help me God," though it also made exceptions for those who preferred to affirm the oath without religious language. Employing this new big-tent approach, the organization met in early 1864 in Allegany, Pennsylvania, and organized the National Association to Secure the Religious Amendment of the Constitution. After ten years, the organization shortened its name to the National Reform Association (NRA). The war, its members proclaimed, was all the proof they needed "that we do not, *as a nation*, possess those moral qualities" a Christian nation must have in order to survive. Their organization made its purpose the Christianizing of the American government.[13]

Out of the gate, the NRA had a message problem. Its goal was ill suited to an American audience who revered separation of church and state, hallowed the Founding Fathers, and held up the Constitution as the highest model of government ever invented. This love for the Constitution, which one movement leader believed "akin to idolatry," caused many citizens to recoil in horror at the idea of it having any religious defect. Yet accusing American Christianity writ large of worshiping false political gods was sure to result in a stillborn movement, and organizers set out to rebrand the Covenanter message.[14]

The NRA tried to persuade their Founders-loving fellow citizens that they must change the Constitution in order to save it. Capitalizing on the American Christian assumption of a shared Protestant foundation, one advocate insisted that the consequence of an amendment would be to make the United States "in fact what in theory we claim to be," namely, "a Christian nation." They muted their traditional criticism of the Founders for not including God in the Constitution. J. R. W. Sloane even began lauding leaders such as "Washington, Adams, Madison, and Lincoln" as "those who [had] in the highest degree adorned and most worthily discharged the functions of this high station." Sidestepping questions about their orthodoxy, he maintained that these four presidents "most frequently declared their dependence upon God for that wisdom which they require in their high and responsible sphere." After the president's assassination, NRA spokesman John Alexander even compared Lincoln with Moses, who passed the nation over into the promised land of freedom, only to die just before entering it. This was a far cry from the earlier generation who had consigned the eighteenth-century paragons to the depths of eternal hell and cast contemporary politicians as manipulative Machiavellians who used religion only to suit their needs.[15]

The NRA argued that contemporary Americans had drifted from the Christian moorings of ancient Western society. They relied on their fellow citizens' sense of shared Protestantism to shape this more palatable message. America's problems were manifold and included Catholic attempts to restrict Bible reading in public schools; the government's Sabbath violations; Mormon efforts to "corrupt the Family" by advocating polygamy; liquor sales; the movement to abolish state- and federally sponsored prayer, fast, and thanksgiving days; and the general attempt "to divorce the American Government from all connection with the Christian religion." Americans were mired in political atheism, and their leaders would not or could not call on God for relief because the nation did not belong to him.[16]

The NRA sought to build "a union of Christian patriots" to support what quickly became known simply as "the Christian Amendment" or "the God Amendment." To this end, they began enlisting volunteers and paid workers, who were encouraged to temper any doctrinal squabbles. Their training manuals insisted that the NRA's main opponents were secular theories of government rather than fellow Protestants. They also tailored their appeal to Christianize America to the broad evangelical message that had been sweeping over the nation during the last century. NRA secretary James Wallace explained to a gathering in Illinois that because individuals must "accept Jesus Christ as [their] only Lord and King, and solemnly promise obedience to him in all things," then they must also allow God to "reign over them in their civil relations." To deny God's authority politically when you accepted it personally was "as strange as it was lamentable," Wallace argued. Other messages focused on the personhood of the nation. Just as the person was condemned by sin and must confess faith to be saved, so the nation stood judged by God until it called out publicly to Christ for salvation. For this reason, the NRA continued to insist on including Jesus, and not just God, in the proposed amendment. To do otherwise, they insisted, would be to substitute national Deism for national atheism.[17]

The most difficult thing to explain to American Christians was how the God Amendment would not conflict with the First Amendment. In 1873 A. A. Miner, Unitarian president of Tufts College in Massachusetts and an NRA supporter, expressed this new language about the protection of Christian heritage and the hallowing of the Constitution. "What was meant as a toleration of differences between Christians" in the First Amendment, he argued, was now "interpreted as a rejection of Christianity itself." Freethinkers had perverted the Founders' intentions and instigated a culture war on Christian elements of American society. Removing the Bible from schools, opening public institutions on the Sabbath, and rejecting biblical morality all evidenced this moral backsliding. Miner wondered aloud if "this noble theory of toleration" now implied its equal and opposite necessity, "the duty of suppressing, in all its laws," anything that offended any conscience no matter how gross a violation of Christian morality it might be. The goal of the NRA, he asserted, was not the combination of church and state but the salvation of the Christian culture of the United States.[18]

In a letter to the editor of the *New-York Tribune*, an anonymous essayist laid out a complementary case for a Christian amendment. After disavowing any desire for a narrow sectarian state, he argued that morality laws already upheld Christian beliefs and it would be a good thing if they acknowledged as much while they did so. If "we are a Christian nation, as distinguished from pagans and infidels," the writer argued, then he "knew of no reason why our National Constitution should be as much pagan and a *little* more infidel than it is Christian." If God was the source of all authority, America's governmental authority should say so. Then, employing themes that would be echoed in twentieth-century conservatism, he protested that the convictions of America's overwhelming majority were being trampled upon for the benefit of the godless minority. "We who are interested in this movement," he railed, "prefer not to live in silence under a Government where in all State affairs Christianity must be silent, and infidelity have everything its own way." But the editor of the *Tribune*, Horace Greeley, understood and rejected the implications of Covenanter philosophy. In his reply, Greeley said that it was ridiculous to think of America as a Christian nation. "France, Spain, Russia, Austria, Mexico, Portugal, Brazil, &c., *are* Christian nations," he insisted. But in the United States religion was a purely personal matter, and it was best to keep it so lest America revert to the ways of old Europe.[19]

Greeley, a moral political reformer in his own right, displayed the high hurdle of credibility the NRA must clear for their movement to succeed. They thus set out to people their organization with the nation's best and brightest Christian leaders. The first were public faces of the campaign—jurists, academics, and churchmen whose national reputations could help attain instant credibility in the public eye. The vast majority of these hailed from the rainbow of Protestant America, though Presbyterians were more likely to join than were people from other denominations. Second, they sought out the activists—worker bees who universally hailed from the Presbyterian fringe. These people wrote the newsletters, organized the public meetings, and circulated the petitions that kept the movement alive.

Two high-profile political converts gave the movement a quick boost of publicity in late 1864. James Pollock, director of the US Mint in Philadelphia, was the man who put "In God We Trust" on American money. He joined the NRA along with William Strong, an eminent jurist just five years away from being named to the Supreme Court. Strong, a Presbyterian, served at various times as president or vice president of the American Sunday School Union, the American Tract Society, and the American Bible Society. Naturally, the association elected him to the symbolic role of president multiple times throughout the late 1860s and early 1870s.[20]

The list of honorary officers, vice presidents, and secretaries ran the gamut from local to national political and educational leaders. After his appointment to the Supreme Court, Justice Strong highlighted the group. In the US Senate, Charles Sumner, B. Gratz Brown, and John Sherman were all early supporters. Following them were the governors of North Carolina, Missouri, and Nebraska and Kansas senator and future governor James Harvey. Three judges from US circuit and district courts were members, as well as members of the state and territorial supreme courts in Alabama, Dakota, Idaho, Iowa, Louisiana, New Mexico, Utah, Washington, and Wyoming. The president of the University of North Carolina, Solomon Pool, joined the NRA, along with a variety of presidents and professors at state and denominational colleges nationwide. The faculty of Princeton Theological Seminary signed on, as did several prominent denominations, including the northern Methodist Church, Old School Presbyterians, the German and Dutch Reformed, and the Episcopal Church. These memberships and endorsements were solicited for their ability to endow the movement with a patriotic and Protestant respectability.[21]

To further increase the NRA's bona fides, the leaders sought out evangelical godfathers whose reputation transcended denominational labels. Charles Grandison Finney was the image and voice of the Second Great Awakening, the phenomenon that took American evangelicalism from the religious outskirts to the cultural mainstream. The Covenanters had despised both him and his awakening for their excesses in religious emotion and rejection of orthodox Calvinism. By 1869, however, they realized that Finney would be a powerful ally. They met with the fiery-eyed preacher, now president of Oberlin College, and "he heartily endorsed the whole programme." Although he was fighting poor health and old age, in 1872, Finney managed to travel to the association's national meeting in New York City. Jonathan Blanchard was an abolitionist and founding president of Wheaton College, the future alma mater of prominent fundamentalists such as Billy Graham and Bill Gothard. Blanchard wrote to the *Christian Statesman* in 1870 to share his reasons for supporting the amendment. "Buddhism on our western border" had combined with the "deluge of paganized Christianity to the east" to surround American Protestants in an envelope of sin. Meanwhile, Mormons corrupted morality from within, and the stark choice left was between "an Atheistic Government" and a Christian one. "We must put Christ into our Constitution," Blanchard insisted, "or a Mormon will be our prophet . . . [and] priestism our religion." By 1871, the nation's most prominent new evangelist, Dwight Moody, signed on as well.[22]

Talking heads notwithstanding, critical day-to-day leadership still came from within the RP and UP churches. The activists were headed initially by UP John Alexander. RP minister James Wallace was employed by one presbytery to work full-time as a traveling agent for the National Reform Association of Southern Illinois. Because of his efforts, rallies were held in Illinois, Iowa, Michigan, Minnesota, New York, Ohio, and Pennsylvania. For many listeners, his speeches were their first exposure to the movement. T. P. Stevenson and David McAllister were the RP editors of the *Christian Statesman*, whose leadership was also critical. RP minister H. H. George was another key leader; he did double duty as field secretary of the National Sabbath Union. In the South, AR ministers were vocal supporters. Denominational heavyweights W. M. Grier, James Boyce, and Robert Lathan all joined the NRA. After the war, the NRA sent black RP theology student John Quarles on a preaching tour of the South in an attempt to recruit freedmen and -women to the cause. He found an audience among African Methodist Episcopal (AME) churches in the upper South. On the whole, however, the movement struggled to gain footing in the politically weary southern churches; southern Christians were not inclined to embrace another clash with the US Constitution.

The UP Church, formed when the Associate Reformed and Seceders joined just before the Civil War, was the first but not the only denomination to endorse the NRA. In 1864, the General Conference of the Methodist Episcopal Church and the Old School Presbyterian General Assembly both gave their support to the God Amendment, although they excluded language about Christ as mediator and ruler of nations. As the years wore on, the NRA became increasingly tolerant of religious diversity and insistent that it would not seek the disenfranchisement of nonbelievers. This caused many Covenanters to grow wary of their own movement, the RPs in particular, who balked at anything less than "a complete reformation of the Constitution." Their more ecumenical members, in turn, became equally wary of "that terrible old lion, Persecution," on the prowl in the organization. Mostly, though, things built toward a big-tent model.[23]

Through these combined efforts, the NRA's popularity rose dramatically across the 1860s and 1870s. Even before the Civil War's end, the association included Quakers and Episcopals and stretched from California to Massachusetts. By 1876, it had amassed more than 10,000 members. Unitarian senator Charles Sumner wrote a letter encouraging the cause. "It can never be out of season," the nation's leading abolitionist politician stated, "to explain and enforce mortal dependence on Almighty God." Timothy Vinton, rector of New York City's Trinity Church, considered it a "blot on our nation" that the United States was "the only civilized nation on Earth that does not acknowledge God in its fundamental law." Missouri senator Benjamin Gratz Brown stood on the Senate floor and decried the United States' "practical atheism in government." Such high-profile statements served the public awareness campaign the NRA waged on the Constitution's secularism, which then led to its second tactic: petitioning Congress.[24]

Time spent in the abolitionist campaign had taught Covenanters how to effectively organize petition drives, and they used this experience to great effect. The NRA sent out sample congressional petitions for local activists to use, with instructions on how to get them submitted. Congress received 18,500 signatures on hundreds of petitions supporting the God Amendment in 1869 alone. The next year, the number climbed to more than 25,000. Meanwhile, the same congressional session saw just two petitions for an eight-hour workday, six for tighter naturalization legislation, and 700 signatures for female suffrage. In 1874 and 1875, nearly 8,000 people signed their names to temperance petitions, and despite a nationwide organizational effort, the Civil Rights Bill of 1874 received less than half the number of signatures of support as did the God Amendment. In those years, the NRA claimed that it had 50,000 signatures on new petitions and was holding out for more. Enthusiasm was more tempered later in the century, but periodically, the organization renewed its efforts. In the 1890s, one California woman signed up 1,000 petitioners. An Illinois petition stretched twenty-five feet, and another of nearly the same length came in from Ohio.[25]

The amendment movement took a shot at a state constitution in 1861 when RP minister John Crozier began pushing the Indiana legislature to Christianize its government via amendment. A bill successfully came out of a legislative committee to acknowledge God as "the source of all power and authority in civil government" and Christ as ruler of nations whose revelation was "supreme authority." All this, said the committee, was done "in order to constitute a Christian government." An accompanying minority report pointed to the obvious theological problems of Christian state building: "For many ages pas[t] there have been wide differences of opinion among [C]hristian nations and communities themselves" as to what God's revealed will might be. Trading Indiana's current government, which the minority report believed was working just fine, for one "so impractical in its aspects," and in the middle of wartime no less, was neither timely nor wise. Convinced by the minority report, the Indiana Senate rejected the measure, saying, "Errors of faith are not crimes, and of right ought not to be made so." The motion was tabled and died.[26]

The 1863 conference at Xenia, Ohio, proposed that the preamble of the US Constitution should read: "We the people of the United States, (recognizing the being and attributes of Almighty God, the Divine authority of the Holy Scriptures, the law of God as the paramount rule, and Jesus the Messiah, the Savior, and Lord of all) in order to form a more perfect union. . . ." The next year, the NRA officially requested that Congress rewrite the preamble, inserting the clause "humbly acknowledging Almighty God as the source of all authority and power in civil government, the Lord Jesus Christ as the Ruler among the nations, his revealed will as the supreme law of the land and, in order to constitute a Christian government" after the words "We the People." Nationwide efforts to petition Congress followed, and Senator Sumner introduced the association's request on the Senate floor in 1864. The time had come to conform the government "to those divine truths that . . . inspire a devout Christian State," he said. Senator John Sherman also offered his support, acknowledging that "this nation and its institutions, have been built upon Christian civilization." This latest attempt to insert God into the Constitution was also sentenced to death by committee.[27]

A decade passed before a version was sent to the House Judiciary Committee. By now any such draft was popularly referred to as "The God Amendment" or "The Religious Amendment." The committee, much to Covenanter dismay, decided that such an amendment would subvert the intent of the Founders and tabled the vote. This defeat came on the heels of a pyrrhic victory in Pennsylvania's 1873 Constitutional Convention. No state had a higher concentration of Covenanter congregations and voters; AR, RP, and UP churches dotted the landscape from Philadelphia to Pittsburgh. But although they were given a full hearing by the convention, NRA advocates failed to convince the delegates to replace the government by the people of Pennsylvania with one recognizing "Almighty God as the source of all authority." Instead, the delegates ratified a document that thanked God "for the blessings of civil and religious liberty." Even a broadly Christian electorate in a strongly Covenanter state would not stand for a reconceptualization of American government.[28]

Stinging from the association's congressional defeat and its failure to make headway elsewhere, former NRA president and current Supreme Court justice William Strong expressed his disappointment to the students at Union Theological Seminary in New York City. Into an otherwise dry address on church property law, Strong embedded a moving reminder that churches had ongoing legal relationships with both state and federal governments dating back to their conceptions. "The laws and institutions of all the States," Strong insisted, "are built on the foundation of Christianity." He "considered as settled, that the religion revealed in the Bible [was] not to be openly reviled or blasphemed" without punishment by the civil law. Strong's studied and deliberate words were overshadowed later that year, however, by Joseph Cumming's bombastic remarks at the NRA's December 1874 meeting. Cummings claimed that the growing menace of atheism was using church–state separation as a protective shield under which to spread its cancer: "No man has any right to be an infidel," and any freethinker who shared his or her views in wider society "ought to be crushed like a viper." These two speeches captured the Janus-faced nature of the movement, caught between careful appeals to an inclusive Christian heritage and its openness to persecuting those outside it. It was becoming increasingly clear that the NRA could only shape American church–state relations by abandoning Covenanter doctrines of church–state integration. By the 1890s, the movement had done just that.

This strategy of broadened appeal worked; they again found themselves in front of the president, this time Benjamin Harrison, renewing their efforts to gain national support.[29]

Thus watered down, the NRA had its greatest success when its newest champion on the Supreme Court declared, "This is a Christian nation." Justice David Brewer, who never joined the NRA but came out publicly as a supporter, spoke for a unanimous court in *Holy Trinity v. United States* (1892). Brewer had been giving speeches at NRA events for some time and afterward printed a book detailing his own thoughts. There he surveyed colonial church establishments and Christianity's influence over the common law. Although he had trumpeted a Christian America, even Justice Brewer was careful not to overreach the acceptable bounds of the American consensus and explicitly favored the separation of church and state.[30]

Emboldened by the high-profile declaration of Christian nationhood by the Supreme Court, and overjoyed that it came from one of their own supporters, the NRA went back to work getting the God Amendment to Congress. In the Senate, Republican William Frye of Maine attempted without success to reintroduce the language on behalf of the NRA in 1893. Taking cues from their recent success through toned-down rhetoric, in 1894 NRA activists broadened their language to include the word *liberty* and refer to the Bible as God's "guidance." The proposal read: "We, the people of the United States, devoutly acknowledging the supreme authority and just government of Almighty God in all the affairs of men and nations, grateful to him for our civil and religious liberty; and encouraged by the assurances of His Word to invoke His guidance, as a Christian nation, according to His appointed way, through Jesus Christ, in order to form a more perfect union. . . ."

NRA activists and RP ministers testified before the House Judiciary Committee, where they presented letters of support from leaders of various denominations and communities, including twenty-two of the twenty-four state senators of Iowa. They encouraged the congressmen to follow the example of the Supreme Court in *Church of the Holy Trinity v. United States*. RP minister R. J. George claimed that America's inherent Christianity arose from its long Atlantic roots, reminding Congress that "the colonies were Christian, the mother country is Christian, the common law is Christian, our civilization is a Christian civilization." Activists such as George represented a new generation of NRA leadership. They sought to maintain the *longue durée* attempt at Christian statecraft while at the same time loosening the proposed language of the amendment to give it a chance of passage. They were desperately performing, or trying to perform, a nearly impossible task that displayed the challenges of Covenanter identity so far and so long removed from Holy Scotland.[31]

The motion was sent to committee and never returned. So it began. For almost every one of the next twelve congresses, NRA supporters successfully entered the God Amendment into legislative action. Each time the bill died in committee. No version ever made it to the floor for debate or vote.[32]

## *Moral Reform and Its Discontents*

Though they made little legal headway in baptizing the Constitution, Covenanters could take some solace in the many alliances they forged with other moral reformers in the post–Civil War era. Together with these friends, they founded the National Reform Bureau, which historian Gaines Foster has called the first organized Christian lobby in Washington, D.C. The National Reform Bureau was headed by Wilbur Crafts, the first editor of the *Christian Statesman* not to be part of an explicitly Covenanter church. Using its ties to members of Congress, the bureau coordinated the activities of the many organizations advocating for moral legislation—including the NRA, the National Temperance Union, the Woman's Christian Temperance Union, and the National Sabbath Union. The bureau's ties to congressional leaders from their offices in the capital advanced the causes of these organizations well. Yet such high-profile success brought equally high-profile resistance; in the process of creating a network for national morality, Covenanters and their allies helped birth the American liberal Left. As they quickly gave modern liberalism a specter to be feared, Covenanters only too late realized that the cost of public engagement would be burying the ghosts of a National Covenant forever. Covenanter agitations over the constitutional basis for public morality began to show the boundaries beyond which American political consensus could not be pushed.[33]

The Covenanters' first extradenominational cultural connections came through their participation in Sabbatarian and abolitionist societies in the antebellum era. When radical abolitionists such as William Lloyd Garrison and the American Anti-slavery Society began joining the Covenanters in labeling the US Constitution a deal with the devil, the RP Church believed that its message was finally getting through. "Covenanters are now not alone in their condemnation of the spirit, acts, and tendencies of the government of the United States," the RP Church rejoiced in 1858. After the war, Covenanters were not shy about reminding the nation that they had held the moral high ground on slavery well before most denominations. Like their abolitionism, their Sabbatarian efforts also took on an increasingly ecumenical cast, although distinctively Covenanter elements remained in their rhetoric. The NRA launched a successful public campaign against the plans to keep the 1876 Philadelphia Centennial Exhibition open on Sundays; its high-profile victory set the stage for more than a decade of Sabbatarian reform. In 1888, Senator Henry Blair chaired the Senate Committee on Education and Labor, which brought witnesses to testify for the passage of the Sunday Rest Bill. Most reformers, especially labor unions, emphasized the social and psychological benefits of a mandatory day of rest. RP and new NRA chair T. P. Stevenson went further, however, calling the bill a "sacred obligation" of God's law, which was binding on "nations and governments as well as individuals." Covenanter groups also pushed against public transit on Sundays, something with which other reformers were less concerned. They made significant headway. President Harrison agreed to curtail military drilling on Sundays, and the Postmaster General's office, after nearly a century of prodding, significantly restricted Sabbath mail activity. The Covenanters supported many of the wider moral issues advocated by their fellow religious crusaders, yet differed markedly in their logic. For good reason, many Covenanters in the postwar years began to hope that cross-denominational cooperation was working and might just push the nation to more comprehensive constitutional solutions.[34]

Pursuing similar ends for different purposes made for strange bedfellows, and nowhere more so than in the temperance movement. Francis Willard was one of nineteenth-century America's most famous temperance reformers. Willard presided over the Woman's Christian Temperance Union (WCTU) for nearly twenty years and developed a professional friendship with NRA activist T. P. Stevenson. The two could not have been more different. Willard was a liberal Methodist, an avowed suffragette, and almost certainly a lesbian. Stevenson, a Covenanter, approved of none of these things. But their politics of moral reform aligned. After several meetings in 1886 and 1887, Willard allowed Stevenson to use the WCTU mailing list, and she was a featured speaker at the 1887 NRA meeting. From 1889 on, the WCTU received delegates from the NRA. In

1893, the WCTU declared that its "aim [was] identical" with the NRA's: to "enthrone Christ the King of the cloister, the camp, and the court." Still, Willard and the WCTU politely refused NRA attempts to woo them into a formal union.[35]

The NRA also became a primary vehicle for marriage advocacy. The institution of marriage was under attack, Covenanters felt, and they stood their ground for a traditional marriage agenda against divorce and polygamy. Polygamy was an especially attractive issue for Covenanters; it gave them the opportunity to argue that if only the nation would officially establish traditional Protestantism, then Mormons could not freely engage in immoral acts under the mantle of religious liberty. Religious freedom became bold-faced moral license. The First Amendment was the problem, Covenanters argued, hoping that the shock of an openly polygamous society out West had finally prepared the public to listen. Leaders were simultaneously encouraged and saddened, however, when in 1878 the Supreme Court ruled against both polygamy and the Covenanters' First Amendment logic in *Reynolds v. United States*. The First Amendment was no shield against immorality after all. Yet Covenanters continued to raise hue and cry regarding the issue anyway. In 1883, the *Christian Statesman* supported President Arthur's initiative to combat polygamy by sending a presidentially appointed commission to Utah. Even though Mormons ostensibly changed their polygamous teachings, Covenanters opposed statehood for Utah up until its eventual passage in 1896.[36]

The NRA also pushed for a uniform divorce law, rather than the "present loose and conflicting and unscriptural legislation on the subject" that varied from state to state. In 1892, the NRA lobbied heavily in favor of a proposed amendment to the Constitution that would outlaw divorce. As with slavery and secession, theirs was a call for a Christian federal government against the godlessness that arose from states' rights. Divorce mill states such as Oklahoma and the Dakotas illustrated perfectly the need for a Christian Constitution that could curb the moral degeneracy of the frontier.[37]

In 1873, an exhibition of sex toys and pornography on display in the vice president's Senate office showed that moral degeneracy was not relegated to the Wild West. These were from the collection of Anthony Comstock, a hitherto-unknown religious enthusiast and moral reformer recently arrived from New York to agitate for antiobscenity laws. Comstock appealed to Supreme Court Justice Strong, the national face of the NRA, who opened the doors to the halls of power for the reformer. By March of that year, legislation had passed prohibiting the distribution of sexually explicit materials—including advice on birth control and abortion. Comstock went on to become the nation's foremost moral reform advocate. Covenanters hailed him as a "heroic guardian of the public virtue," and Comstock, who became equally fond of their activism, was a frequent featured speaker at NRA meetings. Comstock's alliance with the Covenanters demonstrated their new ability to encapsulate mainstream America's longing for a Protestant past. As America's religious conservatives increasingly converged on Washington, D.C., in the late nineteenth century, for the first time groups actually sought the Covenanters out as valued allies. Religious conservatives found the Covenanters as much as the other way around.[38]

In the process, however, Covenanters created as many enemies to the cause of Christian nationhood as they did friends. Resistance came in two forms. The first was from fellow religious reformers who felt that Christian nationalism moved in the opposite direction of good sense and American values. The second came from secularists who for the first time began organizing under the banner of "liberalism" to resist the very concept of a Christian nation.

Separation of church and state was dogma for most Protestant Americans in the nineteenth century. This was made clear in the 1870 confirmation hearings for Justice Strong after his nomination to the Supreme Court. Strong faced stiff questioning about his role in a group determined to insert religious language into the Constitution, coming from senators whose own religious credentials were unquestioned. Many American denominations were in the process of vying for the honor of having been the first to support the separation of church and state. Quakers and Baptists did so most loudly. Political tensions between nativist Protestants and immigrant Catholics ran high, and attempts to codify Christian nationalism seemed decidedly out of touch. Not unlike in the seventeenth and eighteenth centuries, Covenanter cries for church–state alliance seemed like the Protestant version of a Catholic menace at a time when Catholicism was very much on Americans' minds.[39]

Nowhere was the American euphoria over church–state separation more evident than in the debate, dubbed the Cincinnati Bible War, over religion in public schools. In 1872, the Ohio Supreme Court ruled in favor of a Bible-reading ban in Cincinnati schools. The passages the schools had selected, pulled exclusively from the Protestant King James version, were judged an affront to the religious freedom of Catholic students. The emotional politics of "the School Question" immediately became a national issue. Fueled by anti-Catholic animus, Protestant parents demanded that their tax dollars go only to nonsectarian education. Meanwhile, Catholic families advocated for public money to support the parochial schools of their choice. Although some evangelicals worried that divorcing Bible reading from the schools would create moral chaos, on the whole, they stood against supporting religious education with tax funds. Few political issues ever so clearly divided Americans along religious lines; pro-secular-school Protestants on one side opposed pro-Christian-school Catholics on the other. The Covenanters, however, broke ranks with their Protestant brethren by favoring tax support for Christian schools. Only three nineteenth-century groups petitioned the New York legislature to use state funds for religious education: the Jewish synagogue, the Roman Catholic diocese, and the "Scotch Presbyterian Church," another term for New York City's RP congregations. Covenanters were no fans of Catholic education but on principle had no problem with the state supporting religious education—just so long as it was theirs. Moreover, they successfully used the exclusion of the Bible as fodder for their God Amendment argument, an argument that appealed to evangelicals. Secularists were throwing the Christian baby out with the Catholic bathwater, they complained. They wanted Bible reading *and* teaching in the classroom, both of which, they felt, would more directly confront the Catholic menace.[40]

Nationally, these fights culminated in the failed 1875 Blaine Amendment. At the very moment NRA membership was swelling and dreams to Christianize the Constitution seemed attainable, President Grant called for an amendment to permanently secure the separation of church and state. This move could not have been more diametrically opposed to the NRA's efforts. Beating Grant to the punch, Republican presidential hopeful James Blaine immediately introduced his own such amendment, which passed overwhelmingly in the House but fell just shy of the two-thirds supermajority in the Senate. Both Grant and Blaine eyed the upcoming Republican presidential nomination, hoping to ride waves of popular fervor in the wake of the Cincinnati Bible Wars. As the issue raged, Republican politicians fumbled over one another trying to display their credentials on church–state separation. One RP lamented that, despite generations of Covenanter efforts, "the axiom of statesmen that religion should have no place in public affairs" remained overwhelmingly compelling to most voters.[41]

Initially, Covenanters were horrified by Grant's amendment proposal. UP minister David Wallace said that by privileging a corrupted state over true religion, President Grant "out Herods Herod." In relegating faith to the realm of Sunday mornings, the amendment effectively elevated the Constitution's atheism over Christianity. If the amendment passed, Wallace predicted, "God cannot be legally worshiped, nor his name mentioned, nor a word uttered to persuade the children of the country to love or obey him, in any public school." The *Christian Statesman* said that the state, rather than running from a religious fight, should admit frankly that "we oppress the Catholic, and so to a higher degree the Jew, and so to a still higher degree the infidel" by using their tax dollars to expose those people's children to doctrines parents' believed were wrong. Bluntly put, "the Bible in public schools . . . is a tyranny." Yet the answer to that tyranny was not neutrality, because "no Bible is just as fully sectarian as the Bible itself." Privileging secular neutrality assumed that all religions were equally valid (or invalid), which they plainly could not be. Therefore, if religion in the public schools was oppressive, the state must either embrace religious coercion or abandon public schools altogether. "There is no middle ground," Covenanters declared openly: "Let us educate, and let the creed come."[42]

Ironically, the Blaine Amendment became the closest that Covenanters ever came to making a dent in the Constitution. Covenanters, mobilizing through the arm of the NRA, effectively co-opted the Blaine Amendment, editing its language and then lobbying on its behalf. Fearful that its passage might forever close the door on their Christianization agenda, at the eleventh hour the NRA successfully lobbied for a change in the amendment's wording in order to protect Bible reading in public schools. T. P. Stevenson met personally with Blaine and sent a letter to every member of Congress demanding language specifying that the amendment "shall not be construed to prohibit the reading of the Bible in any school or institution." The letter, accompanied by a list of the NRA's most prominent supporters, had the desired effect; the Senate inserted the NRA's language word for word into the amendment.[43]

This move was cleverly designed to win widespread support for politicians and strategic advantage for Covenanters. By amending the Constitution to explicitly protect Bible reading in public schools, the Blaine Amendment would implicitly protect Christianity in the public sphere. The NRA, meanwhile, gave Republican politicians the perfect opportunity to be simultaneously pro-Bible and antireligion in schools. Although the amendment failed, well over half of all states eventually amended their constitutions to outlaw the public support of church schools—and to protect Bible reading in public schools. In fact, the Blaine Amendment's popularity helped propel Ohio governor and Bible-reading supporter Rutherford B. Hayes to the White House. This was another instance in which Covenanter involvement in national reforms did far more for their colleagues than for their own cause. The nation's legislative body consistently considered and overwhelmingly rejected the Covenanters' attempts to Christianize the nation. But with the Covenanters' own help, the first and only attempt to make the nation explicitly secular failed by the narrowest of margins.[44]

Though their national campaigns for a Christian Amendment continued, Covenanter calls for such legislation met with increasing resistance from avowedly Protestant voices. This was especially evident during their 1894 attempt to get the God Amendment through Congress. Who, hostile congressmen asked NRA supporters, were the "Christians" referred to in the amendment? Given that "those organizations of men called the churches have shown their inability to determine who are the Christians," legislators wondered how the republic was to come up with the answer. They speculated that should the amendment pass, a new series of amendments would be required to clarify who was constitutionally a Christian and which books should be included in God's word. And "all of this to what end?" one congressman asked, pulling back the NRA's veil of ecumenicalism to expose its Covenanter foundations. Why would the NRA labor for thirty long years for the passage of this one amendment, he wondered, if they did not expect that they could follow it with future religious legislation that would "employ force to compel acceptance and obedience by the people"?[45]

As they put on display the outer boundaries of Christian conservatism, Covenanters paradoxically also helped galvanize definitions of the American Left. One of the lasting impacts of the NRA's efforts was to spur secular Americans to embrace the term *liberal* to advance their cause against the long shadow of Old World religious persecution in a modern America. Calling the God Amendment a "keg of theological gunpowder," editors at the freethinking journal *Index* garnered their own prominent supporters, including Wendell Phillips and Charles Darwin. Editor Francis Abbot condemned the God Amendment as being driven by "fanatics of the old, Inquisitorial stamp who, if they had the power," would institute capital punishment for religious heresy, all the while believing that they were doing God's work. In 1872, Abbot was given the floor at an NRA convention to speak his mind; he rebuked their "dangerous fires of religious bigotry," a move that established him as the public face of the very radical secularism that NRA members believed was misleading the American people. Out of the *Index*'s readership came the National Liberal League, founded in 1874. Calling themselves simply "Liberals," these secularists set out to secure their own modification of the Constitution in response to the then-viable Christian Amendment being considered in Congress. The Religious Freedom Amendment would make explicit the separation of church and state, at both the state and federal levels. When the Religious Freedom Amendment failed to pass, the Liberals gave their support to the Blaine Amendment and its prohibition on state funds for religious schools. When the Blaine Amendment failed, however, the *Index* still rejoiced. The last-minute Bible-reading provision, sponsored by the NRA, was a piece of "Machiavellian ingenuity" that narrowly missed baptizing the nation with Protestantism. Recognizing the validity of Stevenson's logic, Liberals likened the last-minute word changes to a camel's nose beneath the constitutional tent. Covenanters, through the NRA, were dangerous opponents of a secular state. Ongoing opposition to the NRA and its "Theological Amendment" helped birth the Liberal League and remained crucial to its organizing and recruiting efforts.[46]

NRA leaders explicitly positioned themselves as conservatives fighting this liberal, secular cancer that had infected the federal government. The two sides duked it out in the public square, both fighting for the soul of America's electorate. During the NRA's critical amendment efforts, in 1874, Abbot's Liberals organized a counterattack, gathering enough individual signatures to create a petition stretching a quarter of a mile. Jewish citizens were especially enraged by the NRA's efforts and similarly began pressuring prominent leaders to back away from the amendment. Even more crushing, the 35,000 signatures were introduced by Charles Sumner, whose Jewish and liberal constituents had become rattled over accusations that his amendment support equated to religious persecution; Sumner now attempted to tack away from what some labeled a fanatical movement. Stung by such perceived losses, T. P. Stevenson spoke out vehemently against the new and equally oppressive "demands of liberalism" that insisted every American citizen "conform to secular ideas." The NRA published pamphlets arguing that instead of the American Christian majority ruling the nation as "We the People," the nation was controlled by a small minority of Jews and freethinkers spuriously crying out for religious freedom. American politicians were so careful "not to discriminate against Jew, atheist, or infidel, in the laws of the land, that they shut out Jesus Christ." Unlike these anti-Christian liberals, the NRA had "truly conservative aims": to protect the American society's Christian character from an aggressive, secular state.[47]

Laying claim to the Founding Fathers had always been an integral strategy for gaining the moral high ground in America's culture wars. When liberal secularists began celebrating the words of Thomas Jefferson and identifying their stance with his championing of religious freedom, conservatives needed to come up with an alternative history of America's religious foundation that corresponded with their own claims. Covenanters, who arrived late and reluctantly to the ranks of those hallowing the Founders' faith, attempted to create a Christian founding narrative during the centennial celebrations of 1876. A thirteen-part series in the *Christian Statesman* highlighted the Christian roots of the colonies and the nation. Inverting the traditional narrative of refugees fleeing religious persecution, Covenanters argued that the colonists fled corrupt states in order to form religiously pure political communities. The series quoted extensively from colonial charters that invoked government based on the authority of God. One such example came from the third Virginia charter in 1611, which identified "the propagation of the Christian religion" as one of the colony's central aims. The series also cited taxpayer establishments of religion in most colonies, Christian oaths for office, and widespread Sabbath laws. Moving into the Revolution, the narrative began with the Quebec Act and the First Continental Congress's reaction against the establishment of "false religion" in the colonies. Afterward the Second Continental Congress opened in prayer, voted to hear sermons, called for fast days, employed military chaplains, regulated the religious lives of Continental soldiers, and arranged to import Bibles due to wartime shortages. In view of this history, the editors felt that it was beyond doubt that "the religion of the country was Protestant Christianity."[48]

The NRA also made a concerted effort to rehabilitate their troubled relationship with George Washington, reframing him as a man of intense Christian values. They recounted popular stories of Washington's inaugural ceremony, complete with "so help me God" and a postinauguration worship service. They tallied up the first president's references to "Almighty God" and "Divine Providence" in letters and addresses. And although the Covenanters were still loathe to praise Jefferson, they took perverse joy in pointing out that in his last report to Congress, he "forgot his secular theory of government" and acknowledged that God controlled the fate of nations. The serialized editorial closed with an overview of every state constitution, reviewing their Christian requirements for holding office and swearing oaths. The Covenanter "Centennial Papers" celebrated a history of America's close connection between church and state—a connection they claimed secularists had revised and good citizens had forgotten.[49]

The moral battles between liberals and conservatives in the late nineteenth century resulted in a mixed assortment of successes and failures. Historian Gaines Foster has identified 1,538 acts of moral legislation introduced before Congress from 1841 to 1921. Although less than 7 percent were passed into law, nearly every category saw some level of legislative success. Restrictions on gambling, polygamy, divorce, obscenity, prostitution, Sabbath breaking, narcotics, cigarettes, and prizefighting all made at least some legal gains in Congress. By the early twentieth century, religious reform reached its high-water mark when temperance was ensconced in the Constitution. In contrast, the fight for the God Amendment can only be labeled a complete failure. It was the sole initiative of the nineteenth century that failed to effect a single change to existing laws, despite repeated petitioning, politicking, public rallies, pamphleteering, and high-profile supporters. God, Jesus Christ, and the Bible never came close to being recognized in the Constitution. The Covenanters provided a tremendous amount of political smoke with their God Amendment, but in the end, there was no fire.[50]

In its dying efforts, however, the NRA planted the seeds of modern American conservatism and its efforts to keep religious discourse and rituals in political life. Far from a response to the rapid secularization of society after World War II, the story most often portrayed in popular narratives, the Covenanter-inspired reformers had been calling Americans' attention to political secularity since the nation's first days. The movement established a culture war divided between those who would protect the church in the public square and a liberal Left that would remove it. They condemned the amoral federal government while simultaneously demanding that it act arbitrarily to certify the nation's Christianity and enforce their vision on moral issues. As they looked back over their failed efforts, NRA leaders called themselves the "organized opposition to the encouragements of the secular theory of government." They would not accept that religion had no place in public life, and they squared off against the "revolutionary demands of secularism" even as the tide of battle turned against them. In this clash of cultural values, liberals successfully fought for freedom *from* rather than freedom *of* religion. Defeated Covenanters hoped that, phoenix-like, their old arguments might one day rise again to gain a hearing among American Christians.[51]

## *From Scottish Radicals to Southern Conservatives*

If the fight on the Constitution presented Covenanters at their most historically consistent, on issues of race they were less so. Especially in the South the Presbyterian fringe abandoned its once-radical racial egalitarianism, completing its absorption into southern orthodoxy. There were several causes for this shift. The first was the Civil War itself, in which ARs served, even if reluctantly. AR young men developed a heightened sense of shared southern identity with fellow soldiers. This identity survived the war, even though—and, in some cases, because—many of the men themselves did not. Second, Reconstruction destroyed the economy for many southern whites, increasing their resentment against Northerners and free blacks. Covenanters were hardly immune to these woes, and they joined their fellow Southerners in viewing the Reconstruction governments as morally corrupt precipitators of economic decay. Third, with the issue of slavery now moot, southern Covenanters lost an essential distinctive element distinguishing them from other southern Christians. Finally, and in a development unique to those on the Presbyterian fringe, the success of their educational institutions had filled their pulpits nearly to capacity. This meant that there was little need for the old lay-led Society Meetings that actively reared adherents in the processes of peculiarity. As their religious life began to increasingly mimic that of other southern Presbyterians, the only thing remaining unique about the Covenanters was their psalm singing.

On the Presbyterian fringe there were two casualties of the war and Reconstruction: the biracial churches Covenanters had established and the institutional memory of Holy Scotland. While the Associate Reformed Church continued on as a distinct denomination in the South, its organizational independence had less to do with distinctive views of society and theology than with ethnic and family ties and its congregations' psalm singing. Those who sat in the pews operated almost identically to other southern evangelicals, in particular as they began to use the Bible to support a "law and order" racism relegating newly freed blacks to second-class citizenship. Such developments placed them sharply at odds with northern Covenanters, who proclaimed that "the battle for freedom is not fought entirely through—will not be until our statute-books no longer know the word 'white.' "[52]

In southern AR churches, however, whiteness now counted for quite a lot. Prior to the war, AR congregations consisted of both white and black members. It was an especially attractive denomination for nearby slaves to join, since their literacy-based devotionals advocated teaching slaves to read. Church discipline was administered with an egalitarian spirit. In Chester's AR churches, free white and enslaved black members received equal treatment from church elders, regardless of race. Some examples are illustrative. In 1841, the Hopewell AR church admitted Burrells Hemphill, a slave, to full communion but in the same meeting denied admission to enslaved Jinney Neal on grounds of "her former behavior." In a meeting the following year, the same treatment was meted out to two white entrants. Joseph Wylie was admitted to communion, but Margaret Williford was put off for a time because of "the peculiar circumstances of her former loose conduct." After the war, blacks continued to join AR churches, probably hoping that these prewar arrangements gave precedence for creating a genuinely equal, biracial religious fellowship. They were sorely disappointed.[53]

The first few years of Reconstruction in AR churches saw not only a decrease in the session prosecutions of white members but also sharp increases in policing the moral lives of black members. Before the war, AR churches in the South had disciplined white and black members equally, with the sessions' ire falling more often on white and black women for dancing and fornication than on men of either race. Now, in a desperate attempt to maintain a white social order, sessions lashed out against black members. One telling example is from the New Hope AR church in Blackstock, South Carolina. On May 18, 1866, the session admonished and restored a white man named John Douglas for the sin of profane language and "the indulgence of his passions." He was the last white congregant disciplined for three years. The next day the session met to discuss "the colored members. As there had been some irregularity in their attendance upon public ordinance and some falling away." Thirty-five former slaves came before the session "and after being interrogated and their conduct inquired into" were brought back into good standing. Two women,

Isabella and Emiline Brice, had their communion privileges delayed. In October, freedman Lyttleton Bell was denied the sacrament for allegations of theft. Following that, "Lucinda, a colored woman," another female labeled simply "a colored girl," and a black male named Simpson applied for admission and were denied. None were mentioned by last name. The parents of baptismal candidates had always been mentioned, but now black baptisms were simply noted as an "infant of color." By 1868 the session records were obsessed with matters of black congregants, while white members scarcely appeared. The list of colored members was divided up, and each elder was assigned a group "so that he might observe their deportment" and tell them that any perception of moral failings would entail consequences. In May of that year, there were eight black applicants for membership. Only three were received. Between 1866 and 1868, no white person was debarred from privileges, but nearly 90 percent of the fifty-nine black applications were challenged or denied.[54]

One of the most surprising examples of the effects of the Civil War on biracial Christianity is found in the Bethany AR church near the South Carolina–North Carolina border. In that church, there were no discipline cases against black members until 1860, when the session noted that they had "appointed a patrol to attend to the servants" during worship. After that, cases against black members spiked and far outpaced discipline of whites. By the early 1870s, the cases disappeared because black members fled their formerly biracial churches in favor of more equitable and independent places of worship. The AR congregation in Due West, South Carolina, maintained its prewar black majority of nearly two to one all the way to 1869, when an all-black congregation was formed to separate the races. In the immediate aftermath of war, black Christians seemed willing to give biracial Christianity as ARs. When they fled these congregations in preference for black churches, that preference was the creation of white animosity.[55]

Though they began the Civil War as southern Republicans, ARs ended Reconstruction as southern Democrats. Initially, white Democrats wooed ARs to run for office as Democrats in hopes that their prewar reputation as racial moderates would allow them to serve as a bridge between the two races—whites capable of being elected in districts with black majorities. In Abbeville District, South Carolina, the Democratic Party attempted to co-opt the racial moderation of the ARs by nominating J. N. Young for state senate in 1869. In the days before the election, either Young or one of his supporters issued an editorial that denounced politics "so thoroughly imbued with the Jefferson, Madison, and Calhoun theory of our government." Those exponents of nullification and states rights were fossils best left dead and in the past. The new southern Democratic Party should appeal to the black freedmen as equals. There was nothing to be gained by opposing black suffrage and equality. The time had come for politics of "conciliation, concession, or compromise." Young lost, however, and with that loss, both the South Carolina Democratic Party and southern ARs began to lose faith in racial cooperation.[56]

Accusations that biracial Reconstruction governments were filled with corruption and fraud fell easy on the ears of southern Covenanters, who were accustomed to pushing government to be more Christian in its character. As Reconstruction wore on into the 1870s, their activism became increasingly militant. AR layman and South Carolina state senator J. C. Hemphill waxed poetic on the need for a Christian nation where the Bible formed the cornerstone of "the great law lexicon of eternity." By then, however, the ARs had cemented their vision of biblical law within the southern principle of racial order. ARs joined "rifle clubs," organized militia wings of the Democratic Party, and later participated in the Ku Klux Klan. Robert Reid Hemphill, whose father had done so much to encourage racial moderation and subvert pro-slavery Christianity, was an active member of Wade Hampton's "Home Rule" redemption campaign in South Carolina, which featured violent intimidation of black voters. He was elected as a representative in the controversial 1876 election in which Democrats took back the governor's mansion and state legislature. Hemphill served as captain of the local rifle club. In 1886 he was elected to the state senate, and he remained there until 1894.[57]

This new racial activism for the Democratic Party included violent altercations between white ARs and local former slaves. One such clash became known as the Battle of Wimbushville. Exactly one mile due east of the town of Due West, where the AR Seminary was located, African Americans founded their own village where they could live and raise their families free of white control. The area took on the name of the most prominent African American freedmen in the area, the Wimbush family. They were also the town's most active Republicans. In 1868, several dozen freedmen and freedwomen left the AR Church to found their own Methodist congregation in Wimbushville. By 1872, the area was growing. It had a new schoolhouse, homes, and plans to build a sanctuary for the Mt. Lebanon AME church. That new town—black, Republican, and Methodist—was an island of black independence in the district and a sore spot for white Democratic Covenanters. One Abbeville newspaper dubbed it "this little pent up Africa."[58]

The tensions between Due West and Wimbushville turned violent in the hotly contested 1876 election. White AR congregants "marched" on the black town to break up a Republican rally. Intimidation of black voters, including threats of reprisal, continued through the Democrats' success on Election Day. But these conflicts were about more than politics. The following spring, as black residents were in the middle of raising the new sanctuary for their Mt. Lebanon AME church, an invading posse of AR church members surprised them. At that moment, acting on an anonymous letter that claimed local corn thieves were hiding in the black town, five deputized Due West residents attempted to arrest Cyrus and Jesse Wimbush. The local newspapers labeled them "the bitterest Radical negroes in the county." A fight erupted, and the black residents of Wimbushville successfully defended both their neighbors and their new Methodist sanctuary from the Covenanter invasion. The "battle," however, continued for several more days.[59]

Most of those now coming to blows over Reconstruction politics had once read, prayed, and sung alongside one another as members of the biracial devotional groups that were the heartbeat of Covenanter piety for two centuries. As the conflict now made clear, those days of intimacy had past. Resolution only came when AR Confederate veterans marched as one to finalize the arrests of the Wimbush family, whose local convictions were overturned by the state's supreme court. White ARs resented blacks' rejection of their paternalistic racial moderation and radical religious heritage. By embracing Methodism and supporting the "godless" federal government's policies, freedmen and freedwomen did just that. But it was actually the ARs themselves who had changed—and drastically. Their former brethren and slaves exposed the thin and eroding veil covering a postwar generation. ARs were now more southern than Scottish and more Confederate than Covenanter.

By the turn of the twentieth century, few Southerners could point to anything distinctive about the Associate Reformed Church, other than the oddity of their psalm singing. On the night of the 1924 presidential election, AR Robert Lathan penned an editorial for the Charleston *News and Courier.* Lathan pined for the day when the South included a "school politically which sought as a rule the middle of the road, eschewing ultra-conservatism on the one-hand and radicalism on the other." His essay, entitled "The Plight of the South," won the 1924 Pulitzer Prize.

He was right to say that those days were gone. Oral histories recorded in the mid–twentieth century pointed to Klan participation among AR church leaders from the late nineteenth century and into the early twentieth. Some prominent members of upstate South Carolina AR churches were Klansmen. In the early 1900s, the session of a rural Piedmont South Carolina congregation met to discipline a white member for drunkenness. While they were waiting in the session room, they were overheard to say, "The last time all of us was together was when we hung that nigger down on the creek." The old vestiges of Covenanters in the South, whose antislavery activism and biracial Bible schools once made them so unique, had not simply faded. They had given up on remaining a distinct religious people reckoning themselves among the nations. In the Jim Crow South, they joined the nation.[60]

## *A Legacy Rejected*

As southern Covenanters rejected their old radical faith in favor of a conservative one, so the nation at large rejected the NRA's calls to create a Covenanter America. The moment of Covenanters' greatest organizational strength was also the moment American Protestants were least inclined to tear down the wall of separation between church and state. Nativist resistance to Catholic immigration and the coalescence of liberalism allowed little room for Old World solutions to the problems of a modern society. In failing to amend the US Constitution, the Covenanters set the acceptable limits for American fundamentalists in national reform. America might be bent to the will of Christians, but not through constitutional amendments. In order to become politically relevant, conservatives would have to jettison such fringe positions in favor of those reforms mainstream Americans felt were less threatening and more practical. Historians mention the amendment movement only in passing, mostly citing its failure to exert lasting influence. When they are remembered at all, Covenanters are generally deemed outside the bounds of legitimate Christian reform movements before *and* after the American Civil War. That the movement failed, though, is precisely what makes it historically significant.

The Covenanter-organized, -led, and -populated NRA facilitated the rise of American fundamentalism well into the twentieth century. Historian George Marsden has identified four separate streams in early twentieth-century fundamentalism. The third stream, identified most prominently with William Jennings Bryan and the Winona Bible Conference, sought to preserve Christian civilization through the political sphere. These fundamentalists did not retreat from the political world, as did other twentieth-century religious traditionalists. At Winona, politically active conservative Christians went through weeks of spiritual renewal and political recommitment. Their 1911 meeting focused on the literature of the NRA regarding the Christianization of the Constitution. At such gatherings, the emerging political language of Christianization could be shared, while specific platform planks could be ignored. For example, the argument that freedom *of* religion had been skewed into freedom *from* religion had more resonance once detached from its original Covenanter moorings.[61]

Nowhere did this become more evident than in another series of meetings, the last major show of Covenanter force in American history. The early twentieth century was a period of internationalization in Western organizations, and the new NRA national field secretary, J. S. McGaw, sought to take part in this global vision. McGaw, Stevenson, and Wooster University president Sylvester Scovel devised a series of international conferences on Christian citizenship. As Christian mission work spread the Gospel across the globe, they contended, the problems that confronted "Christian patriots in [the United States were] fast becoming problems in all countries." These goals of global godly citizenship and government reform included Sabbath laws, divorce restrictions, public Christian education, and a host of other church–state points of contact. The first World's Christian Citizenship Conference, held in 1910, was attended mostly by Americans from Covenanter denominations intermingled with visiting Presbyterian missionaries.[62]

The second World's Christian Citizenship Conference, in Portland, Oregon, was a grander affair. It was held in the summer of 1913, and crowds were estimated between 12,000 and 25,000. President Woodrow Wilson sent his regrets and an encouragement to "help the country think out the applications of true Christianity to the problems of citizenship." The speakers represented a broader and more truly international gathering of evangelical Christian activists than the first meeting, though still around half were of Covenanter persuasions. The meeting displayed the ongoing breadth of the Covenanter reform interests, which had not as yet hardened into modern conservative trajectories. Their long-standing racial egalitarianism was on display in speeches that condemned lynch mobs. A lecture on "the Labor Problem" damned socialism but laid the blame for its growth on capitalist businessmen and their sinful practices. Britain, the United States, and the West in general were roundly castigated for their "might makes right strategies" in China. Local Prohibition advocates rejoiced as municipalities passed ordinances outlawing the sale of alcohol in the wake of the conference, and many referred to the antiliquor talks at the event as the catalyst for those changes. The convention ended with everyone in good spirits, having high hopes for the planned 1919 meeting.[63]

Charles Evans Hughes headlined that third and final conference, held in Pittsburgh. He seemed to be the ideal Christian citizen: governor of New York, justice on the Supreme Court, presidential candidate, soon to be appointed secretary of state, and later chief justice of the Supreme Court. But Hughes either completely misunderstood their movement or understood it far too well. He gave what was, functionally, a repurposed stump speech from his failed 1916 presidential bid. He warned against socialism, lauded the effects of capitalism, and encouraged a humane interaction between business and labor. Only at the end did he touch on the subject at hand, making a vague allusion to American democracy's "religious spirit." At a conference aimed at explicitly Christianizing politics, Hughes's afterthought message was a palpable disappointment for the Covenanters. The keynote speaker at their most public event to support Christian nationalism failed even to mention the topic. It was clear testimony that the window of opportunity for a Christian amendment had already closed. Like Christian reformers before him, Hughes was happy to use the Covenanters to advance his own reforms, but he had little interest in advancing theirs. America's most prominent Christian statesman dismissed the Covenanters' objectives by simply ignoring them. Ultimately, so did the nation.[64]

# *Afterword*

## *Holy Scotland in the Contemporary Christian America Debate*

THE HIGH TIDE of Covenanter America has now long receded. Left behind, however, remnants of Holy Scotland remain littered along the shoreline of the contemporary Christian America debate. If one knows what one is looking for, the Covenanters' imprint on the ever-shifting sands of culture war remains clearly evident. Their vision spurred evangelical political mobilization, co-opted Billy Graham's Cold War sermons, and shaped the curriculum of Christian and homeschool culture warriors; and but for reaction against the backwardness of their agenda, the 1980 Reagan Revolution might never have happened. These were the last vestiges of the failed voyage of Holy Scotland across the Atlantic and into modernity, the wreckage strewn along our twenty-first-century debates as reminders that the American past was turbulent and unpredictable.

The efforts of Covenanters merged directly into the political conservatism of the 1940s. The leadership of the New England Federation, organizational forerunner of the National Association of Evangelicals (NAE), included United Presbyterian ministers from the Seceder tradition. And when evangelical icons such as Harold Ockenga and Cornelius Van Til met in St. Louis to form the NAE, they were joined by at least five members of Covenanter denominations, including C. B. Betts, the moderator of the AR Synod, and Erskine College president R. C. Grier. AR J. Alvin Orr helped draft the organization's constitution and bylaws. In 1947, and again in 1954, the NAE supported campaigns to amend the Constitution. Its words borrowed directly from the National Reform Association (NRA): "This nation devoutly recognizes the authority and law of Jesus Christ, Savior, and Ruler of Nations."[1]

Another Covenanter-inspired group, the Christian Amendment Movement (CAM), emerged in 1945. This group worked more explicitly at political lobbying than either the NRA or NAE. Under the leadership of Covenanter Sam Boyle, CAM published the *Christian Patriot*, a monthly bulletin providing tips for political evangelism. By 1954, CAM's cooperation with the NAE began to pay dividends: the Christian Amendment was once again placed before Congress. This version retained the original's emphasis on "the authority and law of Jesus Christ, Savior and Ruler of nations," but it also explicitly protected the civil rights of non-Christians. Appearing before a subcommittee of the Senate Judiciary Committee, NRA and CAM advocates promoted the amendment—and spoke alongside two housewives from the Militant Christian Patriots, who were currently organizing for conservative causes in the California suburbs. They entered into the record documents about the NRA's history, the writings of Senate Chaplain and Scotsman Peter Marshall Sr., and a sermon by the wildly popular Cold War preacher—and former AR—Billy Graham. Graham's sermon, entitled "The Faith of George Washington," rooted its message in an Old Testament verse championed by the American Right for the next half-century: "If my people, which are called by my name, shall humble themselves, and pray, and seek my face, and turn from their wicked ways, then will I hear from heaven, and will forgive their sin, and will heal their land." The senators were unmoved toward such humility. As always, the amendment died in committee.[2]

The Christian Amendment experienced one final high-profile moment, when it disrupted the three-way 1980 presidential race that brought about Ronald Reagan's presidency. CAM leader Sam Boyle's protégé, Howard Elliot, had convinced Illinois congressman John Anderson to try three times, in 1961, 1963, and 1965, to move the God Amendment into the House of Representatives. Anderson was a member of another Calvinist denomination, the Evangelical Free Church, and sympathetic to the Covenanter plea that law was rooted in God. In 1979, Anderson embarked on a remarkably viable third-party bid for the presidency. One early Gallup poll placed him at 26 percent in a virtual dead heat with President Jimmy Carter and California governor Ronald Reagan. His candidacy was irrevocably derailed, however, when the national press discovered Anderson's Christian Amendment activity. Hounded by questions on religion in politics, Anderson came in third, with just over 6 percent of the popular vote. A more robust turnout for Anderson might easily have shifted the balance of electoral votes in 1980, thwarting the conservative resurgence in utero and swinging victory toward Carter. Yet Anderson's turnout was small, in part because the idea of an explicitly Christian Constitution seemed far less thinkable than it had a century before. Even as Reagan reached for a Moral Majority, Anderson's Christian America proved a bridge too far.[3]

Ironically, it was during this very period that Christian America mythology was codified into its present form. One critical component in that process was Francis Schaeffer, the twentieth-century evangelical intellectual whose lifelong battle against secular humanism shaped the worldview of many conservative thinkers even into the twenty-first century. Schaeffer's arguments were written with more nuance than they were read, especially his insistence that Christians should not "wrap Christianity in our national flag." What most readers focused on, however, was Schaeffer's analysis of Covenanter Samuel Rutherford, who had condemned the tyranny of kings (chapter 1). Rutherford claimed that the nation was not merely "the people" but "God's people" and viewed the state as the church politic. According to Schaeffer, Rutherford's work shaped the philosophies of John Locke and the American Founding Fathers. They had intended "We the People" to mean "We the Christian People."[4]

Schaeffer was wrong. Locke was not influenced by Rutherford; in fact he considered all Covenanters to be dangerous theocrats. Rutherford placed the authority of the church above the state, while Locke happily reversed the order to guard against Rutherfordian religious enthusiasm. John Witherspoon, America's most prominent Christian and very Presbyterian Founder, never cited Rutherford despite listing thirty-two specific sources for his Princeton lectures on ethics and politics. Rutherford's works were known in America, but they were entirely associated with the Presbyterian fringe groups whose views on the nation no one wanted to try.[5]

It did not matter that Schaeffer was factually incorrect, however. In the 1970s and 1980s, prominent American fundamentalists looked to him for intellectual leadership and absorbed his argument about the Christian roots of America. Tim LaHaye, who dedicated one of his books to Schaeffer and openly acknowledged an intellectual debt, assumed that American colonists possessed "a Reformation mental attitude" and therefore built a uniquely Christian nation. The "civil laws of the Old Testament formed the basis of our laws and our Constitution," he claimed, evidenced by the fact that the constitutional system of checks and balance was "borrowed directly from Scripture." Also leaning heavily on Schaeffer, fundamentalist leader Jerry Falwell assured his readers that the "Founding Fathers most certainly did not intend the separation of God and government."

Peter Marshall Jr.'s wildly popular 1977 coauthored book *The Light and the Glory* proclaimed that the Constitution was an "institutionalizing of the covenant's legacy." Conservative textbook writers for the budding Christian homeschool movement, inspired by and relying heavily on Marshall's book, believed that the nation rejected the Founders' wisdom during Reconstruction. At that time, "instead of listening to the serious objections" of Christian southern legislators, Congress "made a serious mistake" and passed the Fourteenth Amendment. Now an evil, secular federal government could infringe the rights of Christian citizens. From that point forward, Christian America had been in decline, and it was the cause of the faithful to resurrect it.[6]

The mantle of leadership in this Christian heritage movement now rests with Texas school reformer, history enthusiast, and best-selling author David Barton. Through his organization, WallBuilders, Barton's leadership was instrumental in revising the history curriculum in Texas public schools and through them the national textbook market. He insists that the founding generation was driven by Christian values but that liberal academics, intent on using history for their social agenda, malign the memory of the Founders. *Time Magazine* named Barton one of the nation's twenty-five most influential evangelicals.[7]

Barton regularly leads tours of Washington, D.C., during which he informs attendees that "out of fifty-six signers of the Declaration of Independence, twenty-nine had Bible school or seminary degrees." *Seminary*, it turns out, was a common synonym for *school* or *college* in the Early Republic. In fact, Covenanter James R. Willson bemoaned the sorry state of early American politicians and the atheist colleges that educated them, using the same word. "In our seminaries of learning," he said in 1825, "from the A, B, C, of our primary schools to the highest honors of the university schools . . . the late age of infidelity has almost banished the Bible." Barton's wildly exaggerated claims aside, an underlying suspicion of secular culture out to corrode Christian values is as long-standing as the Covenanters themselves. Willson claimed, in words Barton now echoes, that these seminaries were led by a conspiracy of "heathen poets, philosophers, statesman and historians," who sought to "pollute the imagination, darken the understanding, and corrupt the heart" by requiring students to read "selections from heathen or infidel moralists." It would seem that liberals are always lurking about, ready to corrupt America's youth—no matter in which century one finds them.[8]

The popularity of Christian America continues unabated in the twenty-first century. The relevance of these issues is especially stark in light of the 2013 Defense of Religion Act, which proposed to make Christianity the state religion of North Carolina. Proposed as a means to protect Christian prayers in public meetings, it was supported by multiple elected officials in the Republican-controlled state legislature. The measure died (in committee, of course) when national furor over the issue caused party leaders to quietly drop the issue. The following year, the Supreme Court explicitly protected such sectarian prayers by town governments in *Town of Greece v. Galloway*. Writing for a five-to-four majority, Justice Anthony Kennedy invoked the Founding Fathers' own habits of invoking Christian public prayer. More tellingly, however, national polling in the wake of these controversies revealed that one-third of the American public favored an amendment making Christianity the national religion. Barely half opposed such an amendment, and one in six were unsure.[9]

From extreme conservative Christians such as Barton to solidly mainstream thinkers such as Justice Kennedy, arguments that the separation of church and state is misunderstood and misapplied remain popular. The First Amendment was only intended to keep government out of church life, advocates insist. It was never intended to protect the state from religious influence. According to this narrative, secular liberals have corrupted the Founders' original intentions.[10]

America's original religious Right, the Covenanters, shatter such conservative logic. Their centuries-long struggle contradicts suggestions that the Constitution hallowed Christianity or allowed for the church to influence the state. European nations before and after the founding claimed their nationhood in part from their religious identity. America did not. The implication was clear. Its failure to honor God in the Constitution made the United States the first government in Western history to disassociate itself from Christianity. The Covenanters created the most thorough, logical, and sustained critique of the Christian America thesis in history by assaulting the Constitution on its own terms. Taken as a whole, this logic challenges the religious Right from its own right flank.[11]

Viewed from the vantage point of the twenty-first century, early American history is littered with shocking instances of public religious display, from unopposed public prayers to discrimination against slaves, Catholics, Mormons, and freethinkers. Such observations animate both conservatives' sense of validity and liberals' fear of backsliding. The Constitution, from this perspective, is not nearly as clear on religious questions as it is made to seem. Yet, when viewed from the long arc of history across the Atlantic, it becomes quickly evident that early Americans wrestled with their own past rather than our present. The Founders were far closer in time to Oliver Cromwell's Puritan Commonwealth and the Covenanters' Holy Scotland than to the elimination of prayer in schools. Theirs was a history defined by religion in politics, and there were Covenanters in their midst to prove it. Seen from early America facing its own past, the Constitution created a clean break between Christian Europe and secular America.

After the founding, the Covenanters chastened and motivated both right and left. They defy conventional categories because they belonged to a different age but tried to live in this one. Not all Christian nationalists worshiped America; neither did their ideas cover ulterior motives such as racism. Rather, for them Holy Scotland cast long shadows across the Atlantic and through time. Most clearly, those shadows marked how far Christianization could penetrate, and how far it could not, into American government. Covenanters' ultimate failure is proof of just how secular Americans wanted their government to be. Americans may tolerate multiple gates and doors in the wall of separation, but they have never yet allowed tearing it down.

# *Abbreviations of Archives and Special Collections*

| | |
|---|---|
| BL | British Library. London, England, UK |
| DU | Duke University's David M. Rubenstein Rare Book and Manuscript Library. Durham, NC, USA |
| EC | Erskine College Special Collections. Due West, SC, USA |
| LL | Linenhall Library, Belfast Pamphlet Collection. Belfast, Northern Ireland, UK |
| MC | Montreat Collection, Union Theological Seminary. Decatur, GA, USA |
| NC | New College Library, University of Edinburgh. Edinburgh, Scotland, UK |
| NLS | National Library of Scotland. Edinburgh, Scotland, UK |
| PRONI | Public Record Office of Northern Ireland. Belfast, Northern Ireland, UK |
| PTS | Pittsburgh Theological Seminary, Special Collections. Pittsburgh, PA, USA |
| RPHL | Reformed Presbyterian Historical Library, Reformed Presbyterian Seminary. Belfast, Northern Ireland, UK |
| RPTS | Reformed Presbyterian Theological Seminary. Pittsburg, PA, USA |
| SCDAH | South Carolina Department of Archives and History. Columbia, SC, USA |
| USC | Caroliniana Library, University of South Carolina. Columbia, SC, USA |
| UTC | Union Theological College, Belfast Pamphlets. Belfast, Northern Ireland, UK |
| VSARA | Vermont State Archives and Records Administration. Montpelier, VT, USA |

# *Notes*

## FRONT MATTER

1. Quote found in *Congressional Globe*, 38th Cong., 1st Sess. (February 17, 1864), 693; for Sumner's role, see Stewart Olin Jacoby, "The Religious Amendment Movement: God, People and Nation in the Gilded Age" (PhD diss., University of Michigan at Ann Arbor, 1984), 164–178.

## INTRODUCTION

1. Historical overviews of this debate can be found in John Fea, *Was America Founded as a Christian Nation? A Historical Introduction* (Louisville, KY: Westminster John Knox, 2011), xvi–xviii; Matthew L. Harris and Thomas S. Kidd, *The Founding Fathers and the Debate over Religion in Revolutionary America: A History in Documents* (New York: Oxford University Press, 2011); David Sehat, *The Myth of American Religious Freedom* (New York: Oxford University Press, 2011); Chris Beneke, *Beyond Toleration: The Religious Origins of American Pluralism* (New York: Oxford University Press, 2008); Noah Feldman, *Divided by God: America's Church–State Problem—and What We Should Do about It* (New York: Farrar, Straus and Giroux, 2005); Frank Lambert, *The Founding Fathers and the Place of Religion in America* (Princeton, NJ: Princeton University Press, 2003); Isaac Kranmick and R. Laurence Moore, *The Godless Constitution: The Case against Religious Correctness* (New York: W. W. Norton, 1996); Edward S. Gaustad, *Neither King nor Prelate: Religion and the New Nation, 1776–1826* (Grand Rapids, MI: Eerdmans, 1993); Mark A. Noll, Nathan O. Hatch, and George M. Marsden, *The Search for Christian America* (Colorado Springs, CO: Helmers and Howard, 1989); Thomas J. Curry, *The First*

*Freedoms: Church and State in America to the Passage of the First Amendment* (New York: Oxford University Press, 1987).

2. A simple survey of the indexes of church–state histories will turn up voluminous references to the National Reform Association and Covenanter ministers such as Alexander McLeod, John Mason, James R. Willson, and David McAllister. Most simply subsume these actors within the Protestant mainstream. There are a few recent exceptions to this historical amnesia, in which Covenanters are treated on their own terms within broader studies. Gaines Foster's study of Christian reform lobbyists and the law in post–Civil War America and Steven Green's examination of the evolving processes of disestablishment both take the Covenanter legacy seriously. Several doctoral theses also piece together varieties of elements in the Covenanter story. Gaines M. Foster, *Moral Reconstruction: Christian Lobbyists and the Federal Legislation of Morality, 1865–1920* (Chapel Hill: University of North Carolina Press, 2007); Steven K. Green, *The Second Disestablishment: Church and State in Nineteenth-Century America* (New York: Oxford University Press, 2010). On the Covenanters as an Atlantic and global phenomenon, see Emily Moberg Robinson, "Immigrant Covenanters: Religious and Political Identity, from Scotland to America" (PhD diss., University of California, Santa Cruz, 2004); and Valerie Wallace, "Exporting Radicalism within the Empire: Scots Presbyterian Political Values in Scotland and British North America, c. 1815–1850" (PhD diss., University of Glasgow, 2010). On Pennsylvania, the heartbeat of American Covenanter culture, see Peter Gilmore, "Rebels and Revivals: Ulster Immigrants, Western Pennsylvania Presbyterianism, and the Formation of Scotch-Irish Identity, 1780–1830" (PhD diss., Carnegie Mellon University, 2009). On the issues of church and state involving Covenanters in New York, see James Kabala, "A Christian Nation? Church–State Relations in the Early American Republic, 1787–1846" (PhD diss., Brown University, 2008). On efforts at Constitutional reform, see Stewart Olin Jacoby, "The Religious Amendment Movement: God, People and Nation in the Gilded Age" (PhD diss., University of Michigan at Ann Arbor, 1984). Moberg Robinson's work has subsequently appeared as scholarly articles in the *Journal of Transatlantic Studies* (2013), the *Journal of Scotch-Irish Studies* (2008), and the *Journal of Presbyterian History* (2005). Kabala's work has been expanded in James S. Kabala, *Church–State Relations in the Early American Republic, 1787–1846* (London: Pickering and Chatto, 2013). Wallace's and Gilmore's works are both forthcoming as monographs.
3. Magna Carta, trans. Nicholas Vincent, http://www.archives.gov/exhibits/featured_documents/magna_carta/translation.html. In the nineteenth century, many American jurists argued that America was a Christian nation because portions of the British common law that had been incorporated into American legal practice assumed Christianity throughout. Still other jurists argued that the implication of the Constitution was to radically alter the legal identity of churches, from public entities to private associations. For a discussion of this,

see Green, *Second Disestablishment,* 149–250; Mark Douglas McGarvie, *One Nation under Law: America's Early National Struggles to Separate Church and State* (De Kalb: Northern Illinois University Press, 2004), 3–20, 47–96, 190–192.

4. A common objection raised by other Christians was that Jesus had said his Kingdom was not of this world. Covenanters replied that this was true: Christ's Kingdom was *of* God and *over* the world. To say that Christ's Kingdom was not of this world implied nothing about freeing the world from Christ. J. R. W. Sloane, *A Discourse Delivered before the Reformed Presbyterian Synod* (New York: John A. Gray and Green, 1866), 18; quote from Diary of David Barrow, as quoted in John B. Boles, *The Great Revival: Beginnings of the Bible Belt* (Lexington: University of Kentucky Press, 1972), 10.
5. As Alexander McLeod tried to elucidate, "Coercion, indeed, may never be used in order to make his subjects religious; but it may and must be used in order to suppress immorality, profaneness, and blasphemy; and in order to remove the monuments of idolatry from the land." Alexander McLeod, *Messiah, Governor of the Nations of the Earth* (Glasgow: Stephen Young, 1804), 25; G. A. Edgar, "Right Relation of Church and State," undated pamphlet, 14, EC; David W. Miller, "Did Ulster Presbyterians Have a Devotional Revolution?" in *Evangelicals and Catholics in Nineteenth-Century Ireland,* ed. James H. Murphy (Dublin: Four Courts Press, 2005), 41.
6. Earlier monographs treating Covenanters tend to be nineteenth-century histories built from church records. These books isolate one denomination by following its presbytery and synodical meetings. Twentieth-century histories follow this pattern. There are excellent nineteenth-century examples of these histories for each of the above-mentioned denominations. James Brown Scouller, *A Manual of the United Presbyterian Church of North America: 1751–1881* (Harrisburg, PA: Patriot Publishing, Co., 1881); Robert Lathan, *History of the Associate Reformed Synod of the South, 1782–1882* (Harrisburg, PA, 1882); William M. Glasgow, *History of the Reformed Presbyterian Church in America* (Baltimore, MD: Hill and Harvey, 1888). A more recent attempt also pulled almost exclusively from denominational meeting minutes: William L. Fisk, *The Scottish High Church Tradition in America* (Baltimore, MD: University Press of America, 1994).
7. The borders between Covenanter sects, as well as between Covenanters and other strenuously orthodox Calvinists, were extremely porous. People came and went from one sect to the other with relative ease and to the endless frustration of ministers. This is one reason I treat the groups as part of a broad phenomenon rather than separately—because their members did also. Susannah Raney, for instance, was born Dutch Reformed, married into the ARs, but died an RP. William Findley, a Pennsylvania RP turned AR, fondly remembered listening to Seceder sermons regularly in Ireland. Meanwhile, in Chester, South Carolina, the exodus of RPs northward in protest of slavery led those who stayed behind to join the more moderately antislavery ARs. "Obituary," *Evangelical Witness* 1,

no. 5 (December 1822): 284–285; William Findley, *Observations on "The Two Sons of Oil," Containing a Vindication of the American Constitutions, and Defending the Blessings of Religious Liberty and Toleration, against the Illiberal Strictures of the Rev. Samuel Wylie* (1812), ed. John Caldwell (Indianapolis, IN: Liberty Fund, 2007), 211–215; Peter E. Gilmore, "The Moral Duty of Public Covenanting in the Ante-bellum United States: New-World Exigencies, Old-World Response," *Journal of Transatlantic Studies* 11, no. 2 (June 2013): 186.

8. Though numbers remain nearly impossible to pin down, there were approximately 5,000 Covenanters across the various sects at the time of the American Revolution. By 1822, this number rose to around 15,000. In the mid-1830s, there were approximately 20,000 Covenanters in the United States across three denominations, with the majority of adherents in AR and Seceder congregations. By the Civil War, just under 100,000 adherents kept the faith across five denominational groupings, with the new UP merger constituting over half that number. By the end of the nineteenth century, growth stopped altogether, and their numbers as a percentage of the US population decreased. This was ironic, since it was in the post–Civil War era that Covenanters mounted their most dramatic political assault on the godlessness of the Constitution. By 1896 there were only 120,000 followers, but nearly all of them were in the UP Church, which was shedding its Covenanter heritage by the century's end. There were never more than 10,000 RPs in the nation's first two centuries, and the AR Church entered the twentieth century with fewer people (8,500) than when it entered the Civil War (9,500). An average number of between seventy-five and eighty-five communicants per congregation was suggested to me in conversation by Reformed Presbyterian Church historian Jim Dodson. These numbers proved generally accurate. Reid Stewart estimates around 1,600 RPs at the Revolution. Estimates from 1838 publications suggest an average of approximately 750 people per presbytery. By that time, the ARs were the most populous, followed by Seceder congregations whose numbers were strengthened by recent waves of Irish Protestant immigration. The RPs had particularly slow growth; the denomination has as many members in twenty-first-century America as there were at the time of the Revolution. Their growth outside the United States has been more successful, with active missions to Pakistan, Mexico, and China, to name a few. In fact, there are three times as many Reformed Presbyterians in China today than there are in the United States. Reid W. Stewart, *A Brief History of the General Synod of the Reformed Presbyterian Church in North America* (Lower Burrell, PA: Point Pleasant Ltd., 2011), xi; "Ecclesiastical Statistics," *Evangelical Witness* 1, no. 1 (August 1822): 46; *The American Almanac and Repository of Useful Knowledge* (Boston: Charles Bowen, 1838), 175; *The Presbyterian Historical Almanac and Annual Remembrance of the Church*, vol. 3 (Philadelphia, PA: Joseph M. Wilson, 1861), 327; Robert M. Patterson, *American Presbyterianism in its Development and Growth* (Philadelphia, PA: Presbyterian Board of Publication and Sabbath-School Work, 1896), 82.

## CHAPTER 1

1. Jonathan Swift, as printed in *A Looking Glass for Presbyterians*, no. 2 (Philadelphia, PA, 1764). The poem was modified slightly from "The Life and Character of Dr. Swift." In the original, *Fanatick* is in place of *Presbyterian*, with the same meaning. Jonathan Swift, *The Poems of Jonathan Swift*, vol. 2, 2nd ed., ed. Harold Williams (London: Oxford University Press, 1958), 545–550.
2. David Miller, "Did Ulster Presbyterians Have a Devotional Revolution?" in *Evangelicals and Catholics in Nineteenth-Century Ireland*, ed. James H. Murphey (Dublin: Four Courts Press, 2005), 41; Colin Kidd, "Conditional Britons: The Scots Covenanting Tradition and the Eighteenth-Century British State," *English Historical Review* 117, no. 474 (2002): 1156–1157, 1165–1166; Emily Moberg Robinson, "Sacred Memory: The Covenanter Use of History in Scotland and America," *Journal of Transatlantic Studies* 13, no. 2 (June 2013): 135–157.
3. Geoffrey Parker, "Crisis and Catastrophe: The Global Crisis of the Seventeenth Century Reconsidered," *American Historical Review* 93, no. 3 (October 2008): 1053–1079; Christian Pfister, Rudolf Brázdil, and Rüdiger Glaster, eds., *Climatic Variability in Sixteenth-Century Europe and Its Social Dimension* (Dordrecht: Kluwer Academic Press, 1999), 5–45. This period also coincided with successive poor grain harvests and thus record levels of witch burnings, as witches were thought to be guilty of manipulating the weather. A notable spike in witch accusations also occurred in 1661–62, when Covenanter ministers were being ejected from Scottish pulpits. See Joyce Miller, "Men in Black: Appearances of the Devil in Early Modern Scottish Witchcraft Discourse," in *Witchcraft and Belief in Early Modern Scotland*, ed. Julian Goodare, Lauren Martin, and Joyce Miller (New York: Palgrave Macmillan, 2008), 152.
4. Jenny Wormald, *Court, Kirk, and Community: Scotland, 1470–1625* (Toronto: University of Toronto Press, 1981), 122–125; Alec Ryrie, *The Origins of the Scottish Reformation* (New York: Manchester University Press, 2006), 72–126.
5. Ian B. Cowan, *The Scottish Reformation: Church and Society in Sixteenth Century Scotland* (New York: St. Martin's Press, 1982), 124–138; Gordon Donaldson, *The Scottish Reformation* (Cambridge: Cambridge University Press, 1960), 183–185; Maurice Lee, *Government by Pen: Scotland under James VI and I* (Urbana: University of Illinois Press, 1980), 155–189; Walter Makey, *The Church of the Covenant, 1637–1651* (Edinburgh: John Donald Publishers, 1979), 126–127; Edward M. Furgol, "Scotland Turned Sweden: The Scottish Covenanters and Military Revolution, 1638–1651," in *The Scottish National Covenant in Its British Context*, ed. John Morrill (Edinburgh: Edinburgh University Press, 1990), 139–140; Miller, "Did Ulster Presbyterians Have a Devotional Revolution?" 41; Margo Todd, *The Culture of Protestantism in Early Modern Scotland* (New Haven, CT: Yale University Press, 2002), 97–98, 127–171, 266.

6. *The First and Second Book of Discipline, as it was formerly set forth in Scotland by publicke authoritie, anno 1560 And is at present commanded there to be practiced, anno 1641. Together with some acts of the general assemblies, clearing and confirming the same: and an act of Parliament* (London, 1641), 78–79.
7. David A. Weir, *The Origins of the Federal Theology in Sixteenth-Century Reformation Thought* (Oxford: Clarendon Press, 1990), 4–6.
8. George Buchanan, *De jure regni apud Scotos, or, A dialogue, concerning the due privilege of government in the kingdom of Scotland, betwixt George Buchanan and Thomas Maitland by the said George Buchanan; and translated out of the original Latin into English by Philalethes* (1680), 8–9, 13–14, 19; John Howie, *The Scots Worthies* (1775; repr., Edinburgh: Banner of Truth Trust, 1995), 203.
9. Also noteworthy were the revivals of religion at Shotts in the early 1630s. *First and Second Book of Discipline*, i; *The Pastor and the Prelate, or Reformation and Conformitie shortly compared* (1628), 10–11, 32; *The First and Second Book of Discipline. Together with some Acts of the General Assembly Clearing and Confirming the Same: and an Act of Parliament* (1621), A1–A2; Howie, *Scots Worthies*, 92; Jane Lane, *The Reign of King Covenant* (London: Robert Hale, 1956), 26; Maurice Lee, *The Road to Revolution: Scotland under Charles I, 1625–1637* (Chicago: University of Illinois Press, 1985), 184.
10. The most famous rendition of this story involves the leadership of a common woman named Jenny Geddes. The first mention of Geddes occurred a generation later in the 1670s and appears to collapse two separate incidents reported by contemporaries. Geddes is probably a composite character. Real or imagined though Geddes may be, the riot and the women involved were very real. David Stevenson, *The Scottish Revolution, 1637–1644: The Triumph of the Covenanters* (New York: St. Martin's Press, 1974), 61.
11. The seventeenth-century Puritans also actively made covenants at local levels, especially in the formation of their churches and colonies. See James F. Cooper Jr., *Tenacious for Their Liberties: The Congregationalists in Colonial Massachusetts* (New York: Oxford University Press, 1999); Patrick Collinson, *The Religion of Protestants: The Church in English Society, 1559–1625* (New York: Oxford University Press, 1982); Francis J. Bremer, *The Puritan Experiment: New England Society from Bradford to Edwards* (Hanover, NH: University Press of New England, 1976); Perry Miller, *Orthodoxy in Massachusetts* (Cambridge, MA: Harvard University Press, 1933).
12. James Gordon, *History of Scots Affairs, from MCDXXXVII to MDCXLI*, vol. 1 (Aberdeen: Spalding Club, 1841), 45–47; *The Declinator and Protestation of the Archbishops and Bishops of the Church of Scotland and the others their adherents within that Kingdome, Against the pretended general Assembly holden at Glasgow, November 21, 1638* (1638), 2; James B. Torrance, "The Covenant Concept in Scottish Theology and Politics," in *The Covenant Connection: From*

*Federal Theology to Modern Federalism*, ed. Daniel J. Elazar and John Kincaid (New York: Lexington Books, 2000), 146.

13. "The National Covenant or, the Confession of Faith," in *The Covenants and Covenanters: Covenants, Sermons, and Documents of the Covenanted Reformation*, ed. James Kerr (Middlesex, UK: Echo Library, 2008), 26–28. This language reflects the insights in an Irish context of David W. Miller, *Queen's Rebels: Ulster Loyalism in Historical Perspective*, reprint (Dublin: University College Dublin Press, 2007).
14. "National Covenant," 26–28.
15. Quoted in Crawford Gribben, "The Church of Scotland and the English Apocalyptic Imagination, 1630–1650," *Scottish Historical Review* 88, no. 225 (April 2009): 42.
16. For an overview of the early Scottish elements in the Wars of the Three Kingdoms, see Stevenson, *Scottish Revolution*, 282–286. For an analysis that places nobility at the center and religion as a later-arriving unifying phenomenon, see Lee, *Road to Revolution*, 223–248. On the wars themselves, see Trevor Royle, *The British Civil War: The Wars of the Three Kingdoms, 1638–1660* (New York: Palgrave Macmillan, 2004).
17. "The Solemn League and Covenant," in Kerr, *Covenants and Covenanters*, 77.
18. Gillespie arrived at the year 1643 by placing the reign's beginning at A.D. 383 and interpreting the prophecies of Ezekiel to be 1,260 years. Archibald Johnston, as quoted in S. A. Burrell, "The Apocalyptic Vision of the Early Covenanters," *Scottish Historical Review* 43, no. 135 (April 1964): 20; Gribben, "Church of Scotland and the English Apocalyptic Imagination"; Ann Hughes, "Popular Presbyterianism in the 1640s and 1650s: The Case of Thomas Edward and Thomas Hall," in *England's Long Reformation: 1500–1800*, ed. Nicholas Tyacke (London: University College London, 1998), 235–259; Colin Kidd, *British Identities before Nationalism: Ethnicity and Nationhood in the Atlantic World, 1600–1800* (New York: Cambridge University Press, 1999), 136; Colin Kidd, *Union and Unionism: Political Thought in Scotland, 1500–2000* (New York: Cambridge University Press, 2008), 41, 50–51.
19. Samuel Rutherford, *Lex, Rex: The Law and the Prince, a Dispute for the just PEROGATIVE of King and People* (London: John Field, 1644), 2; John Coffey, *Politics, Religion and the British Revolutions: The Mind of Samuel Rutherford* (New York: Cambridge University Press, 1997), 148–151, 166.
20. Rutherford himself insisted that the two kingdoms were equal, since the civil magistrate could also punish fellow churchmen when they violated civil law. Rutherford, *Lex, Rex*, iii.
21. George Gillespie, "To the Reader," in *Aaron's Rod Blossoming, or the Divine Ordinance of Church Government Vindicated* (1646), 1–38, 51, 224.
22. As George Gillespie put it frankly, toleration would "grant an unbounded liberty unto all sorts of heretics and sectaries [and] is inconsistent with the Solemn

League and Covenant." George Gillespie, *A Late Dialogue betwixt a civilian and a divine concerning the present condition of the church in England* (London, 1644), 3; Samuel Rutherford, *A Free Disputation Against pretended Liberty of Conscience* (London, 1649), preface, 24–26, 145–146, 231; Samuel Rutherford, *A Survey of the Spiritual Antichrist, Opening the Secrets of Familisme and Antinomianisme in the Antichristian Doctrine of John Saltmarsh and Will Del, the Present Preachers of the Army now in England and of Robert Town, Tob. Crisp, H. Denne, Eaton, and others* (London: Andrew Crooke, 1648), 9; George Gillespie, *A Sermon Preached Before the Right Honourable House of Lords, in the Abbey Church at Westminster* (London: Robert Bostock, 1645), 14–18; John Brown, *The Absurdity and Perfidy of all authoritative Toleration of Gross Heresy, Blasphemy, Idoloatry, Popery, in Britain. In Two Letters to a Friend* (1680s; repr., Glasgow, 1780), 5, 14–15; John Coffey, *Persecution and Toleration in Protestant England, 1558–1689* (New York: Longman, 2000), 21–41.

23. *Pamphlet against Dr. Holmes* (October 8, 1650); Thomas Edwards, *The First and Second Part of Gangraena*, 3rd ed., pt. II (London: Ralph Smith, 1646), 13–14.
24. Although the Scots were nonvoting members, they wielded considerable power because of the English Puritans' need for the Covenanter army. Austin Woolrych, *Britain in Revolution, 1625–1660* (New York: Oxford University Press, 2002), 270.
25. *Westminster Confession of Faith*, chaps. 20, 23:3, 30:3; John H. Leith, *Assembly at Westminster: Reformed Theology in the Making* (Richmond, VA: John Knox Press, 1972).
26. John Morrill, ed., *The Scottish National Covenant in Its British Context* (Edinburgh: University of Edinburgh Press, 1990), 13–21.
27. J. G. A. Pocock, *The Discovery of Islands: Essays in British History* (New York: Cambridge University Press, 2005), 139.
28. Thomas Hobbes, *Leviathan, or, The Matter, Form & Power of a Common-Wealth Ecclesiastical and Civil* (1651), 18:3; Sarah Covington, "Royalists, Covenanters and the Shooting of Servants in the Scottish Civil War," *Journal of Scottish Historical Studies* 27, no. 1 (2007): 1–23.
29. George Mackenzie, *Religio Stoici* (Edinburgh, 1663), 1–2; James Sharp to Patrick Drummond, 31 January 1661, in *Lauderdale Papers* (Westminster: Camden Society, 1885), vol. 1; Matthew Wren, *A Brief Theological Treatise Touching the Unlawful Scottish Covenant, Which was in the late ungracious times (with fraud enough, and force), obtruded upon the People of England* (London: D. Maxwell, 1662), 30, NC; John Bramhall, *A Fair Warning to take heed of the Scottish Discipline, As being of all others most Injurious to the Civil Magistrate, most Oppressive to the Subject, most Pernicious to both* (1649), 3–4, NC.
30. Common citations included Exod. 19:1; Deut. 24:10–15, 29:20; Josh. 9:15; 2 Sam. 21:1; 2 Kings 17:15–18; Jer. 11:10, 31:32; and John 23:26. Theophilus Timorcus,

*The Covenanters Plea Against Absolvers, Or, a Modest Discourse Shewing Why those who in England and Scotland took the Solemn League and Covenant cannot judge their Consciences discharged from the Obligation of it* (1661), 51–57; *Three Letters Concerning the Testimony and Obligation of the Covenants Upon Posterity* (undated), un-indexed pamphlet collection, 12, UTC; Robert McWard, *A Testimony against Paying of Ces to an unjust and unlawful Government or wicked Rulers* (ca. 1680), 221, RPHL.

31. Kidd, "Conditional Britons," 1156–1166.
32. Hugh Watt, *Recalling the Scottish Covenants* (London: Thomas Nelson and Sons, 1946), 23.
33. The Committee of the Privy Council for Conventicles to the Duke of Lauderdale, 6 July 1676, in *Lauderdale Papers*, vol. 3; *Pamphlet against Dr. Holmes* (October 8, 1650), 20.
34. "A Letter in Defense of Field-meetings" (June 1678) and "Proclamation against Arms" (May 8, 1679), in Robert Wodrow, *The History of the Sufferings of the Church of Scotland from the Restauration to the Revolution* (Edinburgh, 1721), 1: app. 96, 2: app. 12; Earl of Rothes to the Duke of Lauderdale (undated, ca. 1665), in *Lauderdale Papers*, vol. 1; Jim Smyth, *The Making of the United Kingdom, 1660–1800* (London: Pearson, 2001), 43–52.
35. *Familie Exercise, or, the service of God in Families* (Edinburgh, 1641), NLS; *Directions of the General Assembly Concerning Secret and Private Worship* (1647), ii–iv, NLS; *A Short Directory for Religious Societies* (1782), preface, NLS "For Holy Scotland"; Moberg Robinson, "Sacred Memory."
36. Archbishop of Glasgow to the Duke of Lauderdale, 17 December 1674, in *Lauderdale Papers*, vol. 3; Wodrow, *History of the Sufferings of the Church of Scotland*, 1:3; John Howie, *A Cloud of Witnesses for the Royal Prerogatives of Jesus Christ: Being the Last Speeches and Testimonies of those who have suffered for the truth in Scotland since the year 1680* (Edinburgh: Oliphant, Anderson, and Ferrier, undated), 518–531.
37. Duke of Lauderdale to the King, 2 July 1674, in *Lauderdale Papers*, vol. 3; Earl of Rothes to the Duke of Lauderdale (undated, ca. 1665); Wodrow, *History of the Sufferings of the Church of Scotland*, 2:13–36; Smyth, *Making of the United Kingdom*, 44; David George Mullan, *Narratives of the Religious Self in Early-Modern Scotland* (Farnham, UK: Ashgate, 2010), 56.
38. *Naphtali, or, the Wrestling of the Church of Scotland for the Kingdom of Christ* (1667), 1–25, NLS; Rutherglen Declaration (May 29, 1679), in Wodrow, *History of the Sufferings of the Church of Scotland*, 2:44.
39. John Howie, *Faithful Contendings Displayed* (1780), 10–27.
40. Alexander Shields, *A True and Faithful Relation of the Sufferings of the Reverend and Learned Mr. Alexander Shields, Minister of the Gospel* (1715), 48–49; Alexander Shields, *A Hind Let Loose; or, An Historical Representation of the Testimonies of the Church of Scotland for the Interest of Christ* (Glasgow, 1687), iv, 1, 342–345, 515,

NLS; Wodrow, *History of the Sufferings of the Church of Scotland*, 2:503; Cowan, *Scottish Covenanters*, 118–126.

41. *A proper project for Scotland, to startle fools, and frighten knaves but make wise men happy* (undated), BL; *A Seasonable Admonition and Exhortation to Some who separate themselves from the Communion of the Church of Scotland, wherein is also discovered that the things they complain of, are either false on the Matter, or not sufficient to warrant a Separation* (1698), NLS; Ryan K. Frace, "Religious Toleration in the Wake of Revolution: Scotland on the Eve of Enlightenment, 1688–1710s," *Journal of the Historical Association* 93, no. 311 (July 2008): 355–375. Nationalist rhetoric against the 1707 Act of Union was especially prone to cast the covenants in a nationalistic light: Colin Kidd, *Subverting Scotland's Past* (New York: Cambridge University Press, 1993); Kidd, *Union and Unionism*, 75–80.
42. Ebenezer Erskine, *A Sermon: the Stone Rejected by the Builders exalted as the Head-stone of the Corner* (Henry Hoskins, 1800), 26–27; *Reading no Preaching; or, a Letter to a Clergyman from a Friend in London concerning the unwarrantable Practice of Reading the Gospel, instead of Preaching it* (Edinburgh, 1752), 1–9, RPHL.
43. Watt, *Recalling the Scottish Covenants*, 80–83.
44. William Findley, *Observations on "The Two Sons of Oil," Containing a Vindication of the American Constitutions, and Defending the Blessings of Religious Liberty and Toleration, against the Illiberal Strictures of the Rev. Samuel Wylie* (1812), ed. John Caldwell (Indianapolis, IN: Liberty Fund, 2007), 211; Ray A. King, *History of the Associate Reformed Presbyterian Church* (Greenville, SC: Board of Christian Education Ministries of the Associate Reformed Presbyterian Church, 2008), 39; William L. Fisk, *The Scottish High Church Tradition in America* (Baltimore, MD: University Press of America, 1994), 27; David Stewart, *The Seceders in Ireland* (Belfast: Presbyterian Historical Society, 1950), 98; Ned Landsman, "The Seceders and North America" (paper presented at the Eighteenth-Century Scottish Studies Society, Columbia, SC, April 13, 2012).
45. Norman Davies, *The Isles: A History* (New York: Oxford University Press, 1999), 563.
46. John Abernath, *Reasons for the Repeal of the Sacramental Test* (Dublin, 1733), 66; J. C. Beckett, *Protestant Dissent in Ireland, 1687–1780* (London: Faber and Faber, 1946); Peter Brooke, *Ulster Presbyterianism: The Historical Perspective, 1610–1970* (New York: St. Martin's Press, 1987); I. R. McBride, *Scripture Politics: Ulster Presbyterians and Irish Radicalism in the Late Eighteenth Century* (New York: Oxford University Press, 1989); S. J. Connolly, *Religion, Law and Power: The Making of Protestant Ireland, 1660–1760* (Oxford: Clarendon Press, 1992).
47. William Tisdall, *The Conduct of Dissenters, of Ireland with Respect both to church and state* (Dublin, 1712), Belfast Pamphlet Collection, UTC.
48. William Tisdall, *A Sample of True-Blew Presbyterian Loyalty in all Changes and Turns of Government, Taken chiefly out of their most Authentick Records* (1709), 5,

Belfast Pamphlet Collection, UTC; William Tisdall, *A Seasonable Enquiry into that Most Dangerous Political Principle of the Kirk in Power* (1713), 7, 11, Belfast Pamphlet Collection, UTC; James Fisher, *A View of Seceders in Some Instances of their Usage of the General Synod of Ulster* (Belfast, 1748), 6, Belfast Pamphlet Collection, UTC; Alexander Covill, *The Persecuting, Disloyal and Absurd Tenets of Those who affect to call themselves Seceders Laid Open and Refuted* (Belfast, 1749), 6, Belfast Printed Books, LL.

49. Covill, *Persecuting, Disloyal and Absurd Tenets*, 14; David Miller, "Religious Commotions in the Scottish Diaspora: A Transatlantic Perspective on 'Evangelicalism' in Mainline Denominations," in *Ulster Presbyterians in the Atlantic World: Religion, Politics and Identity*, ed. David A. Wilson and Mark G. Spencer (Dublin: Four Courts Press, 2006), 66; David Hempton and Myrtle Hill, *Evangelical Protestantism in Ulster Society, 1740–1890* (London: Routledge, 1992), 17.
50. Thomas Clarke, "Farewell Letter" (March 15, 1791), as reprinted in *Evangelical Guardian* 1, nos. 7–10 (1843–1844): 324–346.
51. "A Serious Address from the Presbytery of Strabane to the several congregations under their care," *Belfast-News Letter*, March 24, 1772; McBride, *Scripture Politics*, 79–80; Jim Smyth, *The Men of No Property: Irish Radicals and Popular Politics in the Late Eighteenth Century* (New York: Palgrave Macmillan, 1998), 35; Ned C. Landsman, *Scotland and Its First American Colony, 1683–1765* (Princeton, NJ: Princeton University Press, 1985), 9; evidence that Irish Covenanters and Seceders continued this revolutionary activity well into the conflicts of the late eighteenth century exists in the refusal of sessions to discipline rebellious behavior. See Ballybay Session book, 1790–1798, PRONI; Boardmills session book, 1796–1799, PRONI; Joseph S. Moore, "Irish Radicals, Southern Conservatives: Slavery, Religious Liberty, and the Presbyterian Fringe in the Atlantic World" (PhD diss., University of North Carolina at Greensboro, 2011), 321–342.
52. Brycchan Carey, *From Peace to Freedom: Quaker Rhetoric and the Birth of American Antislavery, 1657–1761* (New Haven, CT: Yale University Press, 2012); John Donoghue, "Out of the Land of Bondage: The English Revolution and the Atlantic Origins of Abolition," *American Historical Review* 115, no. 4 (October 2010): 943–974; Joseph S. Moore, "Covenanters and Antislavery in the Atlantic World," *Slavery and Abolition* 34, no. 4 (2013): 539–561; C. Duncan Rice, *The Scots Abolitionists, 1833–1861* (Baton Rouge: Louisiana State University Press, 1981), ix, 28. For broad overviews of antislavery movements, see David Brion Davis, *The Problem of Slavery in the Age of Revolution, 1770–1823* (Ithaca, NY: Cornell University Press, 1977); Christopher Leslie Brown, *Moral Capital: Foundations of British Abolitionism* (Chapel Hill: University of North Carolina Press, 2006); Seymour Drescher, *Abolition: A History of Slavery and Antislavery* (New York: Cambridge University Press, 2009).

53. Rutherford, *Lex, Rex,* 91–92; Rutherford, *Free Disputation Against pretended Liberty of Conscience,* "to the Godly and impartial reader."
54. James VI/I, *The True Lawe of free Monarchies* (Edinburgh, 1598); *Proper project for Scotland,* 23–25; *Testimony and Warning Against the Blasphemies and Idolatry of Popery* (Edinburgh, 1779), title page, 3–4, 32–48, 31, 71.
55. Shields, *Hind Let Loose,* iv; Cowan, *Scottish Covenanters,* 118–126; Donoghue, "Out of the Land of Bondage," 946–949.
56. Reformed Presbytery, *The Act, Declaration and Testimony for the Whole of our Covenanted Reformation* (Edinburgh, 1806), 7–8; Fragment of Address by Delegates from America, ca. 1830, Correspondence with America, no. 1, RPHL.
57. Historian Valerie Wallace ties economic unrest in eighteenth-century Scotland to what she dubs a "Presbyterian moral economy," a sensibility among common Scots about basic fairness and what constituted oppression in local and national affairs. Valerie Wallace, "Presbyterian Moral Economy: The Covenanting Tradition and Popular Protest in Lowland Scotland, 1707–c.1746," *Scottish Historical Review* 89, no. 227 (April 2010): 54–72; Marylyn Westerkamp, *Triumph of the Laity: Scots-Irish Piety and the Great Awakening, 1625–1760* (New York: Oxford University Press, 1988), 1–73, 210–213.
58. On the growth of religious tolerance in this period as a reaction to Covenanters, see Steve Bruce and Chris Wright, "Law, Social Change, and Religious Toleration," *Journal of Church and State* 37, no. 1 (Winter 1995): 103–120; Frace, "Religious Toleration in the Wake of Revolution."

## CHAPTER 2

1. Roger Williams, *The Bloudy Tenet of Persecution, for Cause of Conscience Discussed in a Conference between TRUTH and PEACE,* ed. Richard Groves (Macon, GA: Mercer University Press, 2001), 217, 263, 132. Williams also mentioned the divisions "between the Presbyterians and the Independents, Covenanters and Non-covenanters" in Town of Providence to Sir Henry Vane, 27 August 1654, written in Williams's hand and attributed to him; see also Roger Williams to Governor John Endicott, ca. August–September 1651, both in *The Correspondence of Roger Williams,* vol. 1, ed. Glen W. LaFantasie (Providence: Rhode Island Historical Society, 1988), 398, 338–339.
2. Ned Landsman, *Scotland and Its First American Colony, 1683–1765* (Princeton, NJ: Princeton University Press, 1985), 309, n. 16; Charles H. Lippy, "Chastized by Scorpions: Christianity and Culture in Colonial South Carolina, 1669–1740," *Church History* 79, no. 2 (June 2010): 257; Sir George Mackenzie, as quoted in David Carson, "A History of the Reformed Presbyterian Church in America to 1871" (PhD diss., University of Pennsylvania, 1964), 11.
3. Landsman, *Scotland and Its First American Colony,* 3–4, 179–181, 244; Carson, "History of the Reformed Presbyterian Church in America," 9–14.

4. Recently, historians have shown how rarely the term *Scotch-Irish* was used until the nineteenth century, but as yet, I have not found any thoroughly serviceable replacement. I have retained the term here because of its ubiquity. Culturally popular images of penniless Scotch-Irishmen arriving alone on American shores are generally misleading. Most Scotch-Irish immigrants came as families or churches, and around 80 percent were able to pay their way up front. Many came only after acquiring some degree of means through the linen trade; few, therefore, were destitute. Furthermore, there was no Scotsman prototype, either in Scotland or in America. The same Scotland that produced Richard Cameron also produced the Deist David Hume. For every highland clansman who made his way to places such as North Carolina, there were many more lowland Scots whose immigrant identity was torn between Britishness, Scottishness, and Irishness. In terms of religion, Scotland sent colonists who were Anglican, Quaker, and functionally agnostic along with the varying brands of Presbyterianism. Patrick Griffin, *The People with No Name: Ireland's Ulster Scots, America's Scots Irish, and the Creation of a British Atlantic World, 1689–1764* (Princeton, NJ: Princeton University Press, 2001), 1–8, 65–124; Kerby Miller, "Ulster Presbyterians and the 'Two Traditions' in Ireland and America," in *These Fissured Isles: Ireland, Scotland and the Making of Modern Britain 1798–1848*, ed. Terry Brotherstone, Anna Clark, and Kevin Whelan (Edinburgh: John Donald, 2005); and Kerby A. Miller, "The New England and Federalist Origins of 'Scotch-Irish' Ethnicity," in *Ulster and Scotland, 1600–2000: History, Language, and Identity*, ed. William Kelly and John R. Young (Dublin: Four Courts Press, 2004), 105–118. For the American South, see David T. Gleeson, "Smaller Differences: 'Scotch Irish' and 'Real Irish' in the Nineteenth-Century American South," *New Hibernia Review* 10, no. 2 (Samhradh/Summer 2006): 68–91; on the Covenanters and Irish identity, see Rankin Sherling, "Selective Remembrance: Scottish Sensibilities and Forgotten Irish Contributions to Reformed Presbyterianism in America," *Journal of Transatlantic Studies* 13, no. 2 (June 2013): 158–176; see the note "Terminology," *Journal of Scotch-Irish Studies* 3, no. 3 (Fall 2012): 123. On economics after arrival, see Peter N. Moore, *World of Toil and Strife: Community Transformation in Backcountry South Carolina, 1750–1805* (Columbia: University of South Carolina Press, 2007), 52–53; Landsman, *Scotland and Its First American Colony*, 256–263.
5. In this they were similar to the German Reformed congregations throughout the Conestoga Valley, who pressed pious schoolmasters and tailors into service to work alongside elected elders in supervising the religious lives of the people. Patricia Bonomi, *Under the Cope of Heaven: Society, Religion, and Politics in Colonial America* (New York: Oxford University Press, 2003), 74–75; Leigh Eric Schmidt, *Holy Fairs: Scotland and the Making of American Revivalism*, 4th ed. (Grand Rapids, MI: William B. Eerdmans, 2001), 3–68; Jean Stephenson, *Scotch-Irish Migration to South Carolina, 1772: Rev. William Martin and His Five Shiploads of Settlers* (Washington, DC: Clearfield Company, 1971), 1–21.

6. David Freeman Hawke, *Franklin* (New York: Harper and Row, 1976), 220. For overviews of the Great Awakening that emphasize the dynamics between revivalists and antirevivalists, see Thomas S. Kidd, *The Great Awakening: The Roots of Evangelical Christianity in Colonial America* (New Haven, CT: Yale University Press, 2007); Mark A. Noll, *The Rise of Evangelicalism: The Age of Edwards, Whitefield, and the Wesleys* (Downers Grove, IL: IVP Academic, 2003); Hary S. Stout, *The Divine Dramatist: George Whitefield and the Rise of Modern Evangelicalism* (Grand Rapids, MI: William B. Eerdmans, 1991); George M. Marsden, *Jonathan Edwards: A Life* (New Haven, CT: Yale University Press, 2003). For more skeptical views on the revival that emphasize the roll of early print culture, see Frank Lambert, *Inventing the Great Awakening* (Princeton, NJ: Princeton University Press, 2001); Jon Butler, "Enthusiasm Described and Decried: The Great Awakening as Interpretive Fiction," *Journal of American History* 69, no. 2 (September 1982): 305–325.
7. Craighead required all families to swear the covenants before accepting their children for communion. Richard Locke to Rev. George Craig, as quoted in Alice M. Baldwin, "Sowers of Sedition: The Political Theories of Some of the New Light Presbyterian Clergy of Virginia and North Carolina," *William and Mary Quarterly* 5, no. 1 (January 1948): 52–76; Leonard J. Trinterud, *The Forming of an American Tradition* (Philadelphia, PA: Westminster Press, 1949), 100; Marilyn Westerkamp, *Triumph of the Laity: Scots-Irish Piety and the Great Awakening, 1625–1760* (New York: Oxford University Press, 1988), 198; Michael C. Scoggins, "A Revolutionary Minister: The Life of the Reverend Alexander Craighead," *Journal of Scotch-Irish Studies* 3, no. 3 (Fall 2012): 98–116.
8. Craighead initially insisted that Covenanters were not "obliged to rise in Rebellion against the present Majesty King George." The covenants called for defensive rather than offensive acts. Besides, Covenanters did not possess the sword of the state but, rather, spiritual weapons. They should wage spiritual rather than civil warfare. By 1743, however, his rhetoric was more openly radical. Alexander Craighead, *A Discourse Concerning the Covenants: Containing the Substance of Two Sermons Preached at Middle-Octarara, January 10 and 17, 1741,2* (Philadelphia, PA: B. Franklin, 1742), 32, 38.
9. *Renewal of the Covenants, National and Solemn League; a Confession of Sins; an Engagement to Duties; and a Testimony; as they were carried on at Middle Octorara in Pennsylvania, November 11, 1743* (Philadelphia, PA: Franklin, 1748), 27, 31–32.
10. Ibid., 6, 15–16, 29–32.
11. Ibid., 7, 13, 15, 19, 30.
12. Years after the warring Presbyterians made peace with one another, one minister, under the pseudonym "an old Covenanting, and true Presbyterian layman," continued to chastise the evangelical Tennent brothers and Samuel Davies. *The conduct of Presbyterian-ministers, who sent the letter to the Archbishop of Canterbury, the year 1760, considered, and set in true light: in answer to some*

*remarks thereon. In a letter to a friend. By an elder of the Presbyterian Church* (Philadelphia, PA: Andrew Steuart, 1761); *Records of the Presbyterian Church in the United States of America, 1706–1788* (Philadelphia, PA: Presbyterian Board of Publication and Sabbath School Work, 1904), 165; *Renewal of the Covenants, National and Solemn League*, 23; Samuel Blair, *Animadversions on the Reasons of Mr. Alex. Craighead's Receding from the Judicatures of this Church Together with its Constitution* (Philadelphia, PA: Bradford, 1743), 10.

13. Scoggins, "Revolutionary Minister," 104–107; Baldwin, "Sowers of Sedition," 66–71.
14. John Abernathy, *Reasons for the Repeal of the Sacramental Test* (Dublin, 1733), 66. This view of the connection between the Great Awakening and Revolution was first popularized in Alan Heimert, *Religion and the American Mind from the Great Awakening to the Revolution* (Cambridge, MA: Harvard University Press, 1966). Patricia Bonomi has reasserted this connection by emphasizing religious and cultural networks. Bonomi, *Under the Cope of Heaven*, 132. Opposing this position is Jon Butler, *Awash in a Sea of Faith: Christianizing the American People* (Cambridge, MA: Harvard University Press, 1990); see also Kidd, *Great Awakening*, xii–xix, 288–324; Westerkamp, *Triumph of the Laity*, 34. For an overview of the controversy over Anglican and Presbyterian cooperation in the revivals and beyond, see William Harrison Taylor, "One Body and One Spirit: Presbyterians, Interdenominationalism, and the American Revolution" (PhD diss., Mississippi State University, 2009), 43–51.
15. John Cuthbertson, Personal Diary (September 9, 1753), PTS; *A Warning of the Presbytery of New-Castle, to the people under their care, against several errors and evil practices of Mr. John Cuthbertson; with an appendix relating to the Seceders* (Lancaster, PA: W. Dunlap, 1754); S. Helen Fields, *Register of Marriages and Baptisms performed by Rev. John Cuthbertson Covenanter Minister, 1751–1791, with Index to Locations and Persons Visited* (Baltimore, MD: Genealogical Publishing Company, 1983), viii–xv.
16. Benjamin Franklin, *Narrative of the Late Massacres in Lancaster County, of a Number of Indians, Friends of this Province, By Persons Unknown, With some Observations on the same* (1764); Kevin Kenny, *Peaceable Kingdom Lost: The Paxton Boys and the Destruction of William Penn's Holy Experiment* (New York: Oxford University Press, 2009); Patrick Griffin, *American Leviathan: Empire, Nation, and Revolutionary Frontier* (New York: Hill and Wang, 2007), 46–49, 64–67.
17. Until recently, historians believed that the revolt was led exclusively by Mathew Smith and Thomas Gibson; theirs were the names remaining on the printed petition Franklin distributed. In 2009, the original handwritten document was donated to the Lancaster County Historical Society in Pennsylvania. In that original document, William Brown's name is marked out, and historians have relied most heavily on Franklin's more accessible printed version. Historian Richard MacMaster analyzed biographical data to determine that out of two

William Browns who could have been the third signatory, only Covenanter William Brown had cause to delete his name. Richard K. MacMaster, "The Third Man: William Brown and the Paxton Boys," *Journal of Lancaster County's Historical Society* 115, nos. 1–2 (Fall 2013): 2–13.

18. Alexander Hunt, *A Looking-Glass, &c., No. 2*, in *The Paxton Papers*, ed. John R. Dunbar (The Hague: Martinus Nijhoff, 1957), 301–315; Cuthbertson, Personal Diary (January 27, 1764; March 23, 1759).
19. Cuthbertson, Personal Diary (May 25–31, 1767); John Hughes, as quoted in J. C. D. Clark, *The Language of Liberty, 1660–1832: Political Discourse and Social Dynamics in the Anglo-American World* (New York: Cambridge University Press, 1994), 261.
20. William Saunders, ed., *The Colonial Records of North Carolina*, vol. 1 (Raleigh, NC: P. M. Hale, Printer to the State, 1886). Documenting the American South. University Library, The University of North Carolina at Chapel Hill, 2007.
21. Marjoleine Kars, *Breaking Loose Together: The Regulator Rebellion in Pre-Revolutionary America* (Chapel Hill: University of North Carolina Press, 2002), 42, 126, 155.
22. Others moved into Abbeville, Newberry, and Camden and sometime later into Fairfield, Laurens, and York. Catholic lasted from 1759 to 1773. Stephenson, *Scotch-Irish Migration to South Carolina*, 1–21; Moore, *World of Toil and Strife*, 55–56.
23. Saunders, *Colonial Records of North Carolina*, 9:1282–1285; A. S. Salley Jr., "The Mecklenburg Declaration: The Present Status of the Question," *American Historical Review* 13 (1908): 16–43. The resolves are printed in the *South Carolina Gazette and Country Journal*, June 13, 1775.
24. Clark, *Language of Liberty*, 260–270; William Henry Hoyt, *The Mecklenburg Declaration of Independence: A Study of Evidence Showing that the Alleged Early Declaration of Independence by Mecklenburg County, North Carolina, on May 20th 1775, is Spurious* (New York: G. P. Putnam's Sons, 1907), 22–29; Scoggins, "Revolutionary Minister," 114.
25. The original manuscript contains a footnote stating, "Beswore fidelity to the state with others after speaking of swearing and prayer. J.C." Fisk interpreted this as a quick backtracking against any allegiance to the colonial powers, while Aiken and Adair believed that it represented a breaking of all ties with the British Crown. Aiken and Adair are most likely correct, but more completely it appears that Cuthbertson was convincing the crowd of the justness of renouncing George III's authority. This seems to be the sense of the later words "with others after speaking." Cuthbertson's diary, however, is notoriously cryptic. Cuthbertson, Personal Diary (December 11, 1775, and July 2, 1777); William L. Fisk Jr., "The Diary of John Cuthbertson Missionary to the Covenanters of Colonial Pennsylvania," *Presbyterian Magazine of History and Biography* 73, no. 4

(October 1949): 441–458; Reid W. Stewart, *Rev. John Cuthbertson (1718–1791) First Covenanter Minister to North America* (Lower Burrell, PA: Point Pleasant, 2007), 36; on the ongoing debate by colonial Covenanters about how to apply the covenants, see William Findley, *Observations on "The Two Sons of Oil," Containing a Vindication of the American Constitutions, and Defending the Blessings of Religious Liberty and Toleration, against the Illiberal Strictures of the Rev. Samuel Wylie* (1812), ed. John Caldwell (Indianapolis, IN: Liberty Fund, 2007), 213–215.

26. John Adams to Abigail Adams, 30 March 1777, in *The Adams Papers: Adams Family Correspondence*, vol. 2, *June 1776–March 1778*, ed. L. H. Butterfield (Cambridge, MA: Harvard University Press, 1963), 189.

27. James Hemphill, who had immigrated to Mecklenburg in 1767 from Co. Londonderry, fought in the backcountry campaigns led by Andrew Williamson against the Cherokee. He later served as a lieutenant under guerilla Patriot leader Thomas Sumter. Alexander Craighead's son, Robert, served as captain of the Mecklenburg militia. The fates of the other members of the Chester company were less propitious, however. Within days, one segment was ridden down by British dragoons while drilling in a field; another detachment was surprised while getting their horses shod. Most were taken prisoner. Martin's confrontation with Cornwallis is almost certainly embellished. The more realistic encounter probably involved discussion of the connections between Martin's family and Cornwallis's Irish lands, where the Martins had once kept the stables. The family of Ninian Craig, who arrived with Martin's Covenanters, left behind one of the most thorough accounts of the southern militia campaigns. After captivity in Camden, Martin was released and spent the remainder of the war in Mecklenburg. At the war's conclusion, Martin returned to Chester and pastored the remnants of the ecumenical Presbyterian gathering at Catholic. After being dismissed (and not for the first time) for his chronic alcoholism, Martin oversaw a series of Society gatherings at Long Cane in Abbeville District. From there, he helped form an official RP body—from which he was summarily dismissed for intemperance and selling a slave. "James Hemphill, Rev. Solider," transcription of War Department Pension papers (July 29, 1839), DU; John Craig, "The War in York and Chester," *Chester (SC) Standard*, March 16, 1854; Scoggins, "Revolutionary Minister," 113; David Faris, *The Faris Family of Bloomington, Indiana: A Genealogy of the Descendants of James and David Farrie of Chester District, South Carolina and Their Sister Agnes (Farrie) Smith, Emigrants from County Antrim, Northern Ireland, in 1772* (Baltimore, MD: Gateway Press, 1989), 24; Stephenson, *Scotch-Irish Migration to South Carolina*, 21–24, 84, 87, 91; Robert Lathan, *A Historical Sketch of Union A.R.P. Church, Chester County, South Carolina* (1888), 23; *Biographical Sketch of Rev. William Martin*, undated pamphlet, EC. It is worth noting that Peter N. Moore has argued that the Covenanter-leaning areas around Waxhaw, S.C., were

"reluctant revolutionaries" compared with mainline Presbyterian neighbors and that they were disproportionately likely to side with the Loyalists for reasons of recent immigration and local community conflicts. Yet most of Moore's examples were not explicitly Covenanters; rather, they were Presbyterians who turned to the Associate Reformed Church out of postwar-era frustration with the psalmody question. Moore, *World of Toil and Strife*, 60–75.

28. Fredric Palmer Wells, *History of Barnet, Vermont* (Burlington, VT: Free Press, 1923), 115. Known participants include Irish immigrant John Lytle of Granville, Joseph McCracken, and Lt. John Steel of Camden, N.Y. Donald Smith, ed., "Green Mountain Boy Land Rioters File" (2005), email to the author, February 7, 2013. Dr. Smith has compiled an exhaustive database of agrarian rebels including hometowns and religious affiliations (where known). The database is on punch cards, and Dr. Smith generously searched for known Covenanter and Seceder activists.
29. S. D. Clark, *Movements of Political Protest in Canada, 1640–1840* (Toronto: University of Toronto Press, 1959), 65–71. For these Covenanters in a wider Atlantic context, see Valerie Wallace, "Exporting Radicalism within the Empire: Scots Presbyterian Political Values in Scotland and British North America, c. 1815–1850" (PhD diss., University of Glasgow, 2010), 23–24.
30. Stephen A. Marini, *Radical Sects of Revolutionary New England* (Cambridge, MA: Harvard University Press, 1982), 1–7.
31. Aiding the shift were the decades of internal dialogues in RP congregations about the applicability of the old covenants in the New World. Even John Cuthbertson, who did so much to keep American RPs steadfast in the Good Old Cause, had privately conceded that he would be open to modifying how this political theology worked in American contexts. Lathan notes that there was as much division between members of the same sect as between the sects themselves. Findley, *Observations on "The Two Sons of Oil,"* 211–215; Robert Lathan, *History of the Associate Reformed Synod of the South, 1782–1882* (Harrisburg, PA: published for the author, 1884), 165–184.
32. Lathan, *History of the Associate Reformed Synod of the South*, 165–184.
33. In chapter XX.4, the AR text expanded the original "and by the power of the Civil Magistrate" to "and in proportion as their erroneous opinions or practices, either in their own nature, or in the manner of publishing or maintaining them, are destructive to the external peace of the church, and of civil society, they may be also proceeded against by the power of the civil magistrate." In XXIII.3, it deleted "yet he hath authority, and it is his duty to take order, that unity and peace be preserved in the Church, that the truth of God be kept pure and entire, that all blasphemies and heresies be suppressed, all corruptions and abuses in worship and discipline prevented or reformed and all the ordinances of God duly settled, administered, and observed. For the better effecting whereof he hath power to call synods, to be present at them,

and to provide that whatsoever is transacted in them be according to the mind of God." The replacement language was: "Yet, as the gospel revelation lays indispensible obligations upon all classes of people who are favoured with it, magistrates, as such, are bound to execute their respective offices in subserviency thereto, administering government on Christian principles, and ruling in the fear of God, according to the directions of his word; as those who shall give an account to the Lord Jesus, who God hath appointed to be judge of the world. Hence, magistrates, as such, in a Christian country, are bound to promote the Christian religion, as the most valuable interests of their subjects, by all such means as are not inconsistent with civil rights; and do not imply an interference with the policy of the church, which is the free and independence kingdom of the Redeemer nor an assumption of dominion over conscience." *The Constitution and Standards of the Associate-Reformed Church in North America* (New York: T.&J. Swords, 1799), chaps. XX.4, XXI, XXIII.3; Philip Schaff, ed., *The Creeds of Christendom with a History and Critical Notes*, vol. 3, *The Evangelical Protestant Creeds with Translations*, 6th ed. (1877; repr., Grand Rapids, MI: Baker Books, 1983), 643–655. The ministers who left in protest approached the Reformed Presbytery for a possible merger but were rejected; from this point, their newly created Reformed Dissenting Presbytery continued until it united with the Associate Synod in 1851. Peter Gilmore, "Rebels and Revivals: Ulster Immigrants, Western Pennsylvania Presbyterianism, and the Formation of Scotch-Irish Identity, 1780–1830" (PhD diss., Carnegie Mellon University, 2009), 544–549.

34. States where Covenanter settlements concentrated were more active than most. Pennsylvania had two constitutions, and South Carolina had three. Rhode Island and Connecticut continued to operate under their old colonial charters. Edward Countryman, "Confederation: State Governments and Their Problems," in *A Companion to the American Revolution*, ed. Jack P. Greene and J. R. Pole (Malden, MA: Blackwell, 2004), 362–373.
35. "Sermon on the 5th Commandment: Duties of Citizens" (ca. 1820), DU.
36. David Smith Faris, as quoted in Faris, *Faris Family of Bloomington*, 32; "The Mountain Men," *Evangelical Witness* 3, no. 5 (May 1825): 191–199.
37. Covenanters, Seceders, and the Associate Reformed Church all maintained more stringent adherence to singing only the Westminster Assembly–approved psalm book, known as Rous's Psalter. The psalms were lined out by a song leader and repeated by the congregation during worship. They usually refused to sing hymns. Isaac Watts's Psalter and subsequent hymnals, printed in America by Benjamin Franklin in 1729, caused disruptions throughout American Presbyterianism. Entire congregations withdrew from the mainline Presbyterian Church over the issue, joining various strands of Covenanter denominations from the 1790s through the antebellum period. Taylor, "One Body and One Spirit," 163–165; Raymond Jones Martin, "The Transition from

Psalmody to Hymnody in Southern Presbyterianism, 1753–1901" (SMD diss., Union Theological Seminary, 1963), 1–59; William B. Bynum, "The Genuine Presbyterian Whine: Presbyterian Worship in the Eighteenth Century," *Journal of Presbyterian History* 74, no. 3 (Fall 1996): 157–170. For the ARs on this issue, see Joseph S. Moore, "American Innovations to Scots-Irish Religious Traditions: Rev. John Hemphill and the Covenanter-Seceder Presbyterians in the American South," in *Ulster-Scots and America: Diaspora Literature, History, and Migration, 1750–2000*, ed. Frank Ferguson and Richard MacMaster (Dublin: Four Courts Press, forthcoming).

38. The following episode is treated in depth, with economic and cultural context, in Peter E. Gilmore, *Land of Gospel Light and Liberty: The Irish Presbyterian Diaspora in Western Pennsylvania, 1780–1830* (forthcoming); I am greatly indebted to Dr. Gilmore for allowing me to preview this work as well as to his transatlantic interpretation of the events. Washington was not assured of the grant from Virginia governor Lord Dunmore until July 1774. Charles H. Ambler, *George Washington and the West* (Chapel Hill: University of North Carolina Press, 1936), 177–178.
39. Boyd Crumrine, ed., *History of Washington County, Pennsylvania* (Philadelphia, PA: L. H. Everts and Co., 1882), 859.
40. *The Diaries of George Washington*, vol. 4, *1784–June 1786*, ed. Donald Jackson and Dorothy Twohig (Charlottesville: University Press of Virginia, 1978), 26–29, 37–38; Thomas P. Slaughter, *The Whiskey Rebellion: Frontier Epilogue to the American Revolution* (New York: Oxford University Press, 1988), 84–85, 249.
41. The veracity of the cursing story is dubious, but if there were any poor farmer who would have dared to fine the nation's Revolutionary hero for moral laxity, it would have been a Covenanter church elder. *The Writings of George Washington from the Original Manuscript Sources, 1745–1799*, vol. 28, ed. John C. Fitzpatrick (Washington, DC: US Government Printing Office, 1938), 3–4; local tradition found in Crumrine, *History of Washington County, Pennsylvania*, 859; *The Papers of George Washington*, vol. 4, *April 1786–1787*, ed. W. W. Abbot, Confederation Series (Charlottesville: University Press of Virginia, 1995), 339–342.
42. Luther Martin, "The Genuine Information Delivered to the Legislature of the State of Maryland Relative to the Proceedings of the General Convention Lately Held at Philadelphia, XII" (February 8, 1788), in *The Debate on the Constitution: Federalist and Antifederalist Speeches, Articles, and Letters during the Struggle over Ratification*, pt. 1, ed. Bernard Bailyn (New York: Library of America, 1993), 656. For a broad overview of Anti-Federalism, see Saul Cornell, *The Other Founders: Anti-Federalism and the Dissenting Tradition in America, 1788–1828* (Chapel Hill: University of North Carolina Press, 1999), 1–18.
43. Max Farrand, ed., *The Records of the Federal Convention of 1787*, vol. 1 (New Haven, CT: Yale University Press, 1966), 451–452.

44. "Debate in North Carolina Ratifying Convention" (July 30, 1788), in *The Sacred Rights of Conscience: Selected Readings on Religious Liberty and Church–State Relations in the American Founding*, ed. Daniel L. Dreisbach and Mark David Hall (Indianapolis, IN: Liberty Fund, 2009), 398; Stephen A. Marini, "Religion, Politics, and Ratification," in *Religion in a Revolutionary Age*, ed. Ronald Hoffman and Peter J. Albert (Charlottesville: University Press of Virginia, 1994), 184–217.
45. Presbytery of the Eastward to George Washington, 28 October 1789, in *The Papers of George Washington*, vol. 4, ed. W. W. Abbot and Dorothy Twohig, Presidential Series (Charlottesville: University Press of Virginia, 1993), 275–277; others as quoted in Isaac Kramnick and R. Laurence Moore, *The Godless Constitution: The Case against Religious Correctness* (New York: W. W. Norton and Company, 1996), 37.
46. Their objections were both procedural and ideological; they believed that an antidemocratic government was being pushed through without enough time for consideration. Findley's leadership is evidenced by the published responses of the Constitution's supporters, who named him as the first of the conspirators. *An Address of the Subscribers Members of the late House of Representatives of the Commonwealth of Pennsylvania to their Constituents* (Philadelphia, PA, 1787), and "The Reply to the Six Assemblymen," *Pennsylvania Packet*, October 8, 1787, both in Merrill Jensen, ed., *The Documentary History of the Ratification of the Constitution*, vol. 2, *Ratification of the Constitution by the States, Pennsylvania* (Madison: State Historical Society of Wisconsin, 1976), 112–120; Owen S. Ireland, *Religion, Ethnicity, and Politics: Ratifying the Constitution in Pennsylvania* (University Park: Pennsylvania State University Press, 1995), 19–22, 103, 120.
47. William Findley to John Hemphill, February 1807, DU; *A Draught of an Overture for an Act, Declaration and Testimony of the Reformed Dissenting Presbytery for North America* (Washington, PA: family of the late Colerick, 1806), 26, 64–65.
48. According to the Barnet town records from 1792, an elected committee examined "the accounts of all persons in the town who shall exhibit any accounts against the meeting house and liquidate the same according to equity and good conscience." Quoted in Wells, *History of Barnet, Vermont*, 109–113. "J. Milligan's Petition and Memorial on Behalf of the Covenanters" (October 31, 1833), VSARA; Randolph A. Roth, *The Democratic Dilemma: Religion, Reform, and the Social Order in the Connecticut River Valley of Vermont, 1791–1850* (New York: Cambridge University Press, 1987), 35–36, 42. On New England disestablishment, see Steven K. Green, *The Second Disestablishment: Church and State in Nineteenth-Century America* (New York: Oxford University Press, 2010), 119–143.
49. On Presbyterians in Pennsylvania and whiskey culture, see Peter E. Gilmore, "A Scotch-Irish 'Cultural Revolution': Presbyterians and Temperance in

Antebellum Pennsylvania," *Journal of Scotch-Irish Studies* 2, no. 3 (Fall 2007): 1–15; Fisk, "Diary of John Cuthbertson"; Slaughter, *Whiskey Rebellion*, 190–204.

50. William Findley, *History of the Insurrection in the Four Western Counties of Pennsylvania* (Philadelphia, PA: Samuel Harrison Smith, 1796), 130–139; *Draught of an Overture*, 78–79; *Commemorative Biographical Record of Washington County, Pennsylvania* (Chicago: J. H. Beers and Co., 1893), 863; Dorothy B. Braden, *Presbyterian Churches in Allegheny County, Pennsylvania* (Pittsburgh: Western Pennsylvania Genealogy Society, 1996), 15; see also Gilmore, *Land of Gospel Light and Liberty*. Several recent immigrants who participated in the Whiskey Rebellion and were later buried in the Mingo Creek cemetery probably hailed from Irish Seceder churches. Donald Smith, "Whiskey Rebellion Files," email to the author, February 18, 2013.
51. James R. Willson, "Political Danger. A Sermon preached January 6th, 1825 a fast observed by several churches in Newburgh and its vicinity," reprinted in *Evangelical Witness* 3, no. 4 (April 1825): 156–169; Gilmore, "Rebels and Revivals," 436–438.
52. The phrase substituted here is "general deluge," which was a reference to the Noetic flood. "Negro Slavery," *Evangelical Witness* 3, no. 11 (November 1825): 520–525.
53. Princeton graduate Linn was a Presbyterian who later pastored a Dutch Reformed church in New York City; Mason was a prominent Associate Reformed minister in New York whose overly ecumenical spirit created a denominational rift. The Linn/Lind family were integrated across the Calvinist orthodox spectrum, with many prominent clergymen in the Reformed and AR churches of Pennsylvania and South Carolina. Cuthbertson's diary records multiple encounters with the Linns of Greencastle, Pennsylvania, a family of Covenanter ministers. William Linn, *Serious Considerations on the Election of a President: Addressed to the Citizens of the United States* (New York: John Furman, 1800), in Dreisbach and Hall, *Sacred Rights of Conscience*, 480–492; Grotius, *A Vindication of Thomas Jefferson*, in Dreisbach and Hall, *Sacred Rights of Conscience*, 507; Philip Hamburger, *Separation of Church and State* (Cambridge, MA: Harvard University Press, 2004), 113–117; Fields, *Register of Marriages and Baptisms*, 35, 81, 91, 118, 195, 242.
54. Mason also attacked Jefferson for putting science above biblical creation. Relying on sections from Jefferson's *Notes on the State of Virginia*, Mason portrayed Jefferson as a man who "sneers at the Scripture" by denying the reliability of the Bible on issues such as the common origin of mankind and the Noetic flood. He was particularly appalled at Jefferson's positing of a pre-Adamic race of humans, from whom came Africans and from which their subservient social role derived. John M. Mason, "The Voice of Warning to Christians on the Ensuing Election of a President of the United States," in *The Complete Works*

*of John M. Mason*, vol. 4, ed. Ebenezer Mason (New York: Baker and Scribner, 1849), 522–579.

55. In language that might well be employed in the culture wars of later generations, Mason bemoaned the rise of irreligion among America's youth aged three to thirteen: "Our youth, our hope and our pride, are possessed with the accursed leaven. . . . It is now a mark of sense, the proof of an enlarged and liberal mind, to scoff at all the truths of inspiration and to cover with ridicule the hope of a Christian." Ibid., 522–551, 560–579. For compelling evidence of the early and widespread popularity of stringent church–state division among American evangelicals, see John A. Ragosta, *Wellspring of Liberty: How Virginia's Religious Dissenters Helped Win the American Revolution and Secured Religious Liberty* (New York: Oxford University Press, 2010), 3–13, 137–151.
56. Thomas Jefferson to Doctor Thomas Cooper, 2 November 1822, in *The Works of Thomas Jefferson*, vol. 12, *Correspondence and Papers 1816–1826*, ed. Paul Leicester Ford (New York: G. P. Putnam's Sons, 1905).
57. These suspicions were widespread and ongoing in the Early Republic. As late as 1830, Presbyterians in Kentucky were forced to print pamphlets clarifying that they were not of the same faith as ARs, whose ministers were loudly calling for the joining of church and state. A. Cameron, *Further Exposure of the Folly and Falsehood of the Rev. George C. Light and Others; as Exhibited by Them in a Pamphlet* (Shelbyville, KY: O'b. Pettit, 1830); John Adams to Benjamin Rush, 12 June 1812, as quoted in *The Founding Fathers and the Debate over Religion in Revolutionary America: A History in Documents*, ed. Matthew L. Harris and Thomas S. Kidd (New York: Oxford University Press, 2012), 155–156; James Kabala, "A Christian Nation? Church–State Relations in the Early American Republic, 1787–1846" (PhD diss., Brown University, 2008), 65.
58. Lathan, *History of the Associate Reformed Synod of the South*, 170.

## CHAPTER 3

1. Vermont's RPs, fearful of losing their farms, petitioned the state legislature to guarantee their lands despite their religious objections to full citizenship. The South Carolina RP disagreement arose between followers of the rival pastors of the Beaver Dam and Wateree congregations, the Rev. John Reilly and a Rev. Thomas Donnelly of Old Brick Church. Reilly believed that a distinction should be drawn between serving in state or federal capacities and local judicatories, while Donnelly applied the restrictions universally. Each man had adherents in the other's congregation, and the fallout divided the entire South Carolina RP population. Naturalization oaths were a matter of great concern to recent Covenanter immigrants of all denominational stripes. After debate, RPs finally allowed such oaths so long as they were not construed as approval of the godless Constitution. Resistance was not all-inclusive. Some acts such

as paying taxes were not violations of the principle under the rubric that taxes were themselves moral and the government could take them involuntarily anyway. But voluntary actions were a different matter. Covenanters should not take oaths of allegiance, vote, or serve in militias and juries. Although these were "things not criminal in themselves," such actions should nonetheless be abstained from. To illustrate the danger, Wylie offered the hypothetical of a Pennsylvania Covenanter juror on a case involving the right of a slave owner against a runaway slave. The law of God said that the man was free and could not be returned. But if the slave in question was unfortunate enough to have been born before the emancipation line of March 1, 1780, then the laws of the state clearly made him another man's property. Should the juror rule with God or man? Nonparticipation avoided such moral dilemmas. Divisions among ARs on this issue are evidenced by John Hemphill's letter to William Findley, discussed below. *Minutes of the Reformed Presbytery, 1801–1806* (Pittsburgh, PA: Bakewell and Marthens, 1874), May 10, 1806; David Faris, *The Faris Family of Bloomington, Indiana: A Genealogy of the Descendants of James and David Farrie of Chester District, South Carolina and Their Sister Agnes (Farrie) Smith, Emigrants from County Antrim, Northern Ireland, in 1772* (Baltimore, MD: Gateway Press, 1989), 33; *Reformation Principles Exhibited* (New York: Thomas Seward and Robert Lowry, 1824), 102–105; *State v. Willson*, 13 S.C.L., in D. J. McCord, *Reports of Cases Determined in the Constitutional Court of South Carolina*, vol. 2 (Columbia, SC: D.&J.M. Faust, 1823), 393. For an overview of religious exceptions and the development of the free exercise of religion principle in American jurisprudence that includes this case, see Michael W. McConnell, "The Origins and Historical Understanding of Free Exercise of Religion," *Harvard Law Review* 103, no. 7 (November 1990): 1410–1517, esp. 1466–1473, 1510–1511; Bruce P. Shields, "Scots among the Yankees: The Settlement of Craftsbury East Hill," *Vermont History: The Proceedings of the Vermont Historical Society* 64, no. 3 (Summer 1996): 174–183, n. 18. On the ability to pay taxes, see Samuel Wylie, *The Two Sons of Oil, or Faithful Witness for Magistracy and Ministry upon a Scriptural Basis*, 3rd ed. (Philadelphia, PA: Wm. S. Young, 1850), 63–70.

2. Quoted in James Kabala, "A Christian Nation? Church–State Relations in the Early American Republic, 1787–1846" (PhD diss., Brown University, 2008), 102–103.
3. *An Act of the Reformed Presbytery in North Carolina for a Day of Public Fasting, with the Causes Thereof* (Rocky Creek, SC, 1795), iii, viii–ix; *Reformed Presbyterian Testimony* (1807), 121.
4. *Form of a Covenant in Overture*, pamphlet (ca. 1830), 8, RPTS.
5. They argued that the Bible contained "instructions and reproofs for the prince and the peasant, and for men in every situation. Nations should, therefore, receive the Bible as the supreme law of the land." To those who protested that

government was founded on the law of nature, they retorted, "But what, we ask is the law of nature? It is the law of God." "The Bible the Supreme Law of the Land," *Evangelical Witness* 1, no. 3 (October 1822): 168; John Newell, *The Royal Priesthood of Messiah: A Sermon Delivered before the Society of Inquiry of the Theological Seminary of the Reformed Presbyterian Church* (Pittsburgh, PA: J. T. Shryock, 1858), 18.

6. Thomas Goodwillie, *A Sermon Preached at Montpelier before the Legislature of the State of Vermont* (Montpelier, VT: Geo. W. Hill, 1827), 11; David Scott, ed., *Distinctive Principles of the Reformed Presbyterian Church* (Albany, NY: J. Munsell, 1841), 265; *Act of the Reformed Presbytery in North Carolina*, ix; "Toleration," *Evangelical Witness* 1, no. 9 (April 1823): 410–412.
7. "The Late Alexander McLeod, D.D.," *Christian Magazine of the South* 3, no. 10 (October 1845): 311–313.
8. Alexander McLeod, *Messiah, Governor of the Nations of the Earth* (Glasgow: Stephen Young, 1804), 1–28.
9. Ibid., 24–25, 31–32, 44–45.
10. Samuel B. Wylie, *The Obligation of Covenants: A Discourse Delivered Monday, June 17, 1803 after the Dispensation of the Lord's Supper in the Reformed Presbyterian Congregation, Glasgow*, 3rd ed. (Paisley: Steven Young, 1816), 28–29, 33–34.
11. Zech. 4:14; Wylie, *Two Sons of Oil*, 1–20.
12. Wylie, *Two Sons of Oil*, 10, 37–38, 47.
13. William Findley, *Observations on "The Two Sons of Oil," Containing a Vindication of the American Constitutions, and Defending the Blessings of Religious Liberty and Toleration, against the Illiberal Strictures of the Rev. Samuel Wylie* (1812), ed. John Caldwell (Indianapolis, IN: Liberty Fund, 2007), xix–xx.
14. For instance, Presbyterians in Kentucky became embroiled in a pamphlet war with Methodists between 1829 and 1830. Methodists claimed that an AR minister spoke for Presbyterians when he argued for the union of church and state. Presbyterians accused Methodists of slandering their good American credentials by conflating American Presbyterians with their Covenanter cousins. A. Cameron, *An Exposure of the Folly and Falsehood of the Rev'd George C. Light, as Exhibited in a Pamphlet Published by Him, and Styled "True State of the Case, or Slander Repelled[")* (Shelbyville, KY: Compiler Office, 1829); "Family Prayer," *Christian Magazine of the South* 2, no. 3 (March 1844): 84; Kabala, "Christian Nation?" 65–66.
15. "Pamphlets," *Christian Magazine of the South* 2, no. 7 (July 1844): 220–221.
16. John Cuthbertson ordained Findley as a Covenanter elder. In the conflict with Britain, he served on the Committee of Safety and saw action with the militia. In the 1780s he began serving in the General Assembly; he went on to the Supreme Executive Council and helped write the state constitution guaranteeing universal manhood suffrage and freedom of worship. *Biographical Dictionary of the United States Congress*, http://bioguide.congress.gov/scripts/biodisplay.

pl?index=F000124 (accessed December 3, 2012); Findley, *Observations on "The Two Sons of Oil,"* vii–xv.

17. Findley, *Observations on "The Two Sons of Oil,"* xxi, 220.
18. Ibid., 7–8, 15, 36, 44–48.
19. Ibid., 77–83.
20. Ibid., 86–88, 150–152.
21. Ibid., 211–215, 219–220.
22. William Findley to John Hemphill, February 1807, DU.
23. As Hemphill put it, "It is impossible that people of common sense can believe that there is a toleration where there is no establishment. They certainly might as well say there is a Wife where there is no Husband." Ibid.
24. Ibid.
25. In 1824, the RPs similarly derided Seceders for not allowing resistance to any rightly constituted ruler, regardless of his commitment to Christ's kingship. "The only question which they would permit a christian to ask," they claimed, was, "Is there any person actually in power?" If there was a ruler, any ruler, then Christian citizens must obey him regardless of his religion, behavior, or orders. This, of course, was not true, and the Seceders took great offense. In 1828 they demanded that the RPs recant their spurious allegations, clarifying that "mere usurpers can have no lawful authority." These divisions on government continued well into the century. James R. Willson, *Prince Messiah's Claims to Dominion Over All Governments: and the Disregard of His Authority by the United States in the Federal Constitution* (Cincinnati, OH: Smith and Chipman, 1848), 18–19; "Minutes of Synod of the Reformed Presbyterian Synod, 1828," reproduced in J. E. Boyle and W. Edgar, "The Christian Nation, Part Two," unpublished manuscript (n.d.), III.4, RPTS.
26. Patriotic fealty was a particularly pressing issue for Covenanters in the slave states. "History of Hugh Henry," unpublished paper, EC. For other examples, see "Obituary Notices," *Christian Magazine of the South* 2, no. 9 (September 1844): 288; "Obituary Notices," *Christian Magazine of the South* 3, no. 6 (June 1845): 192. The notice is reprinted from the *Mecklenburg Jeffersonian*; Maurice S. Ulmer, *The Covenanters of South Carolina: A Brief History of the Work of the Reformed Presbyterian Church in the State of South Carolina* (Covington, VA: Standard Printing, 1999), 6–7; "Minutes of the Reformed Presbyterian Synod" (August 12, 1812), reproduced in Gilbert McMaster, *A Brief Inquiry into the Civil Relations of Reformed Presbyterians in the United States According to their Judicative Acts* (Schenectady, NY: S. S. Riggs, 1833), 10–11.
27. Alexander McLeod, *A Scriptural View of the Character, Causes, and Ends of the Present War* (New York: Eastbury, Kirk, and Co., 1815), 1–57, quote from 31.
28. Ibid., 57–60.
29. Ibid., 61.
30. Ibid., 60–235.

31. Thomas Jefferson to P. H. Wendover, 13 March 1815, in *The Writings of Thomas Jefferson*, vol. 14, ed. Andrew A. Lipscomb (1903), 279–281.
32. "The Mountain Man," *Evangelical Witness* 3, no. 5 (May 1825): 191–199.
33. "To the Honourable Senate & House of Representatives of the State of South Carolina now in Session in Columbia," petition from Chester District (November 19, 1819); "J. Milligan's Petition and Memorial on Behalf of the Covenanters" (October 31, 1833), VSARA.
34. "Fourth of July," *Evangelical Witness* 4, no. 8 (August 1826): 357–362.
35. The sermon was preached in 1832 but published in 1848. Willson, *Prince Messiah's Claims to Dominion Over All Governments*, 19, 21, 26–27, 30.
36. Ibid., preface; Kabala, "Christian Nation?" 151–178.
37. Even in the South, John C. Calhoun received similar treatment from South Carolina ARs who insisted that the man was not a believer and that Southerners in their desire for a political hero had "honored the creature more than the Creator." Goodwillie, *Sermon Preached at Montpelier before the Legislature of the State of Vermont*, 23; "On the Death of Calhoun," *Christian Magazine of the South* 8, no. 5 (May 1850): 156; on the growth of early American patriotism, see David Waldstreicher, *In the Midst of Perpetual Fetes: The Making of American Nationalism, 1776–1820* (Chapel Hill: University of North Carolina Press, 1997).
38. Joseph Lowry to John Hemphill, 7 September 1805, DU; Nathan O. Hatch, *The Democratization of American Christianity* (New Haven, CT: Yale University Press, 1989); John B. Boles, *The Great Revival: Beginnings of the Bible Belt* (Lexington: University of Kentucky Press, 1996). For recent challenges to Hatch's democratization thesis, see Amanda Porterfield, *Conceived in Doubt: Religion and Politics in the New American Nation* (Chicago, IL: University of Chicago Press, 2012); and David Sehat, *The Myth of American Religious Freedom* (New York: Oxford University Press, 2011).
39. Covenanters were closely aligned with the Old School Presbyterians in the divisions that occurred, but for reasons far more political. *Act of the Reformed Presbytery in North Carolina*, x; John Cree, *Evils of the Work Now Prevailing in the United States of America, Under the Name of a Revival of Religion* (Washington, PA, 1804); "Items of Intelligence," *Evangelical Witness* 4, no. 2 (February 1826): 139; "Evils Resulting from New Measures in Revivals," *Christian Magazine of the South* 1, no. 1 (January 1843): 11–15; Peter Gilmore, "Rebels and Revivals: Ulster Immigrants, Western Pennsylvania Presbyterianism, and the Formation of Scotch-Irish Identity, 1780–1830" (PhD diss., Carnegie Mellon University, 2009), 477–480.
40. James McGready, as quoted in Boles, *Great Revival*, 128–129.
41. "Fierce for moderation" is a reference to the works of John Witherspoon. "Prospectus," *Evangelical Witness* 1, no. 1 (August 1822): 6; Charles F. Irons, *The Origins of Proslavery Christianity* (Chapel Hill: University of North Carolina Press, 2008); Christine Leigh Heryman, *Southern Cross: The Beginnings of*

*the Bible Belt* (New York: Alfred A. Knopf, 1997); for an interpretation that these developments were postbellum, see Jack Maddex, "From Theocracy to Spirituality: The Southern Presbyterian Reversal on Church and State," *Journal of Presbyterian History* 54 (1976): 438–457.

42. Elias Smith, as quoted in Gordon S. Wood, *Empire of Liberty: The History of the Early Republic, 1789–1815* (New York: Oxford University Press, 2009), 576–619; "Dialogue on Messiah's Headship," *Evangelical Witness* 1, no. 8 (March 1823): 337–348; "Ye Are My Witnesses," *Evangelical Witness* 1, no. 2 (September 1822): 67–68; "Prospectus of the Christian Statesman," *Evangelical Witness* 4, no. 12 (December 1826): 581–582.
43. Ezra Stiles Ely, *The Duty of Christian Freemen to Elect Christian Rulers* (Philadelphia, PA: William F. Geddes, 1828), 1–14; Lyman Beecher, "A Reformation of Morals Practicable and Indispensible," in *Lyman Beecher and the Reform of Society*, ed. Edwin S. Gaustad (New York: Arno, 1972), 16–19. Typically, Covenanters escape mention in most of the major works on the Jacksonian period. Sean Wilentz, *The Rise of American Democracy* (New York: W. W. Norton, 2005), 271–272; William Morse, as quoted in Daniel L. Dreisbach, ed., *Religion and Politics in the Early Republic: Jasper Adams and the Church–State Debate* (Lexington: University Press of Kentucky, 1996), 1–22, 47.
44. Although the postmaster, Hugh Wylie, was related to Covenanter Samuel B. Wylie, he became a firm disestablishmentarian. Hugh Wylie was a New Light Presbyterian who had angered his fellow congregants by vocally attacking the Old World minister-turned-Seceder Thomas Ledlie Birch. Birch sued Wylie for defamation and won $150 in damages. Richard R. John, "Taking Sabbatarianism Seriously: The Postal System, the Sabbath, and the Transformation of American Political Culture," *Journal of the Early Republic* 10, no. 4 (Winter 1990): 555. John observes that the controversy was less an issue of conservatives versus liberals than "a debate among evangelicals over the proper relationship of church and state." Gilmore, "Rebels and Revivals," 588–600.
45. "A Petition of the Inhabitants of Barnet and Vicinity" (September 13, 1804), VSARA; Randolph A. Roth, "The First Radical Abolitionists: The Reverend James Milligan and the Reformed Presbyterians of Vermont," *New England Quarterly* 55, no. 4 (December 1982): 540–563; Randolph A. Roth, *Democratic Dilemma: Religion, Reform, and the Social Order in the Connecticut River Valley of Vermont, 1791–1850* (New York: Cambridge University Press, 1987), 170.
46. The Pittsburgh auxiliary included one minister from each denomination: RP John Black, Seceder Robert Bruce, and AR Joseph Kerr. This auxiliary continued its emphasis on law, while the national organization went about trying to change hearts and minds. "Ye Are My Witnesses," 68; Ezra Stiles Ely to James Renwick Wilson, 13 January 1818, RPTS; *Extracts from the Minutes of the Associate Synod of North America at their meeting at Philadelphia* (Carlisle, PA: William B. and James Underwood, 1818); "The Sabbath," *Christian Magazine of the South* 1,

no. 4 (April 1843): 125; "Observance of the Sabbath," *Christian Magazine of the South* 1, no. 10 (October 1843): 314; Gilmore, "Rebels and Revivals," 602–606, nn. 31, 37.

47. When the telegraph undercut the necessity argument for running mail lines, some regional success occurred in 1841, 1847, and 1850. Only in 1912 did Congress pass legislation closing all post offices on Sunday. Johnson was the face of the Senate report, and Brown was its true intellectual author. *Report of the committee of the Senate of the United States to whom was referred the several memorials on the subject of the transportation of the mails on Sunday 20 January, 1829* (Baltimore, MD: James Lovegrove, 1829); Joyce Appleby, *Inheriting the Revolution: The First Generation of Americans* (Cambridge, MA: Harvard University Press, 2000), 221–223; John, "Taking Sabbatarianism Seriously," 558–559, 562–567; Roth, *Democratic Dilemma*, 171; Wilentz, *Rise of American Democracy*, 389, 405; Daniel Walker Howe, *What Hath God Wrought: The Transformation of America, 1815–1848* (New York: Oxford University Press, 2007), 229–230.
48. James R. Willson, "Political Danger. A Sermon preached January 6th, 1825 a fast observed by several churches in Newburgh and its vicinity," reprinted in *Evangelical Witness* 3, no. 4 (April 1825): 156–169; Willson, *Prince Messiah's Claims to Dominion Over All Governments*, 20.
49. Letter from the America Synod (May 1827), Document no. 3, RPHL.
50. "History of the Formation," *Evangelical Witness* 1, no. 1 (August 1822): 12; David Scott, *Narrative of the Division of the Reformed Presbyterian Church, U.S. 1833* (Rochester, NY: Curtis, Butts, and Co., 1863), 12–16; also Gilbert McMaster, *The Moral Character of Civil Government in Four Letters* (W. C. Little, 1832); Samuel B. Wylie, *Memoir of Alexander McLeod, D.D.* (New York: Charles Scribner, 1855), 447–460.
51. The Engagers formed the Reformed Presbyterian General Synod, and the hard-liners formed the Synod of the Reformed Presbyterian Church. To add to the confusion, the terms *Old Light* and *New Light* were drawn from previous Presbyterian divisions in Ireland and the United States. New Lights, however, rejected the label and argued that they were being consistent with church practice over time. Further obscuring matters, they also used the terms *New School* and *Old School* in these discussions. Thus, I have chosen to call these American groups hard-liners and Engagers. Across the Atlantic the same tensions were apparent. In the closing days of the eighteenth century the RPs of Scotland agreed to allow members to sit on juries and pay taxes. In 1816 the RPs of Scotland used public fasting to deride the failure of the British constitution to conform to biblical principles. It took another five decades before Scottish Covenanters could vote or serve in elected office. In Ireland, meanwhile, RPs split in 1808 on church government principles and endured a schism in 1842 between strict Cameronians led by the Rev. Thomas Houston and a growing Engager strain led

by the Rev. John Paul. *The Original Draft of a Pastoral Address, from the Eastern Subordinate Synod of the Reformed Presbyterian Church, to the People under Their Immediate Inspection* (New York: W. Applegate, 1832), 4; *A Narrative of Recent Occurrences within the Bounds of the Eastern Subordinate Synod of the Reformed Presbyterian Church* (New York: C. A. C. Van Beuren, 1834); *Statement of Some Recent Transactions in the Southern Reformed Presbytery* (New York: Greenwich Printing Office, 1833); McMaster, *Brief Inquiry into the Civil Relations of Reformed Presbyterians in the United States*, 24; Scott, *Narrative of the Division of the Reformed Presbyterian Church*, 18–28. W. M. Glasgow freely interchanged the Light/School terminology as well. William M. Glasgow, *History of the Reformed Presbyterian Church in America* (Baltimore, MD: Hill and Harvey, 1888), 97–105.

52. Gilbert McMaster, *Remarks Offered in Illustration of a Report on the Doctrine of Civil Government before the General Synod of the Reformed Presbyterian Church* (Pittsburgh, PA: Schenectady, 1835), iii–iv; J. S. T. Milligan, *Human Rights and No Rights Reviewed* (1864), 1, RPTS; McMaster, *Brief Inquiry into the Civil Relations of Reformed Presbyterians in the United States*, 20–23; Faris, *Faris Family of Bloomington*, 33.
53. "Causes of Fasting," *Evangelical Witness* 1, no. 7 (February 1823): 305–311.
54. The original character in these travels was named Thomas, before the Titus travels took the concept further. I have collapsed both stories here. "Travels of Titus in the United States," *Evangelical Witness* 3, no. 8 (August 1825): 368; "The Hired Man and His Employer," *Evangelical Witness* 1, no. 3 (October 1822): 136–138.
55. "Hired Man and His Employer."
56. "Dialogue on Messiah's Headship"; "Travels of Titus in the United States," 368.
57. *Original Draft of a Pastoral Address*, 28–29.
58. "A Favorable Indication," *Christian Magazine of the South* 1, no. 2 (February 1843): 61; "Convention of Reformed Churches," *Christian Magazine of the South* 2, no. 6 (July 1844): 219; "The Proposed Union," *Christian Magazine of the South* 3, no. 5 (May 1845): 155; "Unsuccessful Efforts to Unite," *Christian Magazine of the South* 5, no. 7 (July 1847): 215–217. The AR Synod of the South was not invited to participate but expressed hopes that a united church would approach it with the terms of such an opportunity.
59. "Family Worship," *Christian Magazine of the South* 3, no. 5 (June 1845): 165.

## CHAPTER 4

1. Historian Mark A. Noll notes that the only way American Christianity could have prevented the Civil War was the one thing to which Americans would never accede: a Protestant person or body with the power of a pope. This was exactly what the Covenanters had in mind. Mark A. Noll, *The Civil War as a*

*Theological Crisis* (Chapel Hill: University of North Carolina Press, 2006), 157–162.

2. For more thorough studies of Covenanter antislavery, including RP and AR actors, see Daniel Ritchie, "Radical Orthodoxy: Irish Covenanters and American Slavery, circa 1830–1865," *Church History* 82, no. 4 (December 2013): 812–847; Joseph S. Moore, "Covenanters and Antislavery in the Atlantic World," *Slavery and Abolition* 34, no. 4 (December 2013): 539–561.
3. Reformed Presbytery, *The Act, Declaration and Testimony for the Whole of our Covenanted Reformation* (Edinburgh, 1806), 7–8; "The Bible the Supreme Law of the Land," *Evangelical Witness* 1, no. 3 (October 1822): 166–168; Ian B. Cowan, *The Scottish Covenanters, 1660–1688* (London: V. Gollancz, 1976), 118–126; David B. Davis, *The Problem of Slavery in the Age of Revolution, 1770–1823* (New York: Oxford University Press), 44–45; Molly Oshatz, *Slavery and Sin: The Fight against Slavery and the Rise of Liberal Protestantism* (New York: Oxford University Press, 2012), 3–42; James D. Essig, *The Bonds of Wickedness: American Evangelicals against Slavery, 1770–1808* (Philadelphia, PA: Temple University Press, 1982), 3–25.
4. *An Act of the Reformed Presbytery in North Carolina for a Day of Public Fasting, with the Causes Thereof* (Rocky Creek, SC, 1795), iii; William Buell Sprague, *Annals of the American Pulpit*, vol. 9 (New York: Robert Carter & Brothers, 1869), 27.
5. Bethany Associate Reformed Presbyterian Minute Book, MC; *State v. Willson*, 13 S.C.L., in D. J. McCord, *Reports of Cases Determined in the Constitutional Court of South Carolina*, vol. 2 (Columbia, SC: D.&J.M. Faust, 1823), 393; David Faris, *The Faris Family of Bloomington, Indiana: A Genealogy of the Descendants of James and David Farrie of Chester District, South Carolina and Their Sister Agnes (Farrie) Smith, Emigrants from County Antrim, Northern Ireland, in 1772* (Baltimore, MD: Gateway Press, 1989), 25–26; Joyce E. Chaplin, *An Anxious Pursuit: Agricultural Innovation and Modernity in the Lower South, 1730–1815* (Chapel Hill, NC: Institute of Early American History and Culture, 1993), 1–20, 277–329.
6. Surviving church records seem to bear out these accounts of voluntary manumission. For instance, an elder in South Carolina named Robert Beatty agreed to free his slaves Sally, Candace, and Dick. The women would be freed at twenty-five years of age, and the young man, at twenty-eight. In New York, a man in the church was ordered to receive counsel from church elders on the church's position regarding slaveholding. When it was discovered that he had no official membership in the congregation, however, the session had no power to act, and the matter was dropped. *Minutes of the Reformed Presbytery, 1801–1806* (Pittsburgh, PA: Bakewell and Marthens, 1874), July 3, 1801; Coldenham, NY Session Book, November 23, 1801, and May 3, 1802, RPTS; Samuel B. Wylie, *Memoir of Alexander McLeod, D.D.* (New York, 1855), 50–54.

7. Samuel Wylie, *The Two Sons of Oil, or Faithful Witness for Magistracy and Ministry upon a Scriptural Basis*, 3rd ed. (Philadelphia, PA: Wm. S. Young, 1850), 50–53; William Findley, *Observations on "Two Sons of Oil," Containing a Vindication of the American Constitutions, and Defending the Blessings of Religious Liberty and Toleration, against the Illiberal Strictures of the Rev. Samuel Wylie* (1812), ed. John Caldwell (Indianapolis, IN: Liberty Fund, 2007), xix–xxviii, 163–166.
8. The specter of Haiti loomed large for moderates such as William Findley, who saw the killings of whites by their slaves as a cautionary tale for moving too quickly toward emancipation. Radicals tended to view the same events as proof of the need to move more quickly. Findley, *Observations on "Two Sons of Oil,"* x, 162–163.
9. Minutes of the Associate Reformed Synod of the Carolinas, 1804–1806; State v. Willson; "On the Abuse of Oaths," *Evangelical Witness* 8, no. 8 (August 1823): 372–376; Randolph A. Roth, "The First Radical Abolitionists: The Reverend James Milligan and the Reformed Presbyterians of Vermont," *New England Quarterly* 55, no. 4 (December 1982): 549.
10. The elders of the Rocky Creek church are listed as removed to Sparta, Ill.; Morning Sun, Ohio; Cedarville, Ohio; Duck River, Tenn.; Princeton, Ind.; and Bloomington, Ind. Maurice S. Ulmer, *The Covenanters of South Carolina: A Brief History of the Work of the Reformed Presbyterian Church in the State of South Carolina* (Covington, VA: Standard Printing, 1999), 10–11; James Brown Scouller, *History of the United Presbyterian Church of North America*, American Church History Series (New York: Christian Literature Co., 1894), 176–178; Robert Lathan, *History of the Associate Reformed Synod of the South, 1782–1882* (Harrisburg, PA: published for the author, 1884), 359–362; David Ray Wilcox, "The Reformed Presbyterian Church and the Antislavery Movement" (PhD diss., Colorado State College of Education at Greeley, 1948), 61, 96; William M. Glasgow, *History of the Reformed Presbyterian Church* (Baltimore, MD: Hill and Harvey, 1888), 500–501.
11. Faris, *Faris Family of Bloomington*, 25–26.
12. Abolitionism, in Thornwell's mind, was a doctrine in search of a verse; it was born not of the Bible but of the "insane fury of philanthropy." Robert Breckinridge and Charles Hodge later attempted to straddle the space between orthodoxy and antislavery positions. Breckinridge came close to the Covenanter position by arguing that southern slavery was not the same as biblical slavery. Their positions, however, are much different in their underlying logic, historical moments, and audiences. It should also be noted that some ARs held Thornwell in high enough regard to consider offering him the presidency of Erskine College and Seminary; but such sentiments were dangerous and could get an AR accused of latitudinarianism. William Hemphill to R. C. C., 5 March 1847, DU; Mark A. Noll, *America's God: From Jonathan Edwards to Abraham Lincoln* (New York: Oxford University Press, 2002), 386–401, 414–415; Vivien

Sandlund, "Robert Breckinridge, Presbyterian Antislavery Conservative," *Journal of Presbyterian History* 78 (Summer 2000): 145–154; Oshatz, *Slavery and Sin*, 3–42; Essig, *Bonds of Wickedness*, 3–25; J. Albert Harrill, "The Use of the New Testament in the American Slavery Controversy: A Case History in the Hermeneutical Tension between Biblical Criticism and Christian Moral Debate," *Religion and American Culture: A Journal of Interpretation* 10, no. 2 (Summer 2000): 149–186; Robert Bruce Mullin, "Biblical Critics and the Battle over Slavery," *Journal of Presbyterian History* 61 (Summer 1983): 210–226.

13. Alexander McLeod, *Negro Slavery Unjustifiable: A Discourse* (New York: T&J Swords, 1802), 1–37; Larry E. Tise, *Proslavery: A History of the Defense of Slavery in America, 1701–1840* (Athens: University of Georgia Press, 1987), 12–40, 97–182; Lacy K. Ford, *Deliver Us from Evil: The Slavery Question in the Old South* (New York: Oxford University Press, 2009), 19–142.
14. McLeod, *Negro Slavery Unjustifiable*, 1–37, especially 32.
15. Ibid., 32; "Church Libraries," *Evangelical Witness* 1, no. 8 (March 1823): 379–381; "Negro Slavery," *Evangelical Witness* 2, no. 9 (April 1824): 409–419.
16. John Reynolds, review of *Some Remarks on the sinfulness of Slave-holding* 1, no. 12 (May 1844): 560–567; *Evangelical Guardian* 1, no. 8 (January 1844): 413.
17. Polygenesis hypothesized multiple human origins, in contrast to the biblical Adam and Eve; the theory included the not-unsubtle suggestion that these differing human races should be seen hierarchically, with white on top and black at the bottom. On its surface, such theories strongly supported the slave regime, and from the 1840s on, polygenesis was a raging topic in the South. Its biggest challenge, however, came from adamantly pro-slavery monogenesists, who feared the new theory's theological implications rather than its social ones. Covenanter minister John Cuthbertson may have overseen an interracial marriage ceremony between African American Newport Walker and Joan Broadly in 1780. He certainly oversaw marriages between those he labeled "Moor," and he baptized many free blacks and slaves. John Cuthbertson, Personal Diary (October 17, 1780), PTS; James R. Willson, *Prince Messiah's Claims to Dominion Over All Governments: and the Disregard of His Authority by the United States in the Federal Constitution* (Cincinnati, OH: Smith and Chipman, 1848), 33; "The Bible—and the Identity of the Human Species: An Extract from a Sermon—By W.R.H.," *Christian Magazine of the South* 3, no. 9 (September 1845): 257–259; "Negro Slavery"; Andrew Jackson to James Renwick Wilson, 4 October 1831, RPTS; J. R. W. Sloane, *The Three Pillars of a Republic: An Address before the Philo and Franklin Societies of Jefferson College, Canonsburg, Penn. Delivered at the Annual Commencement* (New York: Phair and Co., 1862), 26, 23; Colin Kidd, *The Forging of Races: Race and Scripture in the Protestant Atlantic World, 1600–2000* (New York: Cambridge University Press, 2006), 121–165; Michael O'Brien, *Conjectures of Order: Intellectual Life and the American South, 1810–1860* (Chapel Hill: University of North Carolina Press, 2004), 1:215–252.

18. J. R. W. Sloane, *Review of Rev. Henry J. Van Kyke's Discourse on "The Character and Influence of Abolitionism"* (New York: William Erving, 1861), 6–36. Additional texts in 1 Tim. 1:10 and Luke 4:19.
19. "Slavery in the United States," *Evangelical Witness* 2, no. 3 (August 1823): 133–137.
20. Though Deep South Campbellites belied this pattern, adherents in the Middle South attempted to maintain a position that was "antislavery but not abolitionist." "Evils of the Abolition Association," *American Reformed Covenanter* 1, no. 4 (July 1839): 79–89; William Birney, *James G. Birney and His Times* (New York, 1890), 166; Paul E. Johnson and Sean Wilentz, *The Kingdom of Mathias: A Story of Sex and Salvation in 19th-Century America* (New York: Oxford University Press, 1994), 50–55, 64–66, 78, 177–179; Robert M. Calhoon, *Political Moderation in America's First Two Centuries* (New York: Cambridge University Press, 2009), 240–241.
21. Thomas Goodwillie, *A Sermon Preached at Montpelier before the Legislature of the State of Vermont* (Montpelier, VT: Geo. W. Hill, 1827), 26; Willson, *Prince Messiah's Claims to Dominion Over All Governments*, 24.
22. Samuel Taggart, "The Power for & Against Oppressors" (August 2, 1838).
23. Fergus M. Bordewich, *Bound for Canaan: The Underground Railroad and the War for the Soul of America* (New York: HarperCollins, 2005), 126–146; Wilbur Siebert, *The Underground Railroad from Slavery to Freedom* (New York: MacMillan, 1898), 13–15. Glasgow, *History of the Reformed Presbyterian Church*, 630–631; John Hope Franklin and Loren Schweninger, *Runaway Slaves: Rebels on the Plantation* (New York: Oxford University Press, 2000), 97–208.
24. Siebert, *Underground Railroad from Slavery to Freedom*, 90, 115, 235, 403–438. For Covenanter family names and congregations, see Wilcox, "Reformed Presbyterian Church and the Antislavery Movement," 111–115.
25. Siebert, *Underground Railroad from Slavery to Freedom*, 13–15.
26. Eric Burin, *Slavery and the Peculiar Solution: A History of the American Colonization Society* (Gainesville: University Press of Florida, 2005); Wylie, *Memoir of Alexander McLeod*, 359–360; David Carson, "A History of the Reformed Presbyterian Church in America to 1871" (PhD diss., University of Pennsylvania, 1964), 193.
27. McLeod was vice president of the New York Colonization Society, and his and others' memories of that role may well have morphed into a larger myth. Wylie, *Memoir of Alexander McLeod*, 508–509; Douglas R. Egerton, "Its Origin Is Not a Little Curious: A New Look at the American Colonization Society," *Journal of the Early Republic* 5 (Winter 1985): 463–480.
28. Fragment of Address by Delegates from America, ca. 1830, Correspondence with America, no. 1, RPHL.
29. Wylie, *Memoir of Alexander McLeod*, appendices; J. R. W. Sloane, *The Word: A Discourse Delivered at the Opening of the Reformed Presbyterian Synod* (New York: Thomas Holman, 1859), 16; William Lloyd Garrison, as quoted in

John R. McKivigan, *The War against Proslavery Religion: Abolitionism and the Northern Churches, 1830–1865* (Ithaca, NY: Cornell University Press, 1984), 163; Wilcox, "Reformed Presbyterian Church and the Antislavery Movement," 61–72; William Roulston, "The Abolition Church: Covenanters and the Fight against Slavery in Nineteenth-Century America," *Bulletin of the Presbyterian Historical Society of Ireland* 36 (2012): 16; Carson, "History of the Reformed Presbyterian Church in America," 195.

30. Margaret B. Deschamps, "Antislavery Presbyterians in the Carolina Piedmont," *Proceedings of the South Carolina Historical Society*, 1955: 6–13; on Caruthers, see Jack Davidson, "Eli Washington Caruthers' Unpublished Manuscript against Slavery: An Introduction," *Journal of Backcountry Studies* 6, no. 2 (Fall/Winter 2011), http://libjournal.uncg.edu/index.php/jbc/article/view/375/192.
31. O'Brien, *Conjectures of Order*, 1:14–15; Lacy K. Ford, *The Origins of Southern Radicalism* (New York: Oxford University Press, 1991), 5–96.
32. It is not clear if the petition ever made it to Columbia or if Faris was sent on his way before the petition could be delivered. James Faris, "To the Honorable the Senate and house of Representatives of the State of South Carolina" (ca. 1819), as reproduced in Wilcox, "Reformed Presbyterian Church and the Antislavery Movement," 62; Glasgow, *History of the Reformed Presbyterian Church*, 500–501.
33. "Negro Slavery," 409. Memorial to the Reformed Presbyterian Synod, RPTS; Hugh McMillan to John N. McLeod, 1855, as quoted in Wylie, *Memoir of Alexander McLeod*, 322, 504–505.
34. Douglas Egerton has argued convincingly that the ACS was equally unpalatable to the pro-slavery South as it was to ardent abolitionists in the North. Douglas R. Egerton, "Averting a Crisis: The Proslavery Critique of the American Colonization Society," *Civil War History* 43, no. 2 (June 1997): 142–156; *African Repository and Colonization Journal*, September 1830, 6–7; *African Repository and Colonization Journal*, December 31, 1834, 3; Burin, *Slavery and the Peculiar Solution*, 102–103; Janet Duitsman Cornelius, *When I Can Read My Title Clear: Literacy, Slavery, and Religion in the Antebellum South* (Columbia: University of South Carolina, 1991), 55; Manisha Sinha, *The Counterrevolution of Slavery: Politics and Ideology in Antebellum South Carolina* (Chapel Hill: University of North Carolina Press, 2000), 80; James Henley Thornwell, as quoted in O'Brien, *Conjectures of Order*, 2:1127, 1151; William W. Freehling, "James Henley Thornwell's Mysterious Antislavery Movement," *Journal of Southern History* 57 (August 1991): 383–406.
35. "Contributions" (1825–1849) and "Contributions" (1850–1865), *African Repository and Colonization Journal*; J. D. B. DeBow, *Statistical View of the United States* (Washington, DC: Beverly Tucker, 1854), 45, 63. AR statistics are difficult to come by, but it is doubtful that there were more than 2,000 or 3,000 ARs in antebellum South Carolina. For Vermont, see Randolph A. Roth,

*Democratic Dilemma: Religion, Reform, and the Social Order in the Connecticut River Valley of Vermont, 1791–1850* (New York: Cambridge University Press, 1987), 100.

36. To be sure, he was not always so bold. In Hemphill's earliest days in the ministry, he decided to skip a passage on the correct relationship of servants and masters. He was not "prepared to discuss a topic on which many men are very sensitive without reading more and reflecting more on the matter." William Hemphill, "A Missionary Sermon" (1837), DU; William Hemphill, "Sermon on Matthew 12:41" (Long Cane, SC, July 7, 1839, and Due West, SC, 1852), DU; William Hemphill, "Sermon on the Sixth Commandment," DU.
37. William Hemphill, "Rioting and Suicide, a Sermon on the 6th Commandment" (Long Cane, SC, March 1839), DU; William Hemphill, "Address on Colonization" (July 1, 1840), DU.
38. In 1834, the AR Synod of the South also made inquiries into opening a Manual Labor School as a means to train slaves for trades after they were freed. Reception among the churches for financial support was mixed, and nothing came of the plan. "Minutes of the Associate Reformed Synod of the South," 1834–35; "Minutes of Synod," Associate Reformed Synod of the South, 1828; "Petition of Sundry Citizens of Chester District praying a modification of the Law in relation to teaching slaves" (1838), SCDAH. See also Loren Schweninger, *The Southern Debate over Slavery*, vol. 1, *Petitions to Southern Legislatures, 1774–1864* (Chicago: University of Illinois, 2001), 152–153; Digital Library on American Slavery, PAR 11380107, 11380106, 11383503, 113834406, 11383804, 11383807, http://library.uncg.edu/slavery/ (accessed June 30, 2011); Cornelius, *When I Can Read My Title Clear*, 54–58.
39. *Records of the Session Meetings of Hopewell Associate Reformed Presbyterian Church, 1832–1892* (Richburg, SC: Chester Genealogical Society, 1984), 11–17; *Christian Magazine of the South* 2, no. 9 (September 1844): 284; *Christian Magazine of the South* 5, no. 4 (April 1847): 123; "Report of Rev. T. Turner's Missionary Tour," Minutes of the Associate Reformed Synod of the South, 1836; also Session Book of Cedar Springs Associate Reformed Presbyterian Church, November 1, 1850, MC.
40. "Instruction of Negroes," *Christian Magazine of the South* 5, no. 4 (April 1847): 123–124; Emily Moberg Robinson, "Immigrant Covenanters: Religious and Political Identity, from Scotland to America" (PhD diss., University of California, Santa Cruz, 2004), 23–182; Lowry Ware, *A Place Called Due West* (R. L. Bryan, 2006), 72.
41. "Proceedings of the Meeting in Charleston, S.C. May 13–15, 1845," in *On the Religious Instruction of the Negroes* (Charleston, SC, 1845), 24–26; Ford, *Deliver Us from Evil*, 505–536; Erskine Clarke, *Dwelling Place: A Plantation Epic* (New Haven, CT: Yale University Press, 2005), 247–251.

42. "Proceedings of the Meeting in Charleston, S.C.," 24–26; "A Pastoral Letter," *Christian Magazine of the South* 5, no. 7 (July 1847): 208–209; "Obituary Notices," *Christian Magazine of the South* 2, no. 1 (January 1844): 31–32.
43. A similar speech to the one given to the Abbeville Bible Society was repeated in 1853 and printed. *Minute Book of the Abbeville District Bible Society*, EC; *Our Slaves Should Have the Bible* (Due West, SC: Telescope Press, 1854); Diary of A. E. Lesly, April 4, 1859, EC.
44. "Minutes of Synod," Associate Reformed Synod of the South, 1844, 1845; Irons, *Origins of Proslavery Christianity*, 84–86.
45. "The Religion of Principle," *Christian Magazine of the South* 3, no. 1 (January 1845): 11; "From the General Assembly Presbyterian Church in Ireland, to the Associate Reformed Synod in the South," *Christian Magazine of the South* 5, no. 2 (February 1847): 44–46; "The Late Alexander McLeod," *Christian Magazine of the South* 3, no. 10 (October 1845): 311–313.
46. Ford, *Origins of Southern Radicalism*, 97–144; William W. Freehling, *The Road to Disunion: Secessionists at Bay, 1776–1854* (New York: Oxford University Press, 1990), 211–284.
47. James Harrison to William Hemphill, 10 November 1832, DU; Unknown to William Hemphill, 28 December 1832, DU; *Records of the Session Meetings of Hopewell Associate Reformed Presbyterian Church*, 1–2.
48. *The Original Draft of a Pastoral Address, from the Eastern Subordinate Synod of the Reformed Presbyterian Church, to the People under Their Immediate Inspection* (New York: W. Applegate, 1832), 30.
49. On one particular divide between Vermont Covenanters and Seceders over degrees of radicalism on the slavery question, see Roth, "First Radical Abolitionists."
50. "Negro Slavery"; *Original Draft of a Pastoral Address*, 18–19, 30–31.
51. *Defence of Rev. John Little* (New York: M. W. Dodd, 1851), 1–39, vi.
52. Both William Hemphill and Samuel Taggart attended Jefferson College in Canonsburg, Pa. Samuel Taggart to William Hemphill, January 1840, DU; John Wilson to William Hemphill, 3 September 1833, DU; Helen Turnbull Waite Coleman, *Banners in the Wilderness: Early Years of Washington and Jefferson College* (Pittsburgh, PA: University of Pittsburgh Press, 1956), 7, 171.
53. "Evangelical Repository," *Christian Magazine of the South* 1, no. 10 (October 1843): 316.
54. Pressly was from the Cedar Springs and Long Cane churches. Though he owned slaves, he kept track of his regular payments to slaves for their labors. He was a critic of northern abolitionists on the grounds of their theological liberalism. Daybook, #40a, George W. Pressly Papers, MC; "Evangelical Repository," *Christian Magazine of the South* 1, no. 10 (October 1843): 316; "Evangelical Guardian," *Christian Magazine of the South* 1, no. 8 (August 1843): 252–254.

55. This evidence is tantalizing but far from conclusive. Some ARs did retain a memory of hiring out as a benevolent enterprise in which their slaves were functionally free. A freeman named Isaac, owned by the AR McCain family in Abbeville District, South Carolina, had worked for wages on the side and kept his money hidden throughout the war. When the federal government sold the McCain family plantation for back taxes after the war, Isaac bought the big house and moved in with his family. Memoirs of James Ross McCain, EC; *Day Book Accounts from H. L. Sloan, 1855–1859*, 28, MC; "Evangelical Repository," *Christian Magazine of the South* 2, no. 1 (January 1844): 26; "Minutes of the Associate Reformed Presbyterian Synod of the South" (October 16, 1844); "To the Public," USC; Lowry Ware, *Slaveholders of Abbeville District, 1790–1860 and Largest Property Holders, 1860* (Due West, SC: Lowry Ware, 1997). On the George Grier controversy, see Moore, "Covenanters and Antislavery in the Atlantic World," 553–557; Calhoon, *Political Moderation in America's First Two Centuries*, 228–240.
56. Cuthbertson, Personal Diary (March 23, 1759); Michael C. Scoggins, "A Revolutionary Minister: The Life of the Reverend Alexander Craighead," *Journal of Scotch-Irish Studies* 3, no. 3 (Fall 2012): 112; Kerby A. Miller, Arnold Schrier, Brude D. Boling, and David N. Doyle, eds., *Irish Immigrants in the Land of Canaan: Letters and Memoirs from Colonial and Revolutionary America, 1675–1815* (New York: Oxford University Press, 2003), 140–141, 131 n.; William L. Fisk, *The Scottish High Church Tradition in America* (Baltimore, MD: University Press of America, 1994), 41.
57. Timothy S. Huebner, *The Southern Judicial Tradition: State Judges and Sectional Distinctiveness, 1790–1890* (Athens: University of Georgia Press, 1999), 99–129.
58. Relatives Hemphill visited in 1832 reported that "shortly before he came he had a fight with a Richardson, an Editor of a paper, he was stabbed three times but not very much hurt." Also recreating Covenanter sensibility, his court decisions universally protected the rights of homesteaders to avoid eviction from their properties by rich landholders. This shadow of the old Covenanter agrarian rebels held true even in cases of extreme indebtedness. When the law was not on his side, Hemphill was known to legislate from the bench, as he did in *Sampson and Keene v. Williamson* (1851), when he found that "any forced disposition of the property" of citizens was against Texas law. The judge went so far as to claim that the idea of mortgages themselves was "deceptive and fictitious." Eliza Hemphill to William Hemphill, 22 August 1832, DU; Huebner, *Southern Judicial Tradition*, 125.
59. "Minutes of the Reformed Synod," *Reformed Presbyterian* 11 (1846); "Volunteers," *Christian Magazine of the South* 5, no. 1 (January 1847): 27–28.
60. "Minutes of the RP Synod," *Reformed Presbyterian* 13 (1849): 152; D. S. Faris, paper on slavery (November 1850), as quoted in Wilcox, "Reformed Presbyterian Church and the Antislavery Movement," 62; "Minutes of RP Synod," *Reformed*

*Presbyterian*, 15 (1851), 164–165; "Slavery–The Supreme Court," *The Covenanter* 12 (April 1857): 278.

61. *The Covenanter* 12 (April 1857): 279.
62. Sloane, *The Word*, 15–16, 18–19.
63. A. M. Milligan to Captain John Brown, 24 November 1859, and John Brown to My Dear Covenanter Friend, 29 November 1859, both reproduced in J. Calvin Elder and J. Oliver Beatty, *History of the Reformed Presbyterian Church of New Alexandria, Pa* (1916), 49–50.
64. William Hemphill to Hannah Hemphill, 14 April 1857, DU; Daybook, #33, George W. Pressly Papers, MC: "The Republican party is rapidly drifting into the embrace of ultra Abolitionism."
65. Wilcox, "Reformed Presbyterian Church and the Antislavery Movement," 147; William M. Glasgow, *The Geneva Book, Comprising a History of Geneva College and a Biographical Catalogue of the Alumni and Many Students* (Philadelphia, PA: Westbrook Publishing, 1908), 142–143; Carson, "History of the Reformed Presbyterian Church in America," 209–223.
66. *Review of the Synodical Action on the War*, pamphlet (1863), 1, RPTS; William Milroy, *The Testimony of the Church Respecting Military Associations, &c., with the Wicked and Profane*, pamphlet (ca. 1863), 1, RPTS; Wilcox, "Reformed Presbyterian Church and the Antislavery Movement," 147; Glasgow, *The Geneva Book*, 142–143; Carson, "History of the Reformed Presbyterian Church in America," 209–223.
67. C. S. Young to W. M. Hunter, 23 March 1921, EC; Ware, *A Place Called Due West*, 76; J. Michael Miller, ed., *Echoes of Mercy—Whispers of Love: Diaries of John Hemphill Simpson*, transcribed by Mary Law McCormick (Greenville, SC: Associate Reformed Presbyterian Foundation, 2001), May 10, 1861; Daniel W. Crofts, *Reluctant Confederates: Upper South Unionists in the Secession Crisis* (Chapel Hill: University of North Carolina Press, 1993).
68. Gradualist ARs in Virginia signed a pro-slavery petition in the wake of the Emancipation Proclamation. Abolition, they claimed, "caused the war," and now abolitionists were "trying to destroy religious men who were striving to guide slaves along Scriptural lines." "The Marriage of Slaves," *Due West Telescope*, April 4, 1864; *Due West Telescope*, November 28, 1962; *Due West Telescope*, June 13, 1862; Ernest Trice Thompson, *Presbyterians in the South*, vol. 2 (Richmond, VA: John Knox Press, 1973), 61.
69. James Wallace, *The Amendment of the Federal Constitution: An Address Before the Christian Association for National Reformation of Southern Illinois* (St. Louis, MO: George Knapp, 1865), 6. The actual speech was delivered in November 1864. Glasgow, *History of the Reformed Presbyterian Church*, 126. On the overwhelming consensus among historians that slavery caused the war, see Eric Foner, "The Causes of the American Civil War: Recent Interpretations and New Directions," *Civil War History* 20 (September 1974): 197–214; James

M. McPhereson, "What Caused the Civil War?" *North and South* 4 (November 2000): 12–22; Michael E. Woods, "What Twenty-First-Century Historians Have Said about the Causes of Disunion: A Civil War Sesquicentennial Review of the Recent Literature," *Journal of American History* 99, no. 2 (September 2012): 415–439. Even nonslaveholding soldiers saw slavery as the war's cause and purpose. See Chandra Manning, *What This Cruel War Was Over: Soldiers, Slavery, and the Civil War* (New York: Vintage Books, 2007).

70. Wallace, *Amendment of the Federal Constitution*, 12; Sloane, *Three Pillars of a Republic*, 5, 12–13; John Alexander, *History of the National Reform Movement* (Pittsburgh, PA: Shaw Brothers, 1893), 6.

## CHAPTER 5

1. The president's annual address to congress on the state of the union was presented in written, not spoken form. This account relies on the diary of Secretary of the Navy Gideon Welles. John D. DeFrees, appointed as government printer by Lincoln, remembered that the paragraph made it as far as a printing draft before Lincoln cut it out in the proofing stage. DeFrees remembered that Lincoln "struck it out, remarking that he had not made up his mind as to its propriety." If so, the issue may have lingered on Lincoln's mind past the Cabinet meeting. *Diary of Gideon Welles, Secretary of the Navy Under Lincoln and Johnson*, vol. 2, *April 1, 1864–December 31, 1866* (Boston, MA: Houghton Mifflin Company, 1911), 190; Douglas Wilson and Rodney O. Davis, *Herndon's Informants* (Urbana: University of Illinois Press, 1997), 497.
2. "Interview with the President," *Reformed Presbyterian and Covenanter* 1, no. 1 (January 1863): 16–18; "Interview with the President," *Reformed Presbyterian and Covenanter* 1, no. 2 (February 1863): 48–52; "Christianity and Freedom," *New York Daily Tribune* 23, no. 7, 131 (February 12, 1864): 1; B. F. Morris, *Christian Life and Character of the Civil Institutions of the United States* (Philadelphia, PA: George W. Childs, 1864), 760–763.
3. Richard Carwardine, "Lincoln's Religion," in *Our Lincoln: New Perspectives on Lincoln and His World*, ed. Eric Foner (New York: W. W. Norton, 2008), 223–248; Richard Carwardine, *Lincoln: A Life of Purpose and Power* (New York: Alfred A. Knopf, 2003), 274–282; David Herbert Donald, *Lincoln* (New York: Simon and Schuster, 1995), 336–337, 542.
4. Carwardine, "Lincoln's Religion," 223–248; Abraham Lincoln, "Meditation on the Divine Will," in *The Collected Works of Abraham Lincoln*, ed. Roy P. Basler (New Brunswick, NJ: Rutgers University Press, 1953), 403–404.
5. John Alexander, *History of the National Reform Movement* (Pittsburgh, PA: Shaw Brothers, 1893), 11.
6. J. R. W. Sloane, *A Discourse Delivered before the Reformed Presbyterian Synod* (New York: John A. Gray and Green, 1866), 6; E. D. MacMaster, *The True*

*Life of a Nation: An Address Delivered at the Invitation of the Erodelphian and Eccritean Societies of Miami University* (New Albany, OH: Norman, Morrison, and Matthews, 1856), 7, 9, 19–47; http://www.miami.muohio.edu/University_Advancement/MiamiAlum/history_tradition/presidents/macmaster.html.

7. Stewart Olin Jacoby, "The Religious Amendment Movement: God, People and Nation in the Gilded Age" (PhD diss., University of Michigan at Ann Arbor, 1984), 55.
8. In the midst of the Union's worst days, prominent New England minister Horace Bushnell asserted the Covenanter position that calamity had befallen the nation because it was founded on a secular rather than a Christian basis. His calls for a Christian amendment were short-lived but well received. Morton Borden, "The Christian Amendment," *Civil War History* 25 (1979): 155–167; Mark A. Noll, *America's God: From Jonathan Edwards to Abraham Lincoln* (New York: Oxford University Press, 2002), 423–432.
9. Sloane, *Discourse Delivered before the Reformed Presbyterian Synod*, 7.
10. "Report of the Lakes Presbytery," *Covenanter*, December 1861, 119–120.
11. Alexander, *History of the National Reform Movement*, 6–7; Jacoby, "Religious Amendment Movement," 111–160.
12. Alexander noted that this was an effort to tap into the strength of the "psalm-singing churches." Alexander, *History of the National Reform Movement*, 11; Jacoby, "Religious Amendment Movement," 111–160, n. 20.
13. The name change is also illustrative of the attempt to reach beyond Covenanter borders. For convenience, I use the term *NRA* in the paragraphs that reference the group before and after the 1875 name change. "The Movement to Amend the Constitution," *Reformed Presbyterian and Covenanter*, December 1863, 373; *The National Association for the Amendment of the Federal Constitution* (Philadelphia, PA: Jas. B. Rodgers, 1864), 5.
14. Alexander, *History of the National Reform Movement*, 22.
15. *National Association for the Amendment of the Federal Constitution*, 15; Anonymous, *Our National Obligation* (1873), 13–14, 158; Alexander, *History of the National Reform Movement*, 23; Sloane, *Discourse Delivered before the Reformed Presbyterian Synod*, 31.
16. "Constitution of the National Reform Association," in David McAllister, *The National Reform Movement: Its History and Principles, a Manual of Christian Civil Government* (Philadelphia, PA: Aldine Press, 1890), 7.
17. Alexander, *History of the National Reform Movement*, 11–12, 15–16; *National Reform Manual: Suggestions and Data for District Secretaries and others* (Philadelphia, PA: Christian Statesman Office, 1877), 16; James Wallace, *The Amendment of the Federal Constitution: An Address Before the Christian Association for National Reformation of Southern Illinois* (St. Louis, MO: George Knapp, 1865), 4.
18. Jacoby, "Religious Amendment Movement," 424–490.

19. "State Religion," *New York Daily Tribune* 24, no. 7, 462 (March 7, 1865): 4.
20. Jon C. Teaford, "Toward a Christian Nation: Religion, Law, and Justice Strong," *Journal of Presbyterian History* 54, no. 4 (Winter 1976): 422–437.
21. Many of these supporters would later back off their commitments, most notably Senator Sumner. McAllister, *National Reform Movement*, 11–18; *National Reform Manual*, 1–16; Steven K. Green, *The Bible, the School, and the Constitution: The Clash that Shaped Modern Church–State Doctrine* (New York: Oxford University Press, 2012), 141–143.
22. Jacoby, "Religious Amendment Movement," 413; "Letter from Jonathan Blanchard," *Christian Statesman*, April 1, 1870, 119; *Christian Statesman*, March 1, 1871, 100.
23. James M. Wilson, "The Use of the Elective Franchise," *Reformed Presbyterian and Covenanter*, September 1864, 258–260; J. P. Lytle, "Amendment to the Constitution," *Presbyterian Witness* 12 (December 1864): 202.
24. Edward L. Pierce, *Memoir and Letters of Charles Sumner*, vol. 4 (London: Sampson, Low, Marston, and Co., 1893), 174; Jacoby, "Religious Amendment Movement," 75, 161, 425–450.
25. Gaines M. Foster has identified 128 petitions for the Christian Amendment from 1867 to 1869. Committee on the Judiciary, *Hearings on the Joint Resolution (H. Res. 120) Proposing an Amendment to the Preamble of the Constitution of the United States "acknowledging the Supreme Authority and Just Government of Almighty God in All the Affairs of Men and Nations"* (Washington, DC: Government Printing Office, 1894), 15–16; R. C. Allen, *Fundamental Principles in Civil Government Applied by the Covenanter* (Grove City, PA: Lawrence Printing House, 1901), 31–36; Jacoby, "Religious Amendment Movement," 278–280, 425–450; Gaines M. Foster, *Moral Reconstruction: Christian Lobbyists and the Federal Legislation of Morality, 1865–1920* (Chapel Hill: University of North Carolina Press, 2002), 249.
26. *Journal of the Indiana State House*, 1865, 640–643; *Journal of the Indiana State Senate*, 44th Sess. (1865), 434–435; Jacoby, "Religious Amendment Movement," 251–252.
27. *Congressional Globe*, 38th Cong., 1st Sess. (February 17, 1864), 693; *Christian Statesman*, February 15, 1869, 93; Alexander, *History of the National Reform Movement*, 10; Jacoby, "Religious Amendment Movement," 164–178, also 75, n. 40.
28. Green, *The Bible, the School, and the Constitution*, 137–177, esp. 156–157.
29. Strong himself joked that his lecture would be like drinking sawdust with no butter. William Strong, *Two Lectures upon the Relations of Civil Law to Church Polity, Discipline, and Property* (New York: Dodd and Mead, 1875), 32; Green, *The Bible, the School, and the Constitution*, 166–167.
30. David J. Brewer, *The United States a Christian Nation* (Philadelphia, PA: John C. Winston Company, 1905), 11–41; Morton Borden, *Jews, Turks, and Infidels* (Chapel Hill: University of North Carolina Press, 1984), 73.

31. Committee on the Judiciary, *Hearings on the Joint Resolution (H. Res. 120)*, 1, 4–7, 13.
32. Foster, *Moral Reconstruction*, 107–110.
33. Ibid., 26–46, 110–115.
34. *Covenanter*, January 1858, 146; McAllister, *National Reform Movement*, 9–10; Allen, *Fundamental Principles in Civil Government Applied by the Covenanter*, 7; T. P. Stevenson, as quoted in Foster, *Moral Reconstruction*, 99.
35. Foster, *Moral Reconstruction*, 88–89.
36. *Christian Statesman* 17 (December 20, 1883): 3.
37. McAllister, *National Reform Movement*, 10; Foster, *Moral Reconstruction*, 62–66, 138–139.
38. Foster, *Moral Reconstruction*, 47–71, 89.
39. Jacoby, "Religious Amendment Movement," 227, n. 40; Philip Hamburger, *Separation of Church and State* (Cambridge: Harvard University Press, 2004), 344–352.
40. As one NRA speaker explained in a public school debate in Boston, the Bible was not a sectarian book because its Protestant translations kept it bound to *sola scriptura*. American public schools could use the Bible, unadulterated by Catholic dogma, to inculcate needed morality into America's schoolchildren. Keeping the Bible in public schools was the only sure means to secure the Protestant Christian character of America's future. J. M. Foster, "Can this Nation Live Without Christian Education in our Public Schools," address given at Berkeley Hall, Boston, MA, undated, EC; John Hughes, "The School Question," in *Complete Works of the Most Rev. John Hughes* (New York: Lawrence Kehoe, 1866), 88; McAllister, *National Reform Movement*, 10. For a historical overview of the School Question, see Green, *The Bible, the School, and the Constitution*.
41. James M. Coleman, "Is Jesus King?" undated pamphlet, EC.
42. The language regarding tyranny was taken from a fellow Presbyterian minister who argued that the state should abandon public schools altogether. The editors of the *Christian Statesman* approved of his logic but not his conclusion, instead arguing for Christian public schools. John Miller, as quoted in "The Outlook," *Christian Statesman* 9, no. 16 (December 18, 1875): 121; "The Outlook," *Christian Statesman* 9, no. 18 (January 1, 1875): 137.
43. "The Outlook" and "An Open Letter to Members of Congress," *Christian Statesman* 9, no. 50 (August 12, 1876): 403, 406; Steven K. Green, "The Blaine Amendment Reconsidered," *American Journal of Legal History* 36, no. 1 (January 1992): 38–69.
44. David Sehat, "The American Moral Establishment: Religion and Liberalism in the Nineteenth Century" (PhD diss., University of North Carolina at Chapel Hill, 2007), 266–286.
45. If American Protestants generally feared that the God Amendment would make the nation too conservative, internally, the Covenanters worried that

their efforts had been corrupted in the opposite direction. The RPs, especially, did not universally support the NRA. Some worried that the fundraising was a distraction and laid accusations of mismanagement at the NRA leaders' feet. More worrisome, the NRA asked for flexibility with respect to the ancestral strict theology. Wrestling with Covenanter identity in an age dominated by political engagement to fix the Constitution led RPs to issue an American Covenant in 1871. Hard-liners continued to maintain a testimony of separation, but they reiterated their calls for the Bible to be the supreme law of the land—which, in turn, would fulfill "the obligation of nations to legislate in conformity with the written Word." Just as they demanded complete conformity, the RPs also recommitted to engage and cooperate with other American evangelicals; "Christian friendship" would enable them to "act as one" in their efforts to turn the nation to God. The internal tensions between engager and hard-liner impulses led to yet another schism in 1891. The events became known simply as "the Trial." Several ministers had been attempting to facilitate a reunion between the RPs and the UPs, who agreed on the kingship of Christ but disagreed on the rightness of voting. These Engager ministers felt that the voting issue could be overcome. Dissenters put them on trial, resulting in a mass expulsion of several leading Engagers. Committee on the Judiciary, *Hearings on the Joint Resolution (H. Res. 120)*, 21; Alexander, *History of the National Reform Movement*, 16; *The Covenant Sworn and Subscribed by the Synod of the Reformed Presbyterian Church* (Pittsburgh, PA: Synod of the Reformed Presbyterian Church, 1871), 4–9; *Stenographic Report of the Great "Liberal" Trial in the Covenanter Synod of 1891 with an Introduction* (Allegheny, PA: Covenanter Publishing Company, 1892).

46. "The Defeated Constitutional Amendment," *Index*, August 24, 1876, 402; Steven K. Green, *The Second Disestablishment: Church and State in Nineteenth-Century America* (New York: Oxford University Press, 2010), 302; Hamburger, *Separation of Church and State*, 288–312. This symbiotic relationship between Covenanters and liberals that birthed organized liberalism in America is discussed in Green, *The Bible, the School, and the Constitution*, 150–154.
47. Committee on the Judiciary, *Hearings on the Joint Resolution (H. Res. 120)*, 6; "Is the Constitution of the United States Christian?" undated pamphlet, EC; *National Reform Manual*, 17; Coleman, "Is Jesus King?"; Green, *The Bible, the School, and the Constitution*, 158–159; on Jewish reactions to the NRA, see Borden, *Jews, Turks, and Infidels*, 67–74.
48. "Centennial Papers," *Christian Statesman* 9, no. 42 (July 17, 1876)–10, no. 7 (October 19, 1876); "The Third Charter of Virginia; March 12, 1611," Avalon Project, http://avalon.law.yale.edu/17th_century/va03.asp.
49. "Centennial Papers, X," *Christian Statesman* 10, no. 1 (September 7, 1876): 7.

50. Foster, *Moral Reconstruction*, 238.
51. McAllister, *National Reform Movement*, 21–22.
52. Sloane, *Discourse Delivered before the Reformed Presbyterian Synod*, 6.
53. *Records of the Session Meetings of Hopewell Associate Reformed Presbyterian Church, 1832–1892* (Richburg, SC: Chester Genealogical Society, 1984), 11–17, 26–67.
54. Examination of the session books of the AR Church in the Montreat Collection shows a marked uptick in the prosecution of blacks after the Civil War. The proportion of black to white prosecutions eventually reached at least two to one, precipitating a sudden exodus of black members. New Hope Associate Reformed Presbyterian Church Session Book, MC; Lowry Ware, *A Place Called Due West* (R. L. Bryan, 2006), 100. For similar trends across biracial southern churches, see Charles F. Irons, "Two Divisions of the Same Great Army: Ecclesiastical Separation by Race and the Millennium," in *Apocalypse and the Millennium in the American Civil War Era*, ed. Ben Wright and Zachary W. Dresser (Baton Rouge: Louisiana State University Press, 2013), 194–216.
55. Bethany Associate Reformed Presbyterian Church Session Book, MC.
56. *Press and Banner*, October 8, 1869; "Curtail," *Press and Banner*, October 22, 1869.
57. J. C. Hemphill, "Speech Before the Long Cane and Cedar Springs Bible Society," July 21, 1877, DU; "Gen R. R. Hemphill Editor, Scholar, Soldier, Has Passed to the Great Beyond," *Abbeville Press and Banner*, December 30, 1908.
58. *Press and Banner*, April 11, 1877; *Medium*, April 11, 1877; Ware, *Place Called Due West*, 89–108.
59. Ware, *Place Called Due West*, 89–108.
60. Robert Lathan, "The Plight of the South," *News and Courier* 62, no. 206 (November 5, 1924): 4; Ray A. King, interview with the author, Highlands, NC, March 14, 2012. Names of individuals from these instances, and the name of the particular AR church, have been withheld at the request of the interviewee. These details were compiled by King for his 1966 *History of the Associate Reformed Presbyterian Church*, but he acquiesced to the denomination's demand that they be edited out of the manuscript.
61. McAllister, *National Reform Movement*, 36; George M. Marsden, *Fundamentalism and American Culture* (New York: Oxford University Press, 1980), 133.
62. *World's Christian Citizenship Conference, 1910* (Pittsburgh, PA: National Reform Association, 1910), 1–10.
63. *Second World's Citizenship Conference* (Pittsburgh, PA: National Reform Association, 1913), especially 287–290; *Third World's Christian Citizenship Conference* (Pittsburgh, PA: National Reform Association, 1919), 7.
64. *Third World's Christian Citizenship Conference*, 48–58.

AFTERWORD

1. Executive Committee of the Organization of the National Association of Evangelicals for United Action, *Evangelical Action! A Report of the Organization of the National Association of Evangelicals for United Action* (Boston, MA: United Action Press, 1942), 65, 92–100; Amendment proposal, quoted in Louis Gasper, *The Fundamentalist Movement, 1930–1956*, reprint (Grand Rapids, MI: Baker House Books, 1981), 146. The proposed amendment goes on to read: "through whom are bestowed the blessings of Almighty God." On the NAE, see Joel Carpenter, *Revive Us Again: The Reawakening of American Fundamentalism* (New York: Oxford University Press, 1999), 141–147. Graham left the AR Church because it was too doctrinally restrictive for his more ecumenical, evangelical tastes.
2. Anthony A. Cowley, "From Whence We Came: A Background of the National Reform Association," in *Explicitly Christian Politics: The Vision of the National Reform Association*, ed. William Einwechter (Pittsburgh, PA: Christian Statesman Press, 1997), 10–12; Senate Committee on the Judiciary, *Hearings before a Subcommittee of the Judiciary, United States Senate, Eighty-Third Congress, Second Session on S.J. Res. 87 Proposing an Amendment to the Constitution of the United States Recognizing the Authority and Law of Jesus Christ* (Washington, DC: Government Printing Office, 1954), 1–7, 23, 79–80; 2 Chron. 7:14.
3. Cowley, "From Whence We Came," 10–11; *Covenanter Witness*, November 1980, 2, 14; Jim Mason, *No Holding Back: The 1980 John B. Anderson Presidential Campaign* (Lanham, MD: University Press of America, 2011), 264–308; John B. Anderson, *Between Two Worlds: A Congressman's Choice* (Grand Rapids, MI: Zondervan, 1970).
4. Francis Schaeffer, *A Christian Manifesto* (Wheaton, IL: Crossway Books, 1982), 31–33; Samuel Rutherford, *Lex, Rex: The Law and the Prince, a Dispute for the Just Prerogative of King and People* (London: John Field, 1644).
5. Schaeffer failed to include any supporting quotations for this connection, and Locke makes no mention of relying on the Covenanters in his works. In fact, Locke was entirely put off by religious fanaticism. If he thought about Rutherford at all, he probably saw him as the other extreme of Robert Filmer's divine right of kings treatise *Patriarcha*. Mark A. Noll, Nathan O. Hatch, and George M. Marsden, *The Search for Christian America* (Wheaton, IL: Crossway Books, 1983), 142, n. 12. For ancillary references on Rutherford that are neither causal nor related to *Lex, Rex*, see Ian Harris, *The Mind of John Locke: A Study in Political Theory in Its Intellectual Setting* (New York: Cambridge University Press, 1994), 59, 72. See especially Greg Forster, *John Locke's Politics of Moral Consensus* (New York: Cambridge University Press, 2005), 1–39; Richard Ashcraft, *Revolutionary Politics and Locke's "Two Treatises on Government"* (Princeton, NJ: Princeton University Press, 1986).

6. Tim F. LaHaye, *The Battle for the Mind* (Old Tappan, NJ: Fleming H. Revell Co., 1979), 37–40; Jerry Falwell, *Listen, America!* (Garden City, NY: Doubleday and Co., Inc., 1980), 54. The only people Falwell cites more than once are Francis Schaeffer, Milton Friedman, and John Stormer. Peter Marshall and David Manuel, *The Light and the Glory* (Old Tappan, NJ: Fleming H. Revell Co., 1977), 343. Marshall's emphasis on covenant largely derived from a study of Puritan doctrine, but Marshall himself saw strong connections between Scottish Presbyterianism and American democracy. His mother recalled touring Scotland with his famous Scottish father and hearing about the legacy of "the Covenanters, when dukes and earls, farmers and drapers, merchants and artisans banned themselves into a democracy of the spirit." The Marshalls named their American homestead "Waverley," after Sir Walter Scott's Covenanter novel. Catherine Marshall, *A Man Called Peter: The Story of Peter Marshall* (New York: McGraw-Hill, 1951), 90–101. One particular discussion of such moral declension ends with a sixteen-point personal pledge to help reform the nation for God. Mark A. Beliles and Stephen K. McDowell, *America's Providential History* (Charlottesville, VA: Providence Foundation, 1989), 248–274.
7. David Barton, "The Supreme Court's Decisions on the Separation of Church and State Are Flawed," in *Freedom of Religion*, ed. Gary Zacharias (New York: Greenhaven Press, 2005), 111–118; http://www.time.com/time/specials/packages/article/0,28804,1993235_1993243_1993261,00.html (accessed March 7, 2013). The problems with Barton's work are legion, not the least of which are his academic straw men. Few—if any—historians believe that Jefferson was an atheist, as Barton claims. His citations to this effect consist of obscure quotes from such websites as Ask.com. Historians have long acknowledged Jefferson's deeply informed religious faith, and Barton is either ignorant or lying about that fact. He is correct about one thing, however; Jefferson had "personal theological difficulties over specific religious doctrines." These were the doctrines about the divinity of Jesus, the resurrection of Jesus, and the Trinitarian God. David Barton, *The Jefferson Lies: Exposing the Myths You've Always Believed about Thomas Jefferson* (Nashville, TN: Thomas Nelson, 2012), 196. After selling 20,000 copies, Barton's book was pulled from shelves by the original publisher after numerous inaccuracies were uncovered. The book was named the least credible history book in recent memory by the History News Network. Warren Throckmorton and Michael Coulter, *Getting Jefferson Right: Fact Checking Claims about Our Third President* (Grove City, PA: Salem Grove, 2012), e-book; http://www.publishersweekly.com/pw/by-topic/industry-news/religion/article/53512-nelson-pulls-thomas-jefferson-book.html; http://hnn.us/articles/what-least-credible-history-book-print. See also Randall J. Stephens and Karl W. Giberson, *The Anointed: Evangelical Truth in a Secular Age* (Cambridge, MA: Harvard University Press, 2011), 61–98.

8. James R. Willson, "Political Danger. A Sermon preached January 6th, 1825 a fast observed by several churches in Newburgh and its vicinity," reprinted in *Evangelical Witness* 3, no. 4 (April 1825): 156–169; *The Spiritual Heritage of the United States Capital*, DVD, directed by John Pevoto (Aledo, TX: Wallbuilders, 2002). Barton has also suggested that the number is twenty-four. David Barton, "God: Missing in Action from American History," http://www.wallbuilders.com/libissuesarticles.asp?id=100 (accessed April 18, 2013).
9. In all, nine North Carolina representatives supported the amendment, which died in committee. See http://www.dailytarheel.com/article/2013/04/defense-of-religion-act-denied (accessed March 28, 2015); http://big.assets.huffingtonpost.com/toplines_churchstate_0403042013.pdf; *Town of Greece, New York, Petitioner v. Susan Galloway et al.*, 2014 U.S. Lexis 3110 (2014).
10. This is not to discount the ways in which Protestantism has defined what religion *is* under American law. To the present day, American jurisprudence has defined that freedom as an internal set of core convictions one is free to believe. Religion as outward display, meanwhile, is often judged outside the realm of legal protections. See Winnifred Fallers Sullivan, *The Impossibility of Religious Freedom* (Princeton, NJ: Princeton University Press, 2005).
11. One legal scholar has noted that the Covenanter argument displays "an internal consistency, and within its own frame of reference, an intellectual rigor the most fulminations of the so-called religious right lack." Robert Emery, "Church and State in the Early Republic: The Covenanters' Radical Critique," *Journal of Law and Religion* 25, no. 2 (June 2010): 499.

# Index